Born in 1953, Michael   ⌐ St John's College,
Cambridge, and was called to the Bar by the Inner Temple.
He assisted Suzanne Blum, the French lawyer of the Duke
and Duchess of Windsor, and wrote six books about the
couple. His biography of Ribbentrop was reissued by
Abacus in 2003. He has edited five volumes of the diaries
of James Lees-Milne, and is co-producer of a play based
on those diaries, *Ancestral Voices*. His life of Jeremy Thorpe
awaits publication.

F.M.
THE LIFE OF
FREDERICK MATTHIAS
ALEXANDER

FOUNDER OF THE ALEXANDER TECHNIQUE

to Leah

from

MICHAEL BLOCH

Michael Bloch

Aug. 2011

LITTLE, BROWN

A *Little, Brown* Original

First published in Great Britain in 2004 by Little, Brown

A CIP catalogue record for this book
is available from the British Library.

C-format ISBN 0 316 86048 4
Hbk ISBN 0 316 72864 0

Typeset in Sabon by Palimpsest Book Production Limited,
Polmont, Stirlingshire

Printed and bound in Great Britain by Clays Ltd, St Ives plc

Little, Brown
An imprint of
Time Warner Book Group
Brettenham House
Lancaster Place
London WC2E 7EN

www.twbg.co.uk

*To those without whom
this book would not have happened*

Glynn Macdonald
who suggested I write it

Ursula Mackenzie
my long-suffering publisher

Walter Carrington
my patient mentor

Jean Fischer
my generous historical adviser

Robbie Macdonald
my excellent teacher

and
Daniel F. Barr
who bullied me into starting lessons
in May 1991

Contents

List of Illustrations

With Sir Stafford and Dame Isobel Cripps, 'friends in high places', on F.M.'s 80th birthday, January 1949

At Ashley Place with 80th birthday portrait by Colin Colahan

Cartoon by Ronald Searle in the *News Chronicle*, 26 February 1953: 'He Teaches the Way Back to Health . . .' (Ronald Searle)

F.M.'s hands, 1941 (STAT)

Except where otherwise stated, the above pictures are reproduced by kind permission of Walter Carrington. Thanks are also due to Jean Fischer for providing many of the images on disk.

Foreword

by Walter Carrington

I have eagerly looked forward to this book. F. Matthias Alexander is the most remarkable man I have ever known. I first heard of him when I was a schoolboy in the 1930s. My mother had suffered for years from a debilitating illness: she was so weak as to be practically bedridden. One day, W. H. Eynon Smith, my form master at St Paul's School in London, enquired after her and remarked that he had recently seen a review in the *British Medical Journal* of a book by Alexander called *The Use of the Self*. He suggested that this might be worth looking into.

The result was that my parents read the book and Alexander gave my mother lessons and put her on her feet again: and when he learned that she was the wife of a clergyman of limited means, he charged only a nominal fee. Subsequently he also gave lessons to my father and to me.

I first met him when he invited me to his rooms at 16 Ashley Place, near Victoria Station, and took me out to dinner. He opened the door to me himself and, excusing the absence of servants, said that we were going to the Café Royal. He was then in his middle sixties, white-haired, of medium height, slim, broad-shouldered with slender hips, alert, elegant, with a bright, birdlike eye. He appeared to be the epitome of an Edwardian gentleman of an earlier generation. I found that he had a natural gift for putting a young man at ease. His manner seemed kindness itself; and incidentally, not for a moment did his voice or gesture betray a hint of his Australian origins.

I forget exactly what we talked about that night. He did not seem to have any great literary or intellectual interests, but he spoke nostalgically of the pre-1914 theatre, and he obviously had a fine knowledge of food and wine. He also showed interest in current affairs and in the turf, but it was obvious that his main interest was his work. He had a remarkable empirical knowledge of his own mind–body. Just as shepherds and stockmen know a lot about the health of their beasts, without formal anatomy or physiology, so he knew about his voice and respiratory mechanisms and the proper use and functioning of the human self as a whole. He had a great vision of a future of mankind (or rather for individual members of it), expressed in the title of his first book, *Man's Supreme Inheritance*.

From the moment I met him I wanted to know as much as possible about him, and it was my good fortune to have lessons and train with him, and subsequently to assist him in his practice and on his training course, during the last twenty years of his life.

I have long felt that a biography of Alexander was needed, but although I came to know him quite well and learn quite a lot about his life, I did not feel qualified to write it myself. Fortunately, Michael Bloch, a writer who became my pupil a decade ago, expressed interest in undertaking the task. He has had my help and encouragement during the years he has been working on it, and he has written a splendid book which brings the subject to life.

Prologue

It is notoriously difficult to describe the Alexander Technique: to attempt to do so has been likened to trying to describe a colour to a blind man. Even writers of great talent who were among its followers, such as the American philosopher John Dewey and the English novelist Aldous Huxley, struggled to express it in words. In essence, it is based on the notion that we develop bad habits in our posture which we are often quite unaware of, but which account for much of what goes wrong with us in every department. The Technique provides a practical method of identifying and overcoming these habits. Its founder, the Australian Frederick Matthias Alexander, managed to work it out for himself and apply it to himself after a long, painstaking process of self-examination, described in his book *The Use of the Self* (1932). However, even if one had the insight to grasp its basic principles, and an infinity of time and patience, one would be unlikely to be able to practise it successfully without instruction, for the reason that it is difficult for the uninstructed to know what is wrong with them which needs to be put right. For one's familiar way of doing things feels right, even though it is often wrong. One therefore requires the guidance of a qualified practitioner. As the Technique purports to be a form of training rather than therapy, its practitioners describe themselves as teachers, offering lessons to pupils. Alexander himself gave lessons which essentially consisted of teaching the pupil the correct way of sitting down in and getting out of a chair – for he believed that these two acts encompassed everything that was important in the workings of the postural mechanism. Nowadays, most lessons include an element of 'table work' as well as 'chair work', in which the pupil is subtly manipulated on a massage table: at first sight it resembles a form of physiotherapy, though the object is not curative but educative. A lesson is not a purely passive affair, for it is important that the pupil, while being guided by the teacher, should focus his mind on what he is supposed to be doing (or not doing), with a view to giving (or withholding) consent to any action. In effect, the Technique is a system not just of postural re-education but of mental training, which teaches one to think about whatever one is going to do in the moment before one does it, with a view to refraining from any activity likely to interfere with the efficient realisation of one's goal.

Until I started lessons in the Technique, I knew of it only as an element in the training of actors; and it was a student of acting who introduced me to it. I was then thirty-seven, and had some reason to be happy. I had written five books which had brought me a measure of fame and fortune. I had many friends, and was leading a life which was both exciting and fulfilling. Yet all was not well. I was prey to cold-like infections, which would put me 'under the weather' for about a week a month. I often found myself short of breath, at which times my voice would diminish to a croak. I suffered from various allergies, which would prostrate me during the hay fever season. My love of good food was interfered with by digestive troubles. I had always been a somewhat awkward and malcoordinated individual, and imagined that these conditions would decrease with my experience of life, though in fact they seemed to increase. As a cumulative result of these problems, I tended to feel exhausted and depressed, and had a sense of being on the decline, though I was not yet middle-aged. I consulted many physicians and specialists, but they never seemed to find much wrong with me, and I never seemed to experience much improvement.

This was the situation when, early in 1991, I befriended Daniel F. Barr, a Canadian student at London's LAMDA drama school, among whose many charms was a delightful outspokenness. He expressed the view that I was a wreck, tied up in knots; and he suggested I straighten myself out by taking lessons with his Alexander teacher at LAMDA, Robert Macdonald. I was sceptical and reluctant; and it was only after much bullying by Daniel, as well as several encouraging telephone calls from Robbie, that I went along to submit myself to this experiment. Although I only took a weekly lesson, thought to be the minimum needed for a beginner to derive significant benefit, the results were spectacular. Indeed, one highly visible change manifested itself almost immediately. As a studious boy, I had been in the habit of walking to my day school carrying a heavy bag of books, as a result of which I reached adulthood with my right shoulder almost an inch lower than the left. I had imagined this to be a permanent deformity, was rather self-conscious about it, and had my jackets specially made to hide the discrepancy. But after only a few lessons, the shoulders levelled out. Soon afterwards, friends started remarking that I looked taller and somehow different. In the twelve and a half years since then, I have rarely suffered from a cold or indigestion, and have only twice had serious cause to consult a doctor. My respiratory and allergic problems have not vanished, but only trouble me a fraction as much as they did, clearly because their effects were enormously aggravated by habitual faults in my posture. After six months of lessons, I felt a new man, and was getting much greater enjoyment out of life.

I do not wish to exaggerate, and I cannot claim that the Alexander Technique has provided an answer to all my problems. I also know that, even after practising it for years, I am far from mastering it; and perhaps I shall never do so, for this would involve overcoming a habit which I am rather fond of but which Alexander would have deplored – that of becoming lost in my own thoughts. Yet it has added a new dimension to my life by giving me an awareness of, and an ability to control, those aspects of posture which potentially interfere with efficient functioning and good health. And this awareness continues to grow. A couple of years ago, as I was getting down to serious work on this book, I returned to Robbie for lessons, taking two or three a week in the hope of gaining a greater understanding of the Technique. To my surprise, I have not only gained this understanding but also experienced further improvements in my general functioning, as a result of which I now feel rather fitter at fifty than I did at forty, a medical examination around the time of my fiftieth birthday confirming that, despite the fact that I take little planned exercise, and eat, drink and smoke to my heart's content, I am in pretty good health for my age.

Rooted in the concept of mind–body unity, the Technique brings psychological as well as physical benefits. Before going to Robbie, I had been making slow, unenthusiastic progress with the book I was writing, a biography of the Nazi foreign minister Ribbentrop; but as I took lessons, the writing proceeded with increasing ease, and I even managed to treat this rather depressing subject with a certain verve. When the book appeared in October 1992, it was read by Glynn Macdonald, then Robbie's wife and Chairman of the Society of Teachers of the Alexander Technique. She liked it, and asked if I would consider writing about another figure of whom a biography was needed, F. M. Alexander. Glynn is one of those for whom thought becomes action, and before the end of the year I found myself being introduced to Walter Carrington, who had been Alexander's closest assistant during his later years. As I write, Walter is eighty-eight, but redolent with what can only be described as boyish enthusiasm, despite sustaining injuries as an RAF pilot in his late twenties which would have finished most people off. For the past eleven years, it has been my privilege to have had a monthly lesson with him, as well as many fascinating talks about Alexander, whom he knew and understood as well as anyone. He is a model of patience, for although I told him a decade ago that I intended to write this book, the demands of other projects meant that I was unable to devote myself to it until 2001. On the other hand, the biography of so complex a character is not to be undertaken lightly, and it was perhaps an advantage that I had several years (as Alexander might have put it) to consider the 'means whereby' I was going to accomplish it before 'gaining the end' of writing it.

It is now almost half a century since Alexander (or 'F.M.', as he was generally known) died in 1955; and the fact that no full-length biography of him has yet appeared calls for some comment. There has, in fact, been a good deal of writing about him. Regarding his early life in Australia, two Alexander teachers in that continent, Rosslyn McLeod and Margaret Long, have published interesting findings. There are several vivid accounts of him by men and women who knew him during his last quarter-century – such as Lulie Westfeldt's memoir of training under him in the 1930s, Walter Carrington's diary of teaching in his practice in the 1940s, and Goddard Binkley's journal of lessons with him in the 1950s. Although not much has been written about his life between 1904, when he arrived in London from Australia, and 1931, when he started his first training course, Jean M. O. Fischer, a leading historian of the Alexander Technique, has, through his Mouritz publishing firm and its website, made public an important collection of writings from this period, either by F.M. himself or by others about his work. (He has also produced scholarly editions of two of Alexander's books, full of informative notes, and intends to perform the same service with the other two.) Some books about the Alexander Technique contain valuable summaries of the life of its founder – *Freedom to Change* by Frank Pierce Jones being a notable example – and monographs about various aspects of or episodes in that life often appear in periodicals such as the *Alexander Journal* and *Direction*.

The year 2001 saw the publication by Phillimore of *Frederick Matthias Alexander: A Family History* by F.M.'s great-niece, Wing-Commander Jackie Evans. This painstakingly researched and beautifully illustrated book contains an amazing account of F.M.'s convict ancestry, the best picture we are ever likely to get of his early life in Australia, and a wealth of detail about the rest of his life. As well as being a thrilling read, it is a priceless resource for all who write about F.M. in future; and every chapter of this book owes a debt to it. However, it is what it claims to be – a family history, showing how a clan which emerged from penal servitude during the first half of the nineteenth century became closely involved in the life and work of its leading member, a great and successful man, during the first half of the twentieth. It does not give much idea of F.M.'s personality or thought.

During his lifetime, F.M.'s friends often urged him to write his memoirs. Though reluctant to do so, he did in fact twice embark on such a work – in the early 1930s, at the behest of his adopted daughter Peggy, and in the early 1950s, at the behest of Ron Brown, a journalist pupil who was then writing a book about F.M.'s successful libel action in the South African courts, which he planned to follow with a biography. On the first attempt, F.M. is said to have produced a draft dealing with his life up to his first encounter with one of his greatest supporters, the 2nd Earl of Lytton, in 1926. Unfortunately, all copies of this work, which F.M. evidently decided against publishing, seem to have vanished. One can but hope that a copy survives somewhere, and will emerge some day. All that survives from the second attempt is a fragment of about twelve thousand words dealing with his life up to the time of his leaving Australia in 1904. This fragment (published by Jean Fischer in 1996) consists more of self-serving anecdote than illuminating fact, though it has nevertheless proved a valuable source for the first two chapters of this book.

Ron Brown died before he could get down to his biography of F.M. His friend Edward Owen inherited his research and, during the 1960s, attempted to complete his work, interviewing many who had known Alexander and taking fascinating notes – but he, too, did not finally write his book. Since then, several others have broached the task, at least one of whom, the American Alexander teacher Missy Vineyard, has done considerable research; but no completed work has materialised. (I am indeed fortunate in that I have been able to benefit from the research of these precursors: thanks to Jean Fischer and the late Tony Spawforth, I was able to see many of the notes of Brown and Owen; and Missy Vineyard, when I visited her at Amherst in 2002, was generous in allowing me to see some fascinating material she had collected for her unwritten book.)

No doubt, in each of these cases, there were personal reasons as to why the project was not seen through to completion; but one wonders whether there is also something about the project itself which tends to deter those who attempt it. Looking back on the years of my own life during which I contemplated this account of F.M.'s, it occurs to me that the task is daunting for three (closely related) reasons. First, F.M., largely owing to his sensitivity about his convict ancestry, was highly secretive by nature; and as he was an actor by training (and disposition), what one saw of him did not always correspond to the underlying reality. He tended to cover his tracks, and was cautious in revealing anything of his past, even to members of his own family. Secondly, there is a dearth of original sources. Only ten weeks before he died, F.M. disinherited his loyal assistants, to whom he had intended leaving at least those archives relating to the history of his work, and effectively entrusted his entire estate to his much younger brother Beaumont, a colourful rogue who was uninterested in the Alexander Technique except as a commercial enterprise. Beaumont subsequently became a hotelier, and most of F.M.'s papers are said to have perished when his hotel was ravaged by fire in the 1960s. Nor do other archives reveal much about the first fifty years of F.M.'s life; for although he is known to have befriended many distinguished people, they did not (so far as it has been possible to ascertain) see fit either to keep his letters or write about him in their diaries or memoirs. Thirdly, although F.M. is justly revered by his followers as a genius and a benefactor of humanity who made one of the great discoveries of his time, there are nevertheless aspects of his life and character which can only be regarded as disconcerting.

As one who is neither an Alexander teacher nor a member of the Alexander family, I have perhaps been able to approach the subject with a certain objectivity. I must confess that, at the outset of the project, I felt handicapped by the fact that, although I had greatly benefited from Alexander's work, I had a limited understanding of it from both the practical and the intellectual point of view. Happily, as a result of the research and writing (and my contemporaneous discussions and lessons with Walter Carrington and Robbie Macdonald), my understanding has grown. This may explain the fact that, whereas after finishing all my previous books I have felt somewhat 'down', on completing this one I feel distinctly 'up'.

Such was the help and encouragement I received from Walter Carrington and Jean Fisher in producing this work that I regard it as almost as much theirs as mine (though I naturally take responsibility for all opinions expressed in it). Others who kindly made information or papers available to me include John Best, Dilys Carrington, Professor Peter Clarke, Michael Estorick, Jackie Evans, Clare Felck (archivist at Knebworth House), Clive Fisher, Enid Foster (Librarian of the Garrick Club), Sue Fox, Dr Thomas Frank, Barbara Neil, Nancy M. Shawcross (archivist at the University of Pennsylvania), Tony Spawforth, Dan Stone, Beryl Tolliday (archivist at 18 Lansdowne Road), Missy Vineyard, Elizabeth Walker and Erika Whittaker. I am sorry if I have left anyone out. I am also indebted to Ursula Mackenzie and Tim Whiting, my publisher and editor at Little, Brown; to that most delightful of mentors, Dr R. B. McDowell of Trinity College, Dublin, who read and commented on the chapters around the time of his ninetieth birthday; and to the friends who have heard me talk about the book for more than a decade, often contributing useful suggestions.

I am additionally grateful to Jean Fischer for granting me permission to quote from F.M.'s unpublished letters, in which he owns the rights. He and Missy Vineyard are currently preparing an edition of these letters, which should be essential reading for all who are interested in F.M.'s life and work.

This biography does not claim to be definitive, but aims to give a bird's-eye view of a long and extraordinary life for which, at present, the source material is thin in some parts and quite rich in others. It will have achieved its object if it stimulates further investigation into the career of a still largely unrecognised genius who, almost entirely on his own, discovered a principle which, in the words of John Dewey, 'bears the same relation to education that education bears to all other human activities'.

Michael Bloch
padders@dircon.co.uk
London, December 2003

1

Tasmania

1869–1889

Frederick Matthias Alexander (eventually known to friends and followers as 'F.M.') was born at Table Cape, north-western Tasmania – then one of the remotest corners of the British Empire – on 20 January 1869. During his later years, he rarely mentioned his forebears, except to suggest they were Scottish settlers. In a questionnaire which (at the request of an aspiring biographer[1]) he completed in his eighties, he declared roundly that his father's family came from Scotland; and in conversation and correspondence, he often made some jocular allusion to his Scottish blood.[2] In fact, all four of his grandparents had been transported to Tasmania (then known as Van Diemen's Land) as convicts in the second quarter of the nineteenth century; and there is no evidence of Scots descent. The Alexanders hailed from the West of England.

While it is understandable that F.M. should have been evasive about his origins in a respectability-obsessed age, he had little cause to feel ashamed of his paternal grandfather. Matthias Alexander was born in 1810 in the ancient village of Ramsbury in Wiltshire, where his ancestors had lived for generations. In Tudor and Stuart times, they had probably been agricultural labourers on the local estates of the Earls of Pembroke; but during the eighteenth century – after those estates had been broken up, and Ramsbury had become an 'open' village, unattached to the manor – they established themselves as craftsmen, notably carpenters and wheel-wrights. They prospered to the extent of owning cottages and fields; by the end of the century, some were rich enough to qualify as voters in elections, or have a pew in the village church. It is uncertain whether any of them could read or write, or indeed had any formal education beyond learning their trades. But there is some evidence that they were recep-tive to the radical political ideas then sweeping England: for we know that Matthias's uncle, John Alexander (who later emigrated to America), allowed his carpenter's shop to be used for meetings of the Primitive Methodists, a revivalist sect founded in 1812 which was associated with radical labour movements. Matthias became a hurdle maker, his elder brother Joseph (1806–78), a wheelwright.[3]

In the summer of 1830, agricultural disturbances broke out in several parts of England, known as 'the Swing Riots' as they were sometimes accompanied by threatening letters to landowners and agents signed 'Captain Swing'. They were provoked by the declining lot of the English farm labourer, resulting from the enclosure of land, poor harvests, and the introduction of agricultural machinery. On 22 November, the disturbances reached Ramsbury, where seventeen threshing machines were smashed. Among those arrested as 'machine-breakers' were the brothers Matthias and Joseph Alexander. At their trial before Special Assizes at Winchester on 4 January 1831, the judge took a harsh view of their offence, as 'they belonged to a class of persons who had not even the vain pretence that these machines could affect them in any manner'. As village craftsmen, they had secure liveli-hoods; radical idealism rather than desperate need had driven them to act as they had. They were sentenced 'to be trans-ported to such place beyond the seas as His Majesty should direct for a term of seven years', and found themselves bound for Van Diemen's Land, where they landed at the end of May on the convict ship *Eliza* after a journey of 112 days in grisly conditions. Matthias was twenty years of age; Joseph was twenty-four, and had left behind a wife and three small children.

The British settlement of Van Diemen's Land – an island lying off south-eastern Australia, a little smaller than Ireland – had begun in 1803 with the founding of Hobart. Originally it was an outpost of the convict colony of New South Wales across the Bass Strait; but in 1825, by which time most of the indigenous inhabitants had been exterminated, it became a separate colony with its own governor. In 1831, when the Alexander brothers arrived, it had a population of some 25,000, of whom 10,000 were convicts and 15,000 free settlers, and only about 6000 were women. The first convicts had endured a regime of great harshness; but Governor Arthur had recently established a more humane system which aimed at transforming them into useful citizens. On arrival, they were 'assigned' as labourers either to public works or private employers; if they behaved well, they were eligible after four years for 'tickets of leave', entitling them to work for money while awaiting their eventual freedom. Matthias and Joseph duly received their leave in 1835, and soon afterwards got their freedom too as part of a general amnesty of the Swing rioters. Like other men in their position, they had little thought of returning to England, and hoped to make their fortunes in the rough colonial world with its pioneering opportunities.

They were not alone. In 1832, their younger brother John (1812–98) had also been transported to Van Diemen's Land, for the offence of stealing pigs; and around the same time, a cousin from Ramsbury, John Dowling, had gone out as a free settler working for the Van Diemen's Land Company. The three brothers worked hard to establish themselves, helped by Dowling who became overseer of the important Wickford estate, where he was able to offer them employment. In 1838, Matthias married the convict Mary Redden, an Irish Catholic, born in Limerick and raised in London, who had been transported in 1832, aged sixteen, for stealing a dress worth five shillings. She was a troublesome convict, whose employers repeatedly reported her for drunken and dishonest behaviour; in consequence her term of transportation was extended, and only through marriage to a free man could she regain her liberty. She bore him six sons – of whom F.M.'s father, another John Alexander, born at Wickford in 1843, was the fourth – before dying of consumption in 1850.

In 1849 – by which time the brothers had built up enough capital to buy some fertile land in the inland Deloraine region – the elder John sailed off to try his luck as a prospector in the California gold-rush. Two years later, Matthias followed his example by crossing the Strait and participating in the Victoria gold-rush. They evidently had some success, for in 1852 they purchased several hundred acres of densely wooded Crown land on Table Cape in the remote north-west of Tasmania, including the lower reaches of the River Inglis. The terrain was notoriously difficult; a government report published around this time suggested that

> in no other part of the world . . . are there such formidable obstacles to the clearing and cultivation of land as here besets the settler of small capital, while the difficulties to be encountered in crossing dangerous tidal rivers and traversing forests . . . check all free intercommunication and isolate him almost completely from the notice and sympathy of civilisation.[4]

Undaunted, the brothers laboured to clear the forest and plant crops. They bought a forty-ton schooner to export their timber and grain, for which they found a ready market in the Victoria goldfields. They established the little port of Alexandria on the banks of the Inglis, and sold part of their land at great profit to provide the site for another township, Wynyard, two miles downstream near the mouth of the river. By 1858 – when we get a glimpse of his life from the evidence he gave at a local murder trial[5] – Matthias had become one of the most prosperous citizens of the locality. His land already produced 3000 bushels of wheat a year, sold at twelve shillings a bushel. Alexandria had become the main staging post between the settlements of Stanley to the west and Burnie to the east: Matthias's inn there brought in a further substantial income, as did the rent from his old farm at Deloraine. He had taken a second wife, Anne, who was in the process of bearing him seven more children. His sons by his first marriage helped him run the estate, but also learned useful trades of their own: one became a carter, one a shoemaker, another ran the inn at Alexandria. Young John trained to be a blacksmith – for horses played a vital part in local life, both for communication and recreation: there was already a racecourse in the vicinity run by John Dowling, the Alexanders' relative and former patron.

Had Matthias lived into old age, the life of his grandson F.M. might have been rather different. But in 1865 he suddenly died at the age of fifty-five; and within a short time, his little empire disintegrated. After protracted legal difficulties, compounded by the fact that few of those involved could read or write, his property was divided up between his widow and twelve surviving children. His death coincided with the onset of an agricultural depression in Tasmania (as the colony had been renamed in 1856); for Victoria, its goldfields depleted, no longer provided a market for the island's produce. Matthias's brother John gave up farming and became a shipowner, while his sons struggled to make a living out of the Table Cape estate. Their difficulties were not helped by the building of a new bridge over the Inglis in the late 1860s, which led to Wynyard supplanting Alexandria as the Stanley–Burnie staging post; Alexandria gradually became a ghost town, of which no trace survives today.

Young John eventually inherited £417 from his father, along with a share of the Table Cape estate; but he decided not to join his brothers in farming, and to concentrate instead on his calling as a blacksmith. He was considered a master of his craft, whose services were sought annually across the

Strait for Australia's greatest horse race, the Melbourne Cup. Originally he based himself in Alexandria; but with the decline of that town, he moved to Wynyard in 1870. Meanwhile, he had married Betsy Brown in 1866, when he was twenty-two and she eighteen. Her mother, the London-born Maria Davis, had been transported in 1842, aged sixteen, for receiving stolen silver; like F.M.'s other grandmother, she had got into trouble as a convict, but managed to secure her freedom by marrying an ex-convict – the police constable Thomas Brown, to whom she bore six children before he drowned at sea on a fishing expedition in 1855. F.M. was the first of ten children of John and Betsy, born at Alexandria a few days before the third anniversary of their marriage.

Tasmania in 1869 was an unusual place which marked its offspring in curious ways. It had a population of some hundred thousand, of whom about a third lived in the only two substantial towns, the capital Hobart in the south-east and Launceston in the north-east. Most of the best land lay in the 120-mile belt between these two centres, and had been parcelled out in the second quarter of the century to a few hundred settlers who had been attracted by the availability of convict labour. With the granting of colonial self-government in 1856, this minority settler class had taken power, the majority being excluded from the franchise by a high property qualification. Apart from the excellent convict-built road between Hobart and Launceston, communications in the country were so primitive that it took over a month for returns to come in at elections for the colony's legislature. There were as yet no railways; and a place like Wynyard, a hundred miles west of Launceston, was so remote as hardly to be aware of developments in the capital, several days' journey distant.

The colony lay in the shadow of having been the last and most notorious of Great Britain's penal settlements. Transportation to New South Wales had ceased in 1840, but it had continued until 1853 to Van Diemen's Land, where several thousand transportees-for-life still served at Port Arthur. Whereas the convict element on the mainland had been diluted by large-scale free immigration, former convicts (known as 'Old Hands') still accounted for almost a third of Tasmania's population, much of the rest being the children and grandchildren of convicts. The end of the convict system, though welcomed by most Tasmanians, had led to financial problems: the colony's entire revenue was now substantially less than the £350,000 a year which the British Government had formerly granted it to receive the convicts, who no longer provided free labour for public works. Other legacies of transportation included a continuing shortage of females in the population, an extreme fear of homosexuality, and the existence of a large class of waifs, ageing Old Hands who roamed the country in search of work or charity. Mainland Australians tended to look down on Tasmanians – 'Vandemonians' – as possessing the roughness, dishonesty and vice associated with convicts.

In modern parlance, the entire colony was in a state of 'denial' about the transportation era. Old Hands who had made good (such as the Alexander brothers) simply put their convict pasts out of their minds, often not telling their children about it, or bribing officials to falsify records; similarly, the governing class tried to forget that they had made their fortunes out of convict labour. The name-change which accompanied self-government represented an attempt to 'wash out the stain' and make a fresh start. One way in which Tasmanians tried to exorcise the demons of the past was to stress their 'Englishness'. The climate was similar to England's; the landscape (unlike mainland Australia's) was fairly English, with its lush greenery, lakes and rivers, and picturesque peaks; and the vast majority of the population was English in origin (unlike New South Wales, where a large proportion of both convicts and free immigrants was Irish). The towns, rivers and counties of Tasmania were named after

English counterparts; and English rural traditions were followed, such as the planting of hedgerows. Tasmania was already being marketed to the rich of Sydney and Melbourne as a tourist destination where they might escape the heat of summer in a 'little England'. Most Tasmanians (including Matthias Alexander and his family) were Anglican, and almost all of them were fiercely loyal to the Crown and the mother country, displaying the wildest enthusiasm when Queen Victoria's son Prince Alfred visited the colony in 1870. Thus F.M. was to be brought up to have an almost mystical love of the land which had so brutally exiled his grandparents, and upon which he himself would not set eyes until he was thirty-five.

Economically, the colony was the poor relation of its sister colonies on the Australian mainland, having experienced little of the prosperity and population increase enjoyed by New South Wales and Victoria during the past two decades. It depended overwhelmingly on agriculture for its livelihood; and the agricultural depression of recent years had struck deep, imports falling by one-half, exports by one-third and government revenue to its lowest ever. When the novelist Anthony Trollope visited the island in 1872, he found a prevailing sense of hopelessness. The Tasmanians themselves, he wrote, believed that their colony 'has seen the best of its days, that it is falling into decay, that its short period of importance in the world has already gone . . .'[6] Yet economic salvation lay near at hand with the discovery, in the early 1870s, of massive tin deposits on Mount Bischoff, not far from Wynyard.

F.M. had to struggle to survive from the moment he entered the world; for he was a premature baby, tiny and frail at birth.[7] Only the determination of his strong-willed mother not to lose her first child, and the careful ministrations of the local physician, Dr Wilson, enabled him to pull through the early months. He seemed at first to be faced with starvation, as he was unable to ingest his mother's milk; but he proved able to accept goat's milk – administered, it is said, through a fountain-pen filler. As a result of these precarious beginnings, he became a 'mother's boy': he always remained her favourite child, and she remained in his thoughts even during long years of separation.

He was less close to his father. John Alexander was a religious man, dedicated to his work. But his bearded, unsmiling countenance in family photographs suggests a gruff, melancholy character. He is rumoured to have been a heavy drinker (often the case with blacksmiths, apt to keep themselves cool at the heat of the forge by ordering relays of beer), though he seems to have 'taken the pledge' after the temperance movement reached Wynyard in 1879, and enjoined his children never to touch alcohol. At all events, it can only have come as something of a shock to the earthy blacksmith that his first-born should be a weakling, unlikely to be able to follow him into his trade. Although F.M. seems to have felt for him little of the affection which bound him to his mother, and rarely mentioned him during his years in England (for most of which John was alive, for he lived to a great age and only died in 1936), he nevertheless paid tribute to his father for having brought him up always to be observant and alert.

The Wynyard to which F.M. moved with his parents at the age of one was an isolated spot, not yet served by the telegraph, and connected to the neighbouring townships of Stanley (twenty miles to the west) and Burnie (twelve miles to the east) by roads which were little more than rough tracks and became impassable in wet weather. It had a population of about 150, with perhaps five times as many living in the surrounding countryside: not until the 1880s would it experience any significant further growth. It consisted of a water frontage with wharves and jetties, a few unmetalled streets, a few dozen wooden houses and cottages, two inns (with bars and stables), a general stores and an assembly hall.

There was as yet no Anglican church – the nearest, at which F.M. was baptised, was at Burnie – but it did have a resident Roman Catholic priest, Father O'Callaghan, who took a pastoral interest in all the inhabitants and became a friend of the Alexander family. (Although John Alexander was an Anglican at this time, and would later become a Methodist, it will be recalled that his mother had been an Irish Catholic.) A small government school and reading room was established in 1871, though it took some time to get going, as local farmers were reluctant to lose the labour of their children by sending them to school, and most of the adult population was illiterate.

The John Alexanders lived in a cottage in Hogg Street, with an adjoining smithy and an acre of land. With the arrival of eight more children in the course of the next sixteen years – Arthur (1870), Agnes (1872), Albert Redden (1874), Richard (1876), Amy (1879), May (1881), Horace (1883) and Beaumont (1886) – it must have become a crowded household. However, F.M. had an advantage over other local children in that he was able to roam freely on the Table Cape estate across the river, now farmed by his Uncle Martin. It was there, he tells us in his fragment of autobiography, that he learned to ride, shoot and fish, and 'acquired knowledge of all that concerns agriculture and animals'.[8] In particular he developed an early love and understanding of horses, both his parents being accomplished equestrians.* (His mother had some training as a midwife, and would gallop across the bush, sometimes with the infant F.M. strapped to her back, to attend local births.) Their connections with the family farm also enabled the Alexanders to obtain regular supplies of fresh produce; as Betsy Alexander was a good cook, the family ate well in spite of their modest means, and F.M. and

---

* 'I was born riding gee-gees,' F.M. wrote to Mungo Douglas in April 1945. It has been suggested that his knowledge of horses later gave him certain insights into the workings of the human mechanism.

his siblings grew up with a love of simple good food based on high-quality ingredients.

Betsy, who unlike her husband could read and write, was determined that her children (particularly her eldest and favourite) should receive a decent education, and they were sent first to Sunday school and then to the government school, and encouraged to learn. Though a clever boy, F.M. was not an easy pupil, for he was highly strung and attention-seeking by nature, and had the peculiar trait of being unwilling to believe anything he was told unless it was satisfactorily explained to him. As Walter Carrington recorded in 1946:

> F.M. said that they could never make anything of him at school. He used to . . . dispute every statement that was held up for his belief. If they then referred him to a book, he would ask how the writer of the book knew it to be true. They used to send him up for thrashings but he still came back for more. He would fight anybody and had a terrible temper. Only his mother really understood him . . .[9]

F.M. went on to say that, from the age of sixteen, he 'had never understood how it was possible to believe anything without first experiencing it'. He had thus been unable to swallow the views of his father, 'who believed quite literally in Heaven and Hell and that anyone not of the Church of England faith was utterly lost'. In this early refusal to take anything on trust, and his belief that all knowledge ought to be based on experience, F.M. later claimed to see the beginnings of the thinking which would lead to the development of the Alexander Technique.

Given his unusual temperament, F.M. was fortunate in having a teacher who recognised his abilities and understood his needs. Robert Robertson, who became Wynyard's government schoolmaster in 1879 at the age of twenty-five, was a

Scot who had worked as a law clerk in Stirling before emigrating to Tasmania. He eventually excused F.M. from normal attendance in the schoolroom, where his presence was disruptive, and taught him privately in the evenings. F.M. told Carrington that this 'was all the regular schooling he ever got, and in return, he would win all the prizes and awards for the school when called upon to do so'.[10] Robertson became devoted to the boy, whom he took duck-shooting at weekends; and F.M. in turn came to see the schoolmaster as something of a father figure. (Perhaps it was of Robertson that he was thinking when he later spoke of his 'Scottish' background.) From December 1883 to August 1885 – between the ages of fifteen and sixteen and a half – F.M. officially assisted Robertson as a paid pupil-teacher at the school, his ambition being to qualify as a government school-master himself.[11]

The education which F.M. received from Robertson would have concentrated on a few basics – English language and literature, Bible study, elementary mathematics, and the history and geography of the British Empire. It equipped him well enough for his future career as a book-keeper, without cluttering his mind with abstract ideas. Perhaps most importantly, Robertson imbued F.M. with his own love of Shakespeare, and of the lyrical ballads which were so popular with the Victorians. These would remain F.M.'s favourite form of literature: during his school years, he learned by heart the great Shakespearean monologues and much popular verse, and developed a desire to become at least an amateur declaimer of dramatic poetry.

The world in which F.M. was brought up was strongly religious, the dominant faith being a fierce evangelical Protestantism. (To this day, north-western Tasmania has a reputation as the island's 'Bible belt'.) The Alexanders at first followed a 'low' form of Anglicanism (this being the only form of Protestant worship locally on offer), though they enthusiastically embraced Methodism when it reached

Wynyard in the late 1880s.* Although the adult F.M. would claim to have been sceptical about Christianity from boyhood, and described himself as an agnostic, with little time for organised religion, there can be no doubt that he was deeply affected by his Protestant upbringing. Apart from a thorough familiarity with the scriptures, from which he often quoted in everyday speech, it instilled in him a profound belief in individual responsibility, self-discipline, right and wrong, and personal salvation (though he would develop his own conception of how people ought to be 'saved').

Life in Wynyard for F.M. and his growing band of siblings was simple, but not without its recreations. Apart from the farm, with its opportunities for riding and sport, the creek of the River Inglis, with its comings and goings of sea vessels and its facilities for rowing and sailing, was a constant source of interest. On Saturdays (for the sabbath was strictly observed), public entertainments were organised in the form of regattas, cricket matches and above all horse races: everyone in the district was mad about racing, and F.M. acquired an early fascination for it, together with a gambling instinct, which would remain with him all his life. Occasionally, travelling companies of actors and musicians would perform in the assembly hall, or the much larger exhibition hall built in 1884 for agricultural shows: such performances, which generally took the form of music hall or 'variety', with a succession of short numbers, would have been of a fairly amateurish standard, but must nevertheless have been thrilling for F.M., his interest in poetry and drama aroused by Robertson.

In later life, F.M. would claim to have had an idyllic childhood, only marred by the fact that he suffered periodically from violent internal pains, particularly after prolonged physical exercise. He was clearly unsuited to manual labour, and

---

* Between the wars, family dinners at the Kentish home of F.M.'s brother A.R. would usually end with singing from Moody's and Sankey's gospel hymnal, used by Methodists in the 1890s.

to helping his father in his trade, as would normally be expected of an eldest son. His most striking physical attribute was his beautiful hands, with long, bony, well-articulated fingers – some called him 'the boy with old man's hands'. It is perhaps significant that he was left-handed for most physical activities, such as playing cricket, but taught himself to write with his right hand.*

F.M. grew up in a world largely peopled by his own relations. His father had eleven surviving siblings and half-siblings, his mother twelve, and most of these aunts and uncles lived round about, along with several dozen first cousins. As a boy, F.M. also had contact with three relatives of an earlier generation who had come out as convicts – his maternal grandmother, the erstwhile London silver-receiver Maria Davis, now living in Burnie with her second husband, the sea captain Thomas Lewis; and his great-uncles, the former Swing rioter Joseph Alexander and gold-prospector John Alexander, both living in Wynyard. (Joseph was the free-holder of the cottage in which F.M. was brought up, and himself lived next door. He died in 1878 when F.M. was nine; his brother John survived until 1898.) Did these venerable figures ever speak to him of the old days? All one can be reasonably sure of is that, if they did so, they would have stressed that he should always be secretive about his family's origins when he went out into the world.

Another relative was his uncle James Pearce, married to Betsy Alexander's elder sister Jane. During F.M.'s childhood, he was the landlord of one of Wynyard's two inns; but in the early 1880s the Pearces found their business so affected by the temperance movement, to which much of the local population including the John Alexanders adhered, that they moved to the new mining town of Waratah, which had grown

---

* In his book *Man's Supreme Inheritance* (Part One, Chapter VII), F.M. vehemently criticises the practice of encouraging the naturally left-handed to write with their right hand.

up to serve the great tin-extracting operation on Mount Bischoff. During the last months of 1885, F.M. went out to stay with them at their hotel there. It must have been an adventure for him, as he had probably not previously travelled further afield than Burnie and Stanley; Waratah was almost fifty miles inland from Burnie, connected to it by a steep mountain railway which had been opened to the public just a few months earlier, the journey taking three and a half hours. It happened that the accountant of the mining company, Frank Horne, was a permanent resident at the Pearces' hotel; he was impressed with F.M., and offered him a job in his office at a salary of £2 10s. a week – a princely sum for a youth starting work in that world. On his return to Wynyard, F.M. discussed the offer with his parents, who urged him to accept it: the second son, Arthur, would stay at home to help his father in the smithy. Breaking the news to Robertson that he would not after all be following him into his profession was, as F.M. recalled, 'one of the hardest things he ever had to do in his life', after which the two men sat in silence for a quarter of an hour.[12]

Thus it was that, around the time of his seventeenth birthday in January 1886, F.M. left his childhood home in Wynyard to live and work in Waratah as an employee of the Mount Bischoff Tin Mining Company. As he writes in his autobiographical essay (which prudently says nothing about either the history of his family or the profession of his father*), 'it was not without deep regret that I finished with the way of life I had so enjoyed up to that time, the close touch with nature ... the outdoor experiences in the pure air in the fields and on the river ... The past had to be a memory that cannot fade, and priority given to the future in the making of a career.'[13]

*   *   *

* In the questionnaire he completed for Ron Brown *c*.1950, F.M. said of his father: 'He was a man of many parts, with a history like my own but in different fields.' He also described his publican Uncle James as a contractor, and his policeman maternal grandfather as a magistrate.

The great tin deposits on Mount Bischoff had been discovered by the eccentric prospector James 'Philosopher' Smith in 1871. Mining began the following year, but was at first hampered by the difficulty of conveying the heavy ore across the mountainous terrain to Burnie, whence it was shipped to Melbourne for smelting and trading. This problem was solved by the introduction of horse-drawn trams in 1875, in which year the German engineer 'Bud' Kayser arrived to manage the mine. The early 1880s saw a massive surge in output, making Mount Bischoff the greatest tin mine in the world. Waratah experienced a similar expansion, its population rising from 874 in 1881 to about 2500 in 1885–6, when the new railway opened and F.M. arrived. It was a bustling mining town where men worked hard and played hard, and must have seemed a great metropolis to a village lad like F.M.; its facilities included six general stores, a bank, a hospital, churches of all denominations, a racecourse, a club known as the Mechanics Institute, and four hotels including the Pearces' at which F.M. resided.

F.M. (as he tells us) was given an early chance to prove himself; for soon after his arrival, his boss Horne fell ill and absented himself from the office for a fortnight. By staying up at night, F.M. managed to do much of his superior's work as well as his own. When Horne returned, so impressed was he by F.M.'s efforts that he made the young man a permanent official of the Company so that he might participate in a bonus which was about to be paid. F.M. was duly invited to the dinner given to celebrate the bonus, at which toasts were drunk in champagne. F.M. protested that he did not touch alcohol, but was prevailed upon by his colleagues to join in the carousing and 'seemed to thrive on the wine'. He turned out to have an excellent head, for in the end it was he who helped others home, and together with such of the other diners as remained standing, he climbed to the top of the mountain and back before going to bed.[14]

He seems to have had a great appetite for work, for within a year he had taken on two other jobs in addition to his normal duties. He secured the post of collector of rates for the local road trust, despite requesting more pay than the other applicants; and he became an agent for the life insurance company recommended by the Company to its employees. In order to secure the collector's job, he was required to 'deposit a bond in the sum of £100', which he was evidently able to do.[15] As an insurance agent, he was entitled to a commission of 1 per cent on premiums, and he later recalled his delight when the head of the Company signed a £2000 policy, and F.M. 'went skipping out of the room' having earned the astronomical sum of £20.[16]

He devoted his leisure to three pursuits – learning the violin, horse racing and amateur dramatics. Though he persevered with the first for several years, little was heard of his violin in later life, when he never showed much interest in music. His equestrian enthusiasms, on the other hand, were always passionate. A great moment occurred at Waratah's end-of-the-year meeting in December 1886, when his horse Estelle, which he had trained himself, beat the favourite by a length and a half; his family came from Wynyard to witness the triumph, which brought F.M., not yet eighteen, a prize of £7 10s.[17] On the thespian front, F.M. became an active member of the local dramatic society, based at the Mechanics Institute which possessed theatrical facilities. There he was able to appear in amateur productions, and meet the actors whose companies came to perform. It was probably at Waratah that he first made the acquaintance of an English-born actor based in Melbourne who would later become his teacher – James Cathcart, formerly of the London company of Charles Keane, son of the great Shakespearean actor Edmund Keane. He also had his first encounter with Robert Young, then a Hobart government clerk who performed as a pianist with the travelling Orpheus Company, and his pretty wife Edith, an aspiring actress: Young was destined to become F.M.'s best friend, Edith eventually to become F.M's wife.

These contacts with actors no doubt intensified F.M.'s longing to see something of the world beyond Tasmania. By the beginning of 1889, after three years at Waratah, he had managed to save £500 – a considerable achievement, seeing that the entire accumulated salary of his original job would not have amounted to so much. A year earlier, the Pearces had sold their hotel in Waratah and moved to Melbourne; and F.M. now decided to leave Tasmania and join them there. When he informed his superiors, they were dismayed; the manager Kayser (so F.M. relates) personally begged him to reconsider his decision, pointing out that his prospects with the Company were excellent whereas he would be unlikely to find a comparable position in the competitive atmosphere of the big city. F.M. 'was in the dilemma in which Launcelot Gobbo found himself when in Shylock's employ', but nevertheless stuck to his plan, desiring 'a wider scope of activity, not only in gaining a livelihood but in the fields of art and education in the fullest sense'.[18]

What do we know of the F.M. who set out into the wide world at the age of twenty? No personal account of him (other than his own) survives from this period, but the main outlines of his personality seem fairly clear. He was proud, independent and industrious, prepared to dedicate himself single-mindedly to the achievement of his goals. He was watchful and observant, generally suspicious of his fellow men, though capable of friendship with those who had won his trust. He was disinclined to believe or accept anything unless he had evidence of it from his own senses. Though sceptical of religion, he had a strong sense of right and wrong. He was quick-witted; he was highly strung; and he was apt to lose his temper, particularly if he felt he was being cheated or unjustly accused. He was periodically in-capacitated by health problems which would prove to be the result of 'poor use'.* He enjoyed the good things of life. He was close to his family (or at least to his mother and siblings), though he had not seen much of them for the past few years and would see even less of them for the next few. He had two recreational interests which amounted to obsessions – for the turf and the stage. He may already have begun to see himself as an actor on the stage of life. Conscious of his limitations, he was anxious to improve himself by acquiring more education, polishing his rough manners, broadening his knowledge of the world. Like many Tasmanians, he was touchy and secretive by nature, particularly regarding his background. He must have had marked feelings of being an outsider – for Australians were the outsiders of the British Empire, Tasmanians were the outsiders of Australia, and those from the north-west of the island were the outsiders of Tasmania. But it was with a sense of adventure and full of hope for the future that he landed in Melbourne in 1889.

---

* The term 'use', the verb 'to use oneself', and their derivatives, as later employed by F.M. in his teaching and writing, refer to the way we operate the machine that is ourselves. He probably found inspiration for both the word and the idea in Shakespeare; e.g.: 'Speak the speech . . . tripplingly on the tongue . . . Nor do not saw the air too much with your hand, thus; but use all gently . . .' (*Hamlet*, Act III, scene ii).

2
Australia
1889–1904

Melbourne in 1889 was the greatest city of the Antipodes. A mere village before the 1850s gold-rush, it had grown to have a population of half a million, larger than Sydney's and several times that of the whole of Tasmania. Its economy had been booming for more than a decade, and there seemed no limit to its future expansion. Its prosperity and optimism were reflected in fine public buildings and amenities, and in the recent staging of elaborate celebrations to commemorate Queen Victoria's Golden Jubilee in 1887 and the centenary of Australia in 1888.

On arrival in this fabled metropolis, F.M. went to live with his uncle and aunt, James and Jane Pearce, in the Hawthorne district.[1] He also resumed contact with his ex-convict grandmother Maria, Jane Pearce's mother, who lived in nearby Camberwell with her second husband Captain Lewis. But it was the example of another kinsman which seems to have inspired him at the outset of his life in Melbourne. His late grandfather Matthias (as he would probably have been told by his still-living great-uncle John) had gone on a spree there after making his fortune in the goldfields forty years earlier; and F.M., armed with the £500 he had saved at Waratah, proceeded to do something of the same, devoting himself (as he tells us) to three months of pleasure as he explored the delights of the city. Undoubtedly the main object of his attention was the local stage: Melbourne offered a great variety of theatre, ranging from classical drama to music hall, largely of a high professional standard and often attracting stars from Britain and America. This must have been an experience for a provincial youth who had been stage-struck from childhood, but had hitherto only witnessed amateur productions and the efforts of travelling companies. F.M. tells us that he also spent much time during those months at concerts and art galleries; and it is reasonable to assume that he enjoyed some of the less cerebral pleasures the city had to offer. Certainly he would soon have got to know the famous local racing scene, probably in the company of friends of his father, who (we are told) came over annually in November to shoe the horses for the Melbourne Cup.

At the end of three months, not much of the £500 presumably remaining, F.M. had to think of earning a living. 'By this time,' he writes in his fragment of autobiography, 'I had come to a well-considered decision to train myself for a career as a reciter and to take a position meanwhile in the office of some company.' Curiously, he proceeds to tell us little about his training for a performing career, and much about his work in a succession of dreary clerical jobs. He answered newspaper advertisements for three posts – with an estate agency, a dairy produce auctioneering firm, and a department store. Having been summoned to interviews, he was offered all three jobs; and he proceeded to take up each of them in turn. He decided first to work for the estate agent, as the hours were the shortest, and 'I was at this time . . . much occupied in the evenings in acting and producing plays for an amateur dramatic club.' But after a fortnight he decided that the agent's methods were dishonest, and resigned. He then took up the post with the auctioneers and remained there for about a year, despite once throwing an inkpot at one of the firm's partners after being unfairly accused of incompetence. But the job increasingly involved night-work, which interfered with F.M.'s thespian activities; and so he approached the department store, which duly employed him as a book-keeper.

And what of his preparations for the stage? We know that, having familiarised himself with the city's theatrical scene, he decided that his vocation was not to be an actor so much as a reciter – that is, a declaimer of poetry and dramatic monologues, either in one-man shows or variety performances. This involved training with experts, and appearing in public competitions as he sought to make his name. We also know that he had two eminent teachers – the English actor James Cathcart (formerly of Keane's Company in London), whom he had probably already met in Tasmania, and the Australian elocutionist Fred Hill (son of T. P. Hill, author of *Hill's Oratorical Trainer*). And we know that he became quite close to both these men; for Cathcart eventually presented him with one of his most treasured possessions, Keane's annotated prompt book for *The School for Scandal*,[2] while Hill invited F.M. to live at his house in South Yarra after the Pearce family returned to Tasmania in 1891 or 1892.

Of F.M.'s adventures as he struggled, working at night, to get his first footholds on the ladder of his chosen profession, we know next to nothing. It was not until he had been in Melbourne for almost three years that we find a mention of him in the city's daily press. On 26 November 1891, *The Age*, reporting a variety performance of amateur talent, noted that 'Mr F. M. Alexander gave a tragic recital with great spirit'.[3] We are told no more. We know, however, that he had been inspired, a few months earlier, by Sarah Bernhardt, widely considered the greatest actress of her day, when she and her French company played in Melbourne in the course of an Australian tour; indeed, he later claimed to have attended every performance in which she had appeared.

When F.M. gave his 'tragic recital' in November 1891, his prospects must have looked bleak. In the course of the previous year or so, Melbourne's long boom had given way to a severe economic depression, exacerbated by a spate of epidemics of typhoid and other diseases. Unemployment and bankruptcies soared, and the city's population dropped by fifty thousand. Moreover, around this time, F.M. experienced a breakdown in his own health. What exactly this amounted to is unclear, but he tells us that 'attacks' of the sort from which he had periodically suffered in the past were growing more frequent, resulting in a general condition of 'lowered vitality' which made it difficult for him to cope with his work at the department store. He was fortunate in that his friends now included the store's manager, who allowed him to reduce his workload, and a local physician, Charles Bage, who seems to have taken a close interest in his case. His condition continued to deteriorate, however, and eventually Bage advised him to leave the disease-ridden city for a healthier environment. Experiencing his usual luck in the matter of jobs, F.M. managed to exchange his position in Melbourne for a similar one with a firm of drapers in the seaside town of Geelong, thirty miles to the west. There, he tells us, he made a 'steady improvement towards health and strength', with the result that, after three months, he felt fit enough to return to Melbourne, where he landed yet another book-keeping job, this time with a firm of tea importers. The chronology of all this is rather vague, but he would seem to have returned to the city sometime in the middle of 1892.

Back in Melbourne, F.M. renewed his efforts to establish himself as a reciter, despite the unfavourable economic conditions of the moment, and the interruption to his training caused by his recent illness. On 14 September 1892, the *Herald* reported that the Dramatic Dialogue Contest of the Victoria Amateur Competitions Association had been won by Mr F. M. Alexander and Miss C. Malmgren with a performance from *Macbeth* which was 'listened to with rapt and silent attention', the winners receiving 'a most enthusiastic ovation . . . continuing even as they walked down the hall after leaving the platform'. We hear of him again in May 1893, when he twice appeared in public – at a poetry recital, and an amateur production of scenes from Shakespeare in which F.M. took the title roles of Hamlet, Othello and Macbeth. Both appearances attracted favourable notices. 'A good voice, wide range of emotional expression, and much dramatic force,' wrote the *Sun* of 13 May, 'should, with careful training, carry their possessor to eminence upon the stage.'[4]

At the recital of May 1893, F.M. treated his audience to a dramatic poem of his own devising entitled *The Dream of Matthias the Burgomaster*, available in printed form for sixpence. (The National Library of Australia possesses a copy with a handwritten dedication by F.M. to James Smith, Melbourne's leading theatre critic.) It is based on *The Bells*, a now forgotten melodrama about a guilt-ridden murderer which had been made famous in England by Henry Irving in the 1870s, and which F.M. had recently seen at Melbourne's Theatre Royal with the well-known actor Walter Bentley in the leading role. Though of no great literary merit, F.M.'s verses have a certain verve, and depict in colourful language the 'anguish and remorse' of the tormented criminal:

> He tried to sleep, but all in vain,
> His eyes were hot and red.
> The vision was before him now,
> It hovered round his bed.
> With trembling frame and haggard face
> He moved about the room,
> For the human blood that he had shed
> Now seemed to seal his doom . . .

The narrative switches to the first person:

> 'The scene's before me day and night
> It racks my tortured brain,
> Whate'er I do, where'er I go,
> I bear the brand of Cain . . .

What shall I do? Where shall I go
To rid me of this sight?
Oh God! Have mercy on my soul,
And give me rest this night!
For now my strength is failing fast,
My end is drawing nigh.
Oh help! The vision's there again!
I die! I die! I die!'

Having written this poem, F.M. seems to have included it in virtually every recital he gave. No doubt it provided scope for his histrionic gifts, and was the sort of thing his audiences liked to hear.[5]

It was probably during the second half of 1892 that there began the chain of experiences which F.M. describes in his most famous piece of writing, the opening chapter 'Evolution of a Technique' in *The Use of the Self* (1932). After his recovery from illness, one symptom which persisted was a hoarseness which afflicted him particularly while reciting. Dr Bage prescribed treatment which seemed to have some effect between recitals; but as soon as F.M. returned to the stage, the hoarseness returned, and it became progressively worse over time, to the point where he could sometimes hardly speak after a performance. Seriously worried by a condition which threatened to wreck his reciting career, F.M. embarked on a laborious process of self-observation with the aid of mirrors, gradually making a series of remarkable discoveries. First, he noticed that, in reciting, and to a lesser extent in ordinary speech, he 'tended to pull back the head, depress the larynx, and suck in breath through the mouth so as to produce a gasping sound'. He found that, if he managed to check the pulling-back, the larynx-depression and breath-sucking ceased; but this discovery was initially of little use, as he continued to pull back automatically as soon as he started to recite. His observations did however make him aware that other habits were associated with the pulling-back, notably a lifting of the chest, a shortening of the stature, and a tensing of the muscles in the legs. He remembered that, in his early reciting days, his teacher James Cathcart had told him to 'take hold of the floor with his feet'; F.M. now realised that, in attempting to put this advice into effect, he had developed the habit of tensing his legs when reciting. Indeed, it became apparent to him that the act of recitation triggered a whole series of habitual responses which adversely affected various aspects of his functioning, in which the pulling-back of the head seemed somehow pivotal.

Alexander had identified the nature of his problem, and in so doing had (arguably) stumbled upon a key discovery in physiology, later to be corroborated by the studies of such eminent scientists as Sherrington, Magnus, Coghill and Dart. But it remained to find some way of dealing with the problem; and in his search for a solution, he was initially frustrated by two factors. First, each undesirable action seemed bound up with other undesirable actions, so that by performing one he performed them all. Secondly, all these actions had become so ingrained that they felt familiar and right, and it was practically impossible to overcome any of them by trying to do something else which invariably felt unfamiliar and wrong. Very gradually, after a further, lengthy process of experiment and observation, F.M. found that the solution lay in seeking to 'inhibit' (that is, refrain from doing) what was wrong rather than 'do' what was right, in relying on 'conscious control' rather than unconscious habit, and in focusing the mind on the 'means whereby' rather than 'the end to be gained'. As practice based on these principles enabled him to overcome his vocal problems, he also became 'free from . . . the respiratory troubles which had beset me from birth', and eventually aware that his discovery was not merely applicable to the voice but to overall functioning and the general well-being of mankind.

The Use of the Self was published some forty years after the first events it describes; F.M. gives no dates and no time-scale, and some who were later associated with his work have surmised that his voyage of discovery may have taken place in a rather less systematic way than he would have us believe.* What is certain is that the process he outlines took place over many years. A pamphlet he published in 1900, almost a decade after he had embarked on that process, suggests that he had still not grasped most of the implications discussed in *The Use of the Self*. Even when he left for England in 1904, he had only worked out his ideas in a crude practical form, and it would take him several more years to develop a language in which to express his discoveries. (As we shall see, the earliest writings in which he clearly describes the procedures which we know today as the Alexander Technique date from 1908; and the term 'primary control', which he uses to describe the vital head–neck relationship, does not seem to have occurred to him before 1924.) It is clear, however, that by the beginning of 1894 – after he had perhaps been experimenting for about eighteen months – he had overcome the problem of his hoarseness to the point where he felt confident enough to take the step for which he had been preparing ever since settling in Melbourne, of giving up his clerical work to devote himself professionally to reciting – or rather, to reciting and teaching. For most of those who embark on a career in the performing arts find themselves obliged to teach aspects of their art in order to make a living; and F.M. already felt that he had something new to impart, a method of his own, even if it was still a conception in its infancy, and he could not then have explained exactly what it was.

F.M. decided to launch his new career with a tour of his native Tasmania, five years after he had left it to live in the

---

* 'The early days were probably very different from the legend – more a matter of cheap handbills and quack claims than the step-by-step scientific enquiry and discovery later suggested by the writings of F.M. and others . . .' (F.M.'s former secretary John Skinner interviewed by Edward Owen, November 1961.)

big city. No doubt he felt confident of a favourable reception there as a local boy. No doubt he also looked forward
to seeing his family again, especially his beloved mother –
for although the sea journey from Melbourne to Northern
Tasmania was an easy one, it is unlikely that F.M., as a busy
office worker who devoted his spare time to dramatic pursuits
and an examination of his own health problems, would have
had much opportunity to return 'down home'.

Those five years had been hard ones for Tasmania, which
had suffered severely from the economic depression. John
Alexander's own financial problems were such that he had
been obliged to sell his beloved racehorses to his brother-in-
law James Pearce. John and his wife had also been trauma-
tised by the death, in March 1893, of their tenth and youngest
child Stanley after a life of seven months spent in pain. (F.M.
would later declare that this tragedy had dispelled his belief
in a beneficent God.) These sombre events drove John to
return to the bottle, which he had forsworn on 'taking the
pledge' in 1879. So the atmosphere in the crowded Alexander
household cannot have been altogether cheerful when F.M.
returned to Wynyard early in 1894. He later claimed that,
during this visit, he had a stormy confrontation with his
father, who expressed horror 'that a son of mine should
become a vagabond and strolling player'.[6] This seems to
have resulted in a permanent rupture; and although F.M.
subsequently gave his father some financial help, it is not
certain that they ever met again.*

Notwithstanding these circumstances, the tour went well.
F.M. made his debut at Wynyard on 21 February, contributing

---

* In 'Evolution of a Technique', F.M. refers to his having mentioned his
recent self-investigations to his father, apparently without much response.
'I can remember at this period discussing with my father the errors in use
which I had noticed both in myself and others, and contending that in
this respect there was no difference between us and the dog or cat. When
he asked me why, I replied, "Because we do not *know* how to use ourselves
any more than the dog or cat *knows*."'

nine out of the twenty items at an entertainment in aid of the local brass band, and followed this with appearances at Burnie, Waratah and other centres in the north of the island. It was 'a fascinating experience', he later wrote, and he 'gained confidence with every performance'. On 10 May he appeared at Launceston, reciting Mark Antony's soliloquy and seven long narrative poems, including his own. His crowning moment came on 29 June, when he gave a recital at Hobart Town Hall in the presence of the Governor. Wherever he performed, F.M. won golden opinions in local newspapers (though they would have been naturally generous to a returning son of the colony, and their standards of comparison cannot have been high). They particularly praised his versatility: he seemed equally at home with the humorous and the tragic. However, the inclusion of such comments as 'the strain on the artist must have been considerable' suggests that F.M., while able to put on a good show, may not entirely have overcome his vocal problems at this stage.

As was the custom, F.M.'s recitations were interspersed with items by local 'supporting artists'. At Hobart, he was supported by Robert Young (1856–1910), a jovial government clerk of Belgian ancestry who performed songs at the piano and comic sketches, and his pretty wife Edith Page (1865–1938), the daughter of a prominent settler family who aspired to become a professional actress. F.M. had already met them when they had performed at Waratah in the 1880s; he now became a close friend of them both. He also befriended the editor of the Hobart daily the *Mercury*, whom he met on the train from Launceston to Hobart. The editor took F.M. to his club to introduce him to various local notables, and was subsequently displeased to learn that his young protégé had declined their invitations. 'These people would do anything for you,' he remonstrated. 'You ought to go about and see more of them.' (Relating this story to Walter Carrington half a century later, F.M., who was not clubbable by nature, admitted that all his life he had taken little advantage of such opportunities.[7])

Meanwhile, he had a living to earn; and following his appearances in Launceston and Hobart, he offered what he called 'elocution lessons' (but which sound more like what today would be called 'voice lessons'), charging a guinea a quarter. His friend the editor, in whose paper he advertised these lessons, invited him to contribute an article on elocution, the first known example of his prose writing for publication.[8] Although the style is stilted, and he relies overmuch on quotation from standard works on the subject, the piece is not without interest. He begins by stating that people tend to associate elocution with the production of an artificial voice, whereas it is in fact about making the best use of one's natural endowments. He writes that his own 'system of voice culture' is not just about 'voice production' – pronunciation and the like – but also 'voice building' – transforming a weak voice into one of full power. This aspect, he adds, should be of particular interest to clergymen and barristers who depend professionally on their voices; and in an echo of his own recent troubles, he claims to be able to help sufferers from the condition known as 'clergyman's throat', as well as stammerers. He concludes loftily that 'the study of elocution necessitates the student becoming familiar with the best literature', and that he himself is 'deeply interested in these arts from the educational point of view', hoping that 'the business side of my life will not crush that enthusiasm'.

F.M. remained in Hobart for some months, teaching and giving further recitals. Then, early in 1895, he set out to tour New Zealand, a friend who had emigrated to that colony having assured him that his talents would be appreciated there. This was the first great test of his abilities, for he was operating on unfamiliar territory, no longer able to count on the indulgence of a home audience. By this time, however, he had evidently both mastered his vocal troubles and perfected his recitation act; for he was received every-where with considerable acclaim. At Christchurch, his performances were sold out days in advance, his audiences calling for encore after encore. At Wellington, such was the demand to hear him that a recital was held at the skating rink, the town's largest public space. At Napier, a court summons for a technical breach of the Sunday observance laws only served to give him useful publicity.* Soon, local promoters were competing to represent him.

On 22 June, F.M. made his debut at Auckland, to rapturous press notices. 'Mr Alexander possesses a splendid voice, remarkable for its resonance, power and sympathy, which he uses with great taste,' reported the *New Zealand Observer*. 'His scholarly style is at once apparent, and the manner in which he sinks his individuality is clever.'[9] As at Hobart, F.M. stayed on in the colonial capital for several months giving voice lessons – for which he now charged from three to five guineas a quarter. Here again, he was conspicuously successful: when he entered his pupils for a reciting competition, they won every prize. It happened that three personalities of international reputation were also performing in Auckland at this time – the actor Walter Bentley, the war correspondent and lecturer Frederic Villiers, and the 'memory expert' Professor Loisette; all were persuaded to take lessons with F.M., and were afterwards willing to testify that they had derived benefit from these. Eventually, even the Mayor and Corporation of Auckland enrolled for lessons; and it was at their invitation that F.M. gave a farewell recital at the City Hall on 20 November, the

---

* Having been persuaded to give a Sunday recital, F.M. did not sell tickets, but instead invited his audience to place contributions in a box. At his subsequent trial, he caused a sensation by revealing that the policeman who had issued the officious summons was the father of a local journalist to whom F.M. had recently refused an interview. The judge fined F.M. five shillings, remarking that the publicity generated by the case must have been worth far more to him.

Mayor presenting him with an illuminated address expressing the gratitude of his pupils, an impressive tribute to the young artist of twenty-six.*

Some who heard F.M. recite in New Zealand urged him to take his art across the Pacific to America. In particular, Loisette assured him that he could make his fortune there, and offered to introduce him to a leading impresario who could promote him. F.M. was sorely tempted – at one point he even announced in the press that he intended to join Loisette in New York the following April – but he finally declined the Professor's offer, for two reasons. First, he had received grim news from Wynyard: the economic difficulties of the Alexander household were getting worse, as was his father's drinking, and his favourite sister Amy, ten years his junior, had been injured in an accident. He wanted to be near at hand to help his family in its hour of crisis. Secondly, for all his success as a reciter, the result of his New Zealand experience was that he had become more interested in teaching than performing. (A factor in this, as he wrote ten years later, was his observation of 'that wonderful people, the Maoris', whose remarkable natural breathing control showed what

* 'On being informed that your stay in our city must shortly come to a conclusion, we your pupils feel that we cannot allow the occasion to pass without an expression of regret at your departure, and of appreciation of the services you have rendered us. Of your mastery of the art to which your life is devoted, and your ability as an instructor, we do not feel it necessary to say anything here. Your gifts in both directions are sure to be speedily recognized in whatever English speaking country you may happen to be located. But we feel, Sir, that the relations between us have been something more than those common between master and pupil. Each one of us has been made to feel that you took a personal interest in our progress, and we feel that we cannot allow you to go from amongst us without some acknowledgment of the tireless energy, the ceaseless care and unwearied patience, with which you have directed our studies of an art which is too generally neglected. In thanking you sincerely and wishing you every success coupled with good health, we can only hope you will never entirely forget those who now subscribe themselves – Your grateful pupils.'

human beings were capable of if they used themselves properly.[10]) With a view to concentrating henceforth on establishing his 'method', he therefore returned to Melbourne at
the end of 1895.

Back in Melbourne, F.M.'s friends told him that he must be
mad to give up his now established reciting career for all the
uncertainty and hardship likely to be involved in teaching
his new method. As always, however, he trusted in his own
judgement, and early in 1896 he rented teaching rooms in
the fashionable Australian Building in Elizabeth Street. He
started to advertise, both in the daily press and through a
pamphlet distributed at a well-known music shop: the
pamphlet was originally given away free, but attracted greater
attention when it was later sold for sixpence – confirming
F.M. in his lifelong belief 'that most people's valuation of
anything is determined by the amount they have to pay
for it'.

It is to this advertising that we owe most of our knowledge of F.M.'s teaching in Australia during the years
1896–1903.[11] Throughout the period, he offered 'to culti-
vate and develop the human voice for speaking and singing'
through what he called his 'full-chest breathing method' and
the eradication of such bad habits as shoulder-raising. He
also claimed to be able to 'cure' throat ailments and stam-
mering.* In the various editions of his pamphlet down the
years, F.M. quoted glowing testimonials from named pupils
and patrons. Making allowance for the fact that these had
evidently been solicited by him, probably with the aid of
inducements such as free lessons, they are impressive, and
show that, from the beginning, his 'method' had results

---

* Later, F.M. would insist that he never cured anyone of anything, and
simply helped people stop doing the harmful things which led to their
troubles. This subtle though important distinction had evidently not yet
occurred to him during those early days, nor would it probably have been
appreciated by most of those who came to him seeking relief.

which went beyond the simple improvement of the voice.
Many of his early pupils were clergymen of various denominations, several of whom testified that F.M.'s lessons had
transformed not just their voices but their general health. As
a Congregationalist minister wrote:

> Breathing, once a difficulty, has now imparted to me a new
> life, enabling me to walk a greater distance with less fatigue.
> So perfect is the general equilibrium and control imparted by
> your method that going up and down stairs, which I once
> dreaded, is now performed with ease.[12]

Several doctors, including F.M.'s old physician Dr Bage,
testified that they had sent him patients with throat or
respiratory ailments, with satisfactory results. Other satis-
fied testimonial-writers included such leading citizens as
William McCulloch, Defence Minister in the Government
of Victoria, William Harrison-Moore, Professor of Law at
Melbourne University, and Thomas Kelly, Prior of the
Carmelites.

Of what did F.M.'s 'method' consist during these early
years? His pamphlet tells us much about the benefits to be
expected from it but little about its technicalities, no doubt
partly because he would have found it difficult to put these
into words, partly because he would not have wished to
give away his discoveries. While it is hard to know anything
for certain, it seems reasonable to assume four things. First,
if we are to place any credence in what F.M. tells us in *The
Use of the Self*, his 'full-chest breathing method' must have
been based on the connection he had discovered between
the head-neck-back relationship and the functioning of the
respiratory system. ('Use affects functioning.') Secondly, it
incorporated the idea of checking harmful habits. Thirdly,
it may already have involved some use of the hands to guide
the pupil in the right directions. And fourthly, F.M. was
constantly developing and refining it, in the light both of

his experiences with his pupils and his continuing examination of himself.

During 1896, the first year of his practice, F.M. was joined in Melbourne by most of his immediate family. First, he invited the brother to whom he was closest, Albert Redden (1874–1949), known as 'A.R.', to come over from Wynyard to train as his assistant. Five years younger than F.M., A.R. was an outstanding horseman, but had been unable to find suitable employment in Tasmania owing to the depression; an intelligent and industrious youth, he quickly grasped the essentials of F.M.'s method.* He was followed by their sister Amy, hoping to find relief in Melbourne from persistent medical problems resulting from the accident she had suffered the previous year. The doctors she saw were able to do little for her, but F.M. gave her lessons which enabled her to overcome her lameness and other disabilities. Once she was fit, she, like A.R., was trained by F.M. in his work. Then, shortly before Christmas, their mother Betsy arrived with three more of her children – Agnes (aged twenty-four), May (aged fifteen) and Beaumont (aged ten). They were accommodated, along with Amy (aged seventeen), in a succession of modest rented premises, while F.M. continued to live separately in lodgings with a Captain and Mrs Sinclair.

None of them ever returned to live in Wynyard. Life was no longer tolerable with the moody and heavy-drinking John Alexander; the economic prospects in the area remained

---

* It is not quite clear how F.M. trained A.R. Frank Pierce Jones, who saw much of A.R. in America before and during the Second World War, wrote that A.R. understood F.M.'s work after only six lessons, following which 'the two brothers experimented on each other and worked out various procedures and instructions which were incorporated into the Technique' (Frank Pierce Jones, *Freedom to Change* (Mouritz, 1997) p. 18). On the other hand, Marjory Barlow, the brothers' niece, records A.R.'s boast that 'F.M. never put his hands on him' (Marjory Barlow in conversation with Trevor Allan Davies, *An Examined Life* (Mornum Time Press, 2002) p. 53).

bleak (the Alexander farm on Table Cape was sold around this time); and F.M., the talented eldest son, was now seen as the breadwinner and head of the family. The wretched John, having been abandoned by his wife and all but two of his eight surviving children,* suffered a further disaster in February 1897 when both his cottage and his smithy were destroyed by fire. F.M. helped him rebuild his life by guaranteeing his overdraft, but otherwise there seems to have been no family reconciliation.

With so many mouths to feed, and family debts to shoulder, F.M. devoted himself single-mindedly to building up his practice. It was not until May 1898 that he gave another recital which received notice in the press, and even this seems to have been conceived mainly as a means of publicising his teaching. He hired a large hall, and advertised 'the first appearance in Melbourne of F. M. Alexander, the versatile actor-reciter, entertainer and natural elocutionist'. He was supported by four other artists – his old teacher James Cathcart, who acted a scene from *The School for Scandal*, and three young women, the actress Edith Tasca-Page, the contralto Lillian Twycross, and the violinist Gertrude Summerhayes. Miss Tasca-Page (as she now called herself for stage purposes) was the wife of F.M.'s Hobart friend Robert Young, and had come to Melbourne with his approval to try to establish herself as an actress. Miss Twycross was also from Hobart, while Miss Summerhayes was the daughter of a well-known local piano teacher and accompanist. As his subsequent career would show, F.M. had a talent for attracting women and inspiring their devotion; and he seems by this time to have got to know Edith intimately, while he employed Lillian Twycross as an assistant in his practice. The show attracted a large audience, and reviews which were favourable

* The two remaining were his second son Arthur (born 1870), who continued to assist him in his trade, and his fourth son Dick (born 1876), who eventually emigrated to New Zealand.

if not as enthusiastic as those he had received in New Zealand three years earlier (possibly he was losing some of his freshness as he approached thirty); it was repeated in the same venue six weeks later, and in July ran for two nights at the City Hall in Adelaide, capital of South Australia.

During the first half of 1899, Robert Young retired from his official job as clerk to the Hobart bench and joined his wife in Melbourne. They moved into a house in South Yarra, and F.M. left his lodgings and went to live with them in what seems to have been something of a *ménage à trois*. (In letters written to F.M. in London five years later, Young refers to the three of them as 'the Happy Family', and wonders 'if your thoughts do not occasionally turn to the lovely little boudoir room you so tastefully furnished at No. 89. True, it was small, but then the oriental style of lamp, the papering on the wall, and the Arab tent style of bed all were suited to your luxurious tastes . . .'[13]) In August and September 1899, the Youngs and F.M. jointly produced an ambitious series of entertainments in Melbourne, running for a season of several weeks and involving a professional director: they were based on the shows popularised in England by the German Reed family, consisting of mixed programmes of music, recitations and dramatic sketches which, being both 'light' and 'clean', appealed to people who did not normally attend the theatre. The first night (according to the weekly *Australasian*) 'succeeded in pleasing a large audience': Young was considered to have 'all the fine qualifications for success in this line of business', while F.M.'s 'recitations, grave and gay' were 'commendable both for what he does and he avoids doing'.[14]

F.M. had now been teaching in Melbourne for almost four years. Although he still represented himself as a voice teacher, it must have been increasingly obvious to him – given the relief he had brought to ailing clergymen, to his suffering sister, and to a range of difficult cases sent to him by doctors, including such conditions as curvature of the spine – that the method he had discovered and was continuing to develop was of more general application. His fame, and the demand for his services, was spreading: he sometimes went off to teach in Bendigo, the principal town of Northern Victoria. Finally, in March 1900, he decided it was time for a change: leaving his Melbourne practice, along with the care of their mother and siblings, in the hands of A.R., he moved to Sydney.

Sydney, the capital of New South Wales, was the oldest city in Australia, and during the depression of the 1890s had largely regained its position as the continent's largest and richest city which it had lost to Melbourne in the 1850s. F.M. set about establishing his practice there much as he had done in Melbourne: he rented a teaching studio in the well-known Equitable Building, and began to advertise in the principal daily, the *Sydney Morning Herald*, as well as through the latest version of his pamphlet with its testimonials of his work in Melbourne. He also had a number of useful introductions from influential Melbournians to prominent Sydneians. His pupils in Sydney eventually included Sir George Reid, Premier of New South Wales, who suffered from loss of voice during election campaigns, and Sir Frederick Darley, formerly Chief Justice of the State* and now its Lieutenant-Governor.

F.M. had only been in Sydney a few months when his career took a significant change of direction, largely owing to his close friendship with Robert and Edith. Edith's ambition was to play a leading lady on the professional stage. Shortly before F.M.'s move, she had managed to secure a part in a Melbourne play; but this did not lead to other things, and in the middle of 1900, the Youngs joined F.M. in Sydney, where during September and October the three of them put on a series of light entertainments similar to

* On 1 January 1901, the Commonwealth of Australia came into existence, and the former 'colonies' (including Tasmania) became 'states' of the new federal dominion.

those they had produced in Melbourne a year earlier. Then, early in 1901, F.M. for the first time advertised lessons in acting, offering his students the prospect of appearing in his own production of *The Merchant of Venice*.* Three perform- ances of this production, 'under the patronage of His Excellency the Lieutenant-Governor', duly took place at Sydney's Theatre Royal at the end of June, F.M. playing Shylock, Edith Portia, and F.M.'s students the other parts. The performances were favourably received – though perhaps there was a touch of irony in some of the press notices, which concentrated their praise on 'the rich and splendid costumes' and the fact that all the players were audible. A few weeks later, in September, F.M. hired another theatre, this time for a fortnight. During the first week, he produced *Hamlet* with his student company – in which, naturally, he took the role of the Prince, and Edith played Ophelia; during the second, they repeated *Merchant*.

At the beginning of 1902, F.M. moved to more spacious teaching premises, and joined forces with a conductor of Central European origin rejoicing in the name of Gustav Slapoffski to advertise the grandiloquently named 'Sydney Dramatic and Operatic Conservatorium': F.M. would teach the drama side (that is, his Shakespeare class), charging his students five guineas a year (more if they wanted to be taught the Delsarte system of mime and gesture), while Slapoffski would train students to be opera singers for six guineas. This much-puffed enterprise, again patronised by the indulgent Lieutenant-Governor, does not seem to have lasted long, for its advertisements ceased after a few months, and F.M. had given up his expensive rooms by September. He did, however, produce *Hamlet* and *The Merchant of Venice* again that year

---

* The idea of a training establishment for actors (as distinct from singers) was fairly novel at this time. London's first modern drama school, the Academy of Dramatic Art, was only founded three years later, its founder, Herbert Beerbohm Tree, showing some interest in F.M.'s earlier efforts in Sydney.

with Edith and his students; this time the company went on tour, playing in no fewer than twenty-nine towns in New South Wales between June and September. Although the audiences were rough and sometimes unpredictable (at their first out-of-town venue, Bathurst, the players faced a riot and had to be rescued by the police), the tour was always remembered by F.M. as one of the most interesting experiences of his life.*

For two years – 1901 and 1902 – F.M. had ceased to regard the private teaching of his 'method' as his main business, and had concentrated on his Shakespeare classes and productions, assisted by Edith.† This brought him satisfaction and some fame, but little fortune – in fact it landed him in debt. What, meanwhile, had become of his teaching practice? In Melbourne it disappeared entirely for a time – for A.R., who was in charge there, enlisted for service in the Boer War in February 1901 and did not return until April 1902. In Sydney, F.M. seems to have continued teaching part of the time, and tried to train Robert Young as his assistant – but although Young began to teach in F.M.'s rooms, he proved to be less interested in F.M.'s method than in the very different (and in fact quite incompatible) Sandow system of muscle-building. And when A.R. returned from South Africa, he too began to show interest in the Sandow system.

Just a decade after its fragile conception, the infant Alexander Technique might have petered out at this point – but for a fortunate encounter. Dr W. J. Stewart McKay

---

* The following year, in July 1903, F.M. organised another, shorter tour, much of the cast being the same as in 1902. And more than thirty years later, he would relive his experience as a Shakespeare producer by putting on both *Merchant* and *Hamlet* at the Old Vic in London with the students of his training class, he again playing the title roles: see Chapter 5.

† F.M. later stressed that he had given his drama students 'special training' in his method, which accounted for the fact that none of them suffered from stage fright when appearing in public for the first time (*Man's Supreme Inheritance*, Chapter VI).

(1866–1948) was thirty-six in 1902, three years F.M.'s senior; after medical studies in London, he had become one of Sydney's leading surgeons, as well as a respected textbook writer. He had already heard about F.M. from colleagues in Melbourne, and after hearing him recite at a concert (possibly one of a series which F.M. gave with the Youngs and Slapoffski in October and November 1902), he arranged to take lessons, with the blunt words, 'If your teaching is sound, I'll make you; but if it's not, I'll break you.'[15] McKay was fascinated by F.M.'s method; he understood (possibly the first to do so) that the Tasmanian had made an important original discovery with implications for the prevention as well as the relief of illness. True to his word, he helped F.M. by sending him patients and recommending him to colleagues. Sharing as they did a love of plain speaking and good living, they soon became friends. Indeed, the debonair doctor seems to have become something of a role model for F.M.: he dressed dapperly, indulged a taste for the best food and wine, ran a small farm which supplied him with fresh produce, and devoted his spare time to racing and the study of 'form' – all of which would eventually be true of F.M.

It may have been due to McKay's influence that, during 1903, F.M.'s advertising underwent a change of emphasis: he now claimed that his 'full-chest breathing method' could deal with 'post-nasal growths' and 'throat and chest troubles', while 'the cultivation of the speaking and singing voice' came third on the list. McKay may also have been responsible for improvements to his method which F.M. is known to have adopted that year, making it more useful from the medical standpoint. Feeling that F.M. should acquire some formal knowledge of medicine, McKay encouraged him to attend classes at his medical school, but without much success: F.M. showed little aptitude for academic learning, and was shocked to observe the poor 'use' of the supposedly distinguished doctors who lectured him.[16] McKay did however succeed in persuading F.M. to write something about his theories, and was instrumental in having his article 'The Prevention and Cure of Consumption' published in Sydney's *Daily Telegraph* in December 1903.[17]

Though somewhat prolix, this article is of interest as the first serious exposition of F.M.'s principles. Despite its title, it is in fact an essay on breathing: at that period, forty years before the introduction of antibiotics, the main treatment for tuberculosis was a regime of total rest combined with the deep breathing of fresh air to increase the oxygen intake; and F.M. argued that what was needed was not so much a visit to an expensive sanatorium, nor 'deep-breathing exercises' of the sort then in vogue (which he would later roundly condemn), but the shedding of a number of common 'harmful habits' which had resulted in 'the decay of the breathing power of mankind'. He summarised these as follows:

a. a strong and apparent contraction of the throat and neck muscles

b. a very distinct depression of the larynx

c. raising the shoulders, thus rendering correct respiration impossible

d. a 'sniffing' sound (in nasal breathing), or a 'gasping' sound (in mouth breathing) accompanies [sic] each inspiration

e. the contraction of the nasal passages

f. a very poor thoracic mobility (vital capacity)

g. a habit of mouth-breathing, with its attendant ills.

F.M. contended that 'our mode of life is responsible for the decay in respiratory power', leading to 'chest and lung weakness' which was 'one of the greatest factors in the predisposition of people to plumonary diseases'. Doctors were not generally qualified to understand this, 'for with rare exceptions they are cursed with the same . . . harmful habits'. On the other hand, he congratulated a number of 'liberal-minded, enthusiastic and practical truth-seekers of the medical profession' who had seen the light and sent him patients to rid them of such habits. F.M. concluded that prevention was better than cure, and that many of the ailments from which people suffered could be avoided if they learned to breathe properly, preferably from an early age. In this connection, he added that 'the book I am publishing early next year will, I hope, give the necessary theoretical and practical assistance required by parents and teachers to enable them to carry out this great work'. Within days of his article appearing, he had started advertising this book, which 'embodied the details' of his 'perfect breathing method', and to which the public were invited to subscribe for ten shillings and sixpence – though in fact no book of F.M.'s was to be published until 1910.

By the time the article was published, McKay was urging him to go to London: only there was he likely to achieve proper recognition for his discovery, and the material success he sought. McKay remained in touch with various distinguished London doctors who had been his teachers or colleagues during his student days, and offered to give F.M. introductions to them, which would both help him establish his practice there and enable him to discuss his ideas with some of the brightest medical minds of the day. The problem was money – F.M. was earning enough to maintain himself in Sydney and his mother and sisters in Melbourne, but had no spare cash to speak of, and was still substantially in debt as a result of the guarantee of his father's overdraft and the cost of his Shakespeare productions. He was pondering this problem towards the end of February 1904, when a bookmaker he met on a tram offered to take a 'double bet' at 150–1 on horses which, so F.M. had heard from A.R., were tipped to win two imminent local races – the Newmarket Handicap and the Australian Cup. Both duly won, and F.M. scooped £750 for a £5 stake. This windfall enabled him to pay his most pressing debts, leave a sum for the maintenance of his female relatives, and buy his sea passage to London, with something left over to get him started there.

*   *   *

So far as is known, few personal records survive of the first decades of F.M.'s life: most of his archives are said to have perished in a fire in the 1960s. By some chance, however, we do have several dozen letters written to him by his mother, A.R. and Robert Young in 1904 and 1905, while he was on the sea journey to England and during his first months there; and these give some interesting insights into his relationships, his circumstances and his work on the eve of his departure from Australia.

The letters from his mother (addressed to 'my darling boy') show that, in his mid-thirties, his relationship with her continued to be intensely close, almost oedipal. 'You said . . . I was a queen. I wish I was for your sake . . . You deserve to be the son of a king.'[18] She feels intensely proud of him, convinced that he can do no wrong and is destined for great things. 'Yes, my face does beam with joy when I hear of your wonderful success, and I know you will be "Sir Frederick" one of these days.' 'It is indeed wonderful what you have accomplished, and to think how you studied it all out for yourself.'[19] 'I always looked forward to your being something out of the ordinary, but you have gratified my wish more than I ever expected.'[20] She is free with advice. 'Dear, do not trust strangers too much, for one never knows. I know you are careful, and that is the right thing to be.'[21] She has strong views on 'the accursed drink', hastening to report that someone they knew in Wynyard has been murdered in a drunken brawl.[22] And despite her happy memories of the bet which enabled F.M. to leave Australia – 'it gave me so much joy to see you get the big win . . . I shall always remember that day, the lucky day of our lives'[23] – she also disapproves of racing: she is relieved to hear from F.M. in London that he has given it up[24] (a very temporary intention), but suspects A.R. of being secretly addicted to it, for although he works hard and earns a good living, he makes only modest contributions to her housekeeping bills. She fears that A.R. may be 'like our old man, a money grubber'[25] (the sole reference in these letters to her husband in Tasmania). She also complains that A.R. is 'too bossy altogether',[26] quarrelling at various times with his brother Beaumont and sister Amy.

It cannot have been pleasant for A.R. to hear his mother (with whom he now lived in Melbourne) constantly praising his eldest brother, while treating him as the errant son. His letters to F.M. ('Dear Fred . . . your affectionate and everloving bro Ab') are friendly and fraternal for the most part, but undemonstrative and rather short. He does however explode with anger on discovering that F.M. has been criticising him in letters to their mother. 'You say you have done this or that for me. I know you have, and I have always done whatever was in my power for you . . . a darn sight better than most fellows would have done . . . There's no use my quoting anything else because it only brings bad feeling between us, but I won't be accused of things in mother's letters. Say what you like to me and I will answer you, but don't treat me like a child . . .'[27] In March 1905, A.R. surprises everybody: it turns out that he has been saving money in order to move the family to a beautiful house on the outskirts of Melbourne, set in three acres of grounds.

All three correspondents are filled with a certain awe at F.M.'s making the journey to the old country – his mother (who has of course never been there) calls it 'home'. ('How I have longed for you to go home and make your mark in the world.'[28]) And they all ask themselves whether, one day, they may be joining him there. He has promised his mother and sisters that he will arrange for them to come over as soon as he has established himself.[29] On the other hand, he advises A.R. against coming, provoking the rejoinder: 'You say if I came to London I would have nothing to do. When I come to London it will be for a trip and I won't want anything to do . . .'[30] As for Robert Young ('Dear F.M. . . . yours affectionately, Bobba'), he is already a sick man in his late forties, and wonders if he will ever see his best friend again. 'I feel in a great way the separation which has had to come about . . . the association between us having been of such a binding nature and our thoughts in so many things being as one, our tastes alike . . .'[31]

One person, however, who follows F.M. to England almost immediately is Edith: as soon as she hears of his arrival there (June 1904), she sails by the next boat. What is one to make of this? Before her departure, Edith tells F.M.'s mother (as Betsy writes to her son) that 'she would not have gone only you made her promise . . . She said you would not leave Australian shores until she promised.'[32] Robert's letters, however, suggest that he has encouraged her in the idea of going after F.M., who regards the prospect with mixed feelings. 'Take care of the Little Lady, and no matter how angry you get at times, be forbearing always as you promised me.'[33] Indeed, it seems clear that F.M. and Edith have been conducting a longstanding intimacy with the acquiescence of Robert, who has made F.M. promise not just to 'take care' of his wife in London, but to be faithful to her there. 'I would give all I have to see bright and happy days come to Little Did [Edith] and yourself . . . Always be true, dear F.M. So far as domesticity is concerned, you have all you could wish for . . . Remember that I feel a sacred trust in you, and my last hours will be easy if I feel that you will never cause anyone regret or yourself bitter remorse by drifting ever so little or changing, no matter how old one or the other may look in years to come . . .'[34]

The letters reveal two things about the circumstances under which F.M. left Australia. First, he was not in the best of health. 'I felt so anxious about you when you left,' writes his mother, 'you looked so thin and ill.'[35] She makes him promise to rest during the two-month journey,* so as to arrive in England looking and feeling well. Secondly, although

---

* His ship took the 'long' route round the Cape of Good Hope, rather than the 'short' route through the Suez Canal.

some of his creditors may have been paid out of his racing windfall, others remained unsatisfied, including his landlord in Sydney, the *Sydney Morning Herald* (with whom he was in arrears for his advertising), and the makers of the costumes for his Shakespeare productions. (To these had now been added all those who had sent ten shillings and sixpence for the phantom book.) So fearful was F.M. that these creditors would prevent him from sailing that he left Australia in some secrecy; and lest they pursue him across the world, he continued to behave secretively on his arrival in London, refraining from advertising there for some months. (The debts were eventually dealt with by Robert and A.R., who settled some of them, while persuading other creditors that F.M.'s prospects were excellent and they would do well to wait.)

And what of F.M.'s work? He still has some hankering after the theatre, for his mother writes apprehensively: 'I am delighted that you made such an impression with your Shakespearean work . . . but do not go in for that, it will only get you into debt as you were over here. Go on with your own clever and wonderful methods* and you will make a fortune and God will bless you.'[36] All three correspondents refer to the improvements F.M. has recently made to his teaching for 'treating medical cases'. F.M.'s former assistant Lillian Twycross, still working in his former Melbourne chambers as a singing teacher, feels upset that he did not see fit to impart these to her before his departure.†[37] He has, however, imparted them to A.R., who has mastered them ('they tell me I'm quite a "don" at describing the methods'[38]), and to Robert, who has not yet got the hang of them but will eventually do so with A.R.'s help. A.R.

---

* In these letters, they are generally referred to in the plural.
† Indeed, Lillian behaves like a woman scorned. She is 'jealous and bitter', assuring F.M.'s mother that he will be a failure in London, and soon return (10 June 1904). And she is furious with A.R. and Amy 'because they have your new methods and will not tell her' (23 October 1904).

and Robert, until recently interested in the rival Sandow
system, are now dedicated to keeping alive F.M.'s work in
Australia – though they look upon it more as a business
enterprise than a scientific endeavour, and are always ready
to combine it with other treatments and methods which
promise to bring in the customers.* Robert also keeps in
touch with McKay, 'a card and a real good sort', who
continues to advise F.M. from afar. 'McKay . . . [says] on
no account are you to pull a long face and frighten the
b——y inside out of a patient by telling him he is terribly
bad . . . Rather adopt the method of saying, "Well, your
case is pretty severe, but not so bad that we cannot cope
with it." Mac says he has known several instances where
you have frightened people from coming to you, and if you
do that in London it will be an awful pity . . .'[39]

Having said goodbye to his mother, his two brothers and his
three sisters, F.M. sailed from Melbourne on the *Afric* of the
White Star Line on 19 April 1904. To his surprise, it stopped
at Hobart, giving him a last glimpse of his native Tasmania.
He was never to see Australia again.

* For example, A.R. writes to F.M. (10 October 1904) that 'a chap came
to my rooms the other day with a machine for vibrating. It is worked by
electric current and the effect is like massage only better. It can be worked
with your clothes on and I think it would be splendid in connection with
our breathing [*sic*] for asthma and chronic bronchitis . . .'

3

London

1904–1914

When F.M. landed there aboard HMS *Afric* on 13 June 1904, London was not just the capital of the British Empire but the greatest city in the world. Almost one quarter of the earth's land surface and population was ruled from Whitehall, while the Royal Navy held undisputed sway over the seas. Britain was the leading commercial nation, the 'City' the world's principal financial centre, the pound sterling the global currency for trade. Much magnificent architecture bore witness to this wealth and imperial splendour (though large areas of the metropolis, with its huge population of six million, remained squalid and overcrowded). In numerous fields of science and industry, the arts, letters and ideas, Britain, the cradle of the Industrial Revolution, still led the world. She had recovered from the shock of the Boer War, when her painful victory had dented the myth of her invincibility, and radiated confidence under the shrewd and jovial King Edward VII. The Kaiser's Germany was perceived as a rival (Britain had just come to terms with her traditional rival, France, in the *entente cordiale*), but few imagined this rivalry would lead to war. A long period of Conservative government was drawing to a close, its patrician flavour illustrated by the fact that the Prime Minister, Arthur Balfour, had succeeded his uncle, Lord Salisbury, to the office in 1902. The burning political question of the day was whether Britain should continue her traditional policy of Free Trade or levy tariffs on imports from outside the Empire – a debate which would soon tear apart the Conservative Party and usher in a decade of reforming Liberal government in 1905.*

It was the second time in his life that F.M. had arrived by sea in the city of his dreams. But Melbourne in 1889, a colonial capital less than half a century old, was not to be compared to London; and the circumstances of his arrival were very different. Then he had been a youth of twenty, just a few days' journey from home, free of obligations, with £500 in his pocket, able to call on friends and relations for advice and assistance. Now he was thirty-five; he had crossed to the other side of the world; he had left behind a mass of debts; and he knew virtually no one. Then, while hoping for an eventual career on the stage, he had no immediate ambitions, no sense of urgency, and proceeded to dissipate his capital on three months of pleasure. Now, his aims could not have been clearer or more specific; he had to husband his limited resources; and he had not a day to lose, for he had to start establishing a reputation and earning a living almost immediately if he was not to go down to disaster.

And succeed he did. By the end of June, he had found just the mentor to give him the help he needed. Within a few months, his practice was a going concern. Within a couple of years, he had as many pupils as he could handle, and had won the support of some famous men. By October 1910, when he published his first book, *Man's Supreme Inheritance*, he was something of a celebrity himself, leading the life of a top professional man.

Clearly, the six years between F.M.'s arrival in London and the appearance of his book were crucial to his career; and it is unfortunate that our sources of information about them are so meagre. We have half a dozen pamphlets he

---

* In *Man's Supreme Inheritance* (Part One, Chapter VI), F.M. cites the opposing viewpoints of Free Traders and Protectionists as examples of 'rigid habits of mind'.

published during those years, a few letters by him and notices
about him which appeared in the press, and one report on
his work from another pen. All that seems to survive by way
of personal records are the letters written *to* him from
Australia by his mother, his brother and Robert Young during
the first of those years, up to the spring of 1905. (His own
side of this correspondence would doubtless be more interesting; but we do not have it.) A certain amount of anec-
dotal information has come down to us, mostly recounted
by F.M. himself in the last twenty years of his life and recorded
by his followers. So far as is known, apart from one brief
mention in a volume of theatrical memoirs, none of the
distinguished people he got to know during those years has
left any account of him. Perhaps future research will reveal
further information: letters may yet be discovered among the
papers of the personages he befriended; an unpublished
memoir covering these years which he is known to have
written around 1930, generally believed to have been lost,
may still turn up. For the present, what follows is the picture
which emerges from such material as there is.

The first thing to be noted is that, arriving in London as a
completely unknown colonial, hoping to make a livelihood
out of his equally unknown discoveries, F.M. needed to
impress those people he managed to meet who were in a
position to help him. Among the assets he was able to bring
to this task were a certain distinction of manner and considerable persuasive charm: the editor of Sydney's *Daily
Telegraph* (who had published his article on breathing)
described him as 'an accomplished man of strong magnetic
power, and very earnest'.[1] These qualities were partly natural
to him, but had also developed through his training and
experience as an actor: although he suffered from a degree
of social insecurity, and had as yet no very clear idea how
either to explain or to propagate his discoveries, his acting
ability enabled him to represent himself as a seasoned man

of the world who knew exactly what he was talking about and where he was going. This inevitably involved an element of impersonation: he concealed his convict ancestry, rough Tasmanian upbringing and lack of formal education to act the part of a 'gentleman'. But he can hardly be blamed for such subterfuge, for it was necessary to make the right impression if he was to succeed in the class-conscious world of Edwardian London: as he later told Walter Carrington, 'In those days, you just couldn't get on here unless you appeared to be the right sort . . .'[2]

This need to impress, to act the part, explains the fact that, despite his financially precarious situation, F.M. did not hesitate, during his first weeks in London, to spend such limited funds as he had* on three things. The first was a wardrobe of fine clothes from a good tailor: he was always to be beautifully dressed in a rather dapper, actorish way (and would continue to dress in the same Edwardian style for the rest of his life). As his mother twice wrote to him that summer, 'What a gentleman they will think you with your nice clothes.'[3] The second was a prestigious address: as in Melbourne and Sydney, he sought to rent the smartest rooms he could afford. By the middle of August, he had moved into the impressive-sounding No. 1 Army & Navy Mansions – an apartment in a solid, redbrick building near Victoria Station, next to the famous Army & Navy Stores. The third was a manservant, for no respectable practitioner could be seen opening his own door to his clients; by the end of 1904 he had engaged one William, who would remain in his service for the next ten years.

The most valuable item in F.M.'s luggage consisted of the letters of recommendation to eminent London doctors which

---

* That is, what remained of his racing win of £750 after settling the most pressing debts of himself and his father, leaving some money for the maintenance of his mother and sisters, and buying his sea passage. At a guess, he would have arrived in London with rather less than the £500 with which he is said to have arrived in Melbourne fifteen years earlier.

he had been given by Stewart McKay and his colleagues; and soon after his arrival, F.M., attired in his 'nice clothes', called to present these letters to their addressees. Inevitably, he experienced disappointments. One famous surgeon of whom he had hopes was W. Arbuthnot Lane (1856–1943) of Guy's Hospital, who had developed new treatments for fractures and digestive disorders; as his writings stressed the connection between faulty respiration and other complaints, he might have been expected to endorse F.M.'s methods. Lane, however, only saw F.M. once, showed no great interest in what he had to say, and merely advised him not to advertise. Another distinguished practitioner and writer of medical textbooks, Dr C. W. Mansell-Moullin (1851–1940), gave him a more friendly hearing, but advised him not to bother with doctors and to take his system directly to the public.[4] However, a very different reception awaited F.M. when, within a fortnight of his arrival in London, he went to see R. H. Scanes Spicer (1856–1925), ear, nose and throat surgeon at St Mary's Hospital, Paddington, to whom he had an introduction from Dr Brady, McKay's ENT colleague in Sydney. In his article of 1903, F.M. had already quoted from writings of Spicer stressing the importance of children being taught to breathe properly. Not only did Spicer show an instant appreciation of F.M.'s ideas, but F.M. with equal quickness noticed faults in Spicer's 'use'; their first meeting soon turned into a 'lesson', which brought Spicer, who suffered from poor health, considerable relief. Having called during the early afternoon at his house in Eaton Square, F.M. was prevailed upon to stay on for tea and supper by the surgeon, who was clearly fascinated by his work. So excited was F.M. by the success of the meeting that he could not restrain himself from firing off an expensive telegram about it to Robert Young.[5]

Here, it seemed, was a man who could do for him in London what McKay had done for him in Sydney – a distinguished supporter who could put work his way, help him develop and publicise his ideas, and introduce him to other

potential helpers. Indeed, not only did Spicer almost immediately start sending F.M. patients to see what he could do
with them, but he enrolled himself, his wife and his children
for further lessons;* and in a speech he gave at a meeting
of the British Medical Association at Oxford in July 1904,
he made observations on the mechanics of nasal breathing
which appear to some extent to have been inspired by his
recent meetings with F.M. Later, F.M. would resent such
unacknowledged 'borrowings'; at the time he was flattered,
and hastened to send Young in Sydney and A.R. in Melbourne
copies of the issue of the *British Medical Journal* reporting
Spicer's speech, along with a letter Spicer had written recommending F.M. and his work. 'Dr Spicer is evidently "the right
man in the right place",' replied Young. 'It is splendid luck
to have [found] such a friend.'[6] However, F.M.'s mother, to
whom he had sent a photograph of Spicer, wrote that 'there
is something in it I do not like . . . It is a clever face and yet
it looks as if it wants to get all it can out of you . . .'[7]

Although F.M. had some other sources of work during his
first year in London – at least one other doctor to whom he
had an introduction, the Harley Street surgeon Percy Jakins,
sent him patients, and by 1905 he was getting pupils directly
through press advertising† and word of mouth – it was Spicer

---

* It was almost certainly to Spicer that F.M. was referring when, in a
pamphlet of January 1906, he described one of his earliest London cases in
the following terms: 'In August 1904, I imparted the method to a well known
medical man, who had thoracic rigidity, was subject to laryngeal attacks and
inclined to corpulence . . . yearly visit to Carlsbad necessary. In 1905 he was
in possession of a mobile thorax . . . weight reduced by 13lb . . . had complete
freedom from laryngeal attacks . . . visit to Carlsbad deemed unnecessary.'
† Such was F.M.'s nervousness about his Australian creditors that it was
not until he had been in London for the best part of a year that he started
to advertise in the press. On 2 April 1905, Young wrote to him: 'I think
things will boom now you have put the advt. All along I said you were
restricted in your operations on account of not being able to advertise . . .'
The advertising does not seem to have lasted long, for F.M. soon had a full
practice. It has not yet been possible to trace any of the advertisements.

who brought him most of his early business, who effectively launched him on his career, and whom he came to regard as his chief mentor and friend. As Young's letters reveal, the two men met frequently for discussions, with the result that F.M. was constantly improving his 'general knowledge with respect to the physiology of the matter'.[8] It was a reciprocal relationship, for F.M. was able to give Spicer invaluable assistance with difficult cases. A striking early example – a patient F.M. received from Spicer in August 1904, referred to in the letters from Australia as 'the bad case' or 'the St Mary's Hospital case' – was a lady in the early stages of tuberculosis, suffering from both laryngitis and breathing difficulties. F.M. recognised that her problems were related to 'an undue depression in the clavicular and lumbar region'; by the end of September, he was able to report some success, and after a few months she 'was in excellent health and in enjoyment of adequate respiratory control and vital capacity'.[9]

Spicer was also responsible for the first press publicity F.M. received in England, which gives further insight into their relationship. Another recent Australian arrival was Violet Elliott, a full-throated contralto who had caused something of a sensation in London with her unusually low range. The *Daily Express* was running a series of articles about her; and on 18 October 1904 their reporter accompanied her when she went to have her throat examined by Spicer in Eaton Square.[10] There she met 'Mr F. M. Alexander, the elocutionist, himself an Australian', who wanted to see 'how she breathed'. Spicer explained that F.M. had 'been working for many years on exactly the same lines as himself with regard to proper breathing'. After observing Miss Elliott sing, F.M. declared: 'I could double your power and do away with all the physical and nervous strain you put upon yourself now.' Having examined her, Spicer concurred, saying that despite her remarkable voice 'she does not know how to breathe yet, or how best to use her extraordinary powers'. For the benefit of the newspaper, F.M. then said a few words about his 'system', which freed the thorax and facilitated natural breathing through the nostrils; he praised the 'perfect breathing' of the Maori, and condemned 'so-called physical culture' systems which developed muscular chests at the expense of thoracic rigidity. With all this Spicer 'entirely agreed', adding that 'the lung and heart troubles, the adenoids, the bronchial complaints, the spinal weaknesses, and the generally defective physique of the population' might largely be avoided by the adoption of proper breathing methods such as F.M.'s.

What is remarkable here is that, less than four months after they had first met, one of the leading specialists in his field was giving unqualified approval to an untrained and unknown practitioner, endorsing his methods and virtually treating him as an equal. Though Spicer is not named in the *Daily Express* article (which refers to him simply as Miss Elliott's throat specialist), there were other occasions that autumn when he was happy to use his name to recommend Alexander and his work – from the Australian letters, for example, we learn that he offered to introduce F.M. both 'at the Royal College [of Surgeons]'[11] and 'to the big [ENT] man in America'.[12] It is also said that Spicer took F.M. to a meeting of the British Medical Association at Sheffield, where he sought leave to admit the Australian to the proceedings and invite him to talk about his work; but the reaction of the assembled doctors was one of shocked refusal.[13] Despite Spicer's support, F.M. already found the medical profession closing ranks against him; and the course of his future relations with Spicer himself was not to run smooth.

Undoubtedly, the greatest thrill for F.M. when he came to live in London was his ability to experience the marvellous theatre the metropolis had to offer, about which he had heard so much in Australia from actors such as Cathcart and Bentley who had once belonged to London companies.

The stage remained his greatest love, and he spent most of his evenings at the theatre, to the envy of Young and A.R. who read his accounts of the wonderful performances he witnessed. Nor did he want just to see and hear the legendary performers of the day; he longed to meet them and demonstrate his work. It was therefore with some excitement that he received a new patient from Spicer in October 1904 in the form of the leading young actress Lily Brayton (1876–1953), who together with her husband, the gargantuan Australian actor and playwright Oscar Asche (1871–1936), had taken over the management of the Adelphi Theatre only the previous month.[14] Miss Brayton was in an anxious state since, shortly before she was due to play Katherine in *The Taming of the Shrew*, she had lost her voice. After four days of lessons with F.M., she got it back. She carried on with her lessons, finding that they improved not just her voice but her general health. As she later wrote to F.M.: 'I think your system simply wonderful. It enables one to do the greatest amount of work without fatigue . . .'[15] By the end of November, F.M. was a regular visitor to the dressing rooms of the Adelphi, where he 'imparted breathing' not just to Miss Brayton but other actors of the company. 'Very seldom does one have such a novel post to fill behind the scenes of a London Theatre,' wrote Young approvingly.[16]

It is difficult to overestimate what this experience must have meant to F.M. For him, the greatest things in life were his work and the stage; and both his mother and Young had expressed fears in their letters that, seduced by the brilliant theatrical life of the imperial capital, he would be sidetracked from his work and seek to resume his acting career with all its hardships and uncertainties.[17] And now he had proved to himself that, by helping actors with their problems and putting them in the best condition to satisfy their professional demands, he could combine these two worlds. Just as Spicer became his ally and sponsor in the medical world, so Lily

Brayton and Oscar Asche* seem to have fulfilled a similar role in the theatrical world: they were in a position to introduce or recommend him to many of the thespian icons of the day, and to spread the word that here was the man to call in the event of voice trouble.

The late Victorian and Edwardian periods marked the heyday of the actor-manager; and in that dual profession (in which the Asches had just established themselves) three great names stood out – Henry Irving (1838–1905) at the Lyceum Theatre, Herbert Beerbohm Tree (1853–1917) at Her Majesty's Theatre, and George Alexander (1858–1918) at the St James's Theatre. (All received knighthoods, the first actors to be so honoured – Irving in 1895, Tree in 1909, Alexander in 1911.) Within a short time of his arrival, F.M. succeeded in meeting all three. In fact, he came to London already armed with an introduction to George Alexander† from some Australian contact: Alexander was the godfather of sophisticated drawing-room comedy, who had produced the plays of Oscar Wilde and Sir Arthur Wing Pinero. 'Hope you get G. Alexander,' wrote A.R. to F.M. on 24 October 1904, 'it would be great if you could fix his throat for him after all the specialists had failed.' Apparently George Alexander did have a lesson with F.M.; but he chose not to repeat the experience, and when presented with his bill, accused him of 'practising extortion'.[18] Clearly there would be no support from that quarter.

Sir Henry Irving was considered the greatest actor of his day; F.M. regarded him as little short of God, and later told

---

* Asche later admitted that, when first told about F.M.'s method, he had 'been more than inclined to scoff', but that he had been completely won over by his wife's rapid restoration to vocal health. He became a racing companion of F.M., and reputedly asked F.M.'s opinion about his proposed new musical *Chu Chin Chow*, destined to become the great stage hit of the First World War. Their common Australian background (Asche had been born to Swedish parents in Queensland) was doubtless a factor in their friendship.

† The coincidence of name meant nothing: he had been born George Alexander Samson.

Walter Carrington that his greatest ambition in life had been to meet him.[19] Irving's greatness lay in his projection of personality, his mastery of mannerisms and his ability to create atmosphere; his voice was penetrating rather than powerful, and in fact somewhat thin and reedy. By the time F.M. arrived in London, he was well past his prime: in recent years he had been shaken by a series of financial disasters, given up management to concentrate on acting, and started suffering from the emphysema which would kill him. Having presumably heard about F.M.'s success at the Adelphi or received a recommendation from the Asches, Irving wrote to him asking to try his services. (The handwriting on the envelope was recognised by F.M.'s servant William, who had an aunt on the stage.[20]) From September 1904 to February 1905, Irving toured the provinces in his final role, Becket in Tennyson's historical play of that name; but after Christmas, suffering from exhaustion, he took an extended break in London and Bournemouth. It seems to have been during this period that he first saw F.M.; for F.M. later published a note he had received from the great man dated 19 January 1905:

> I am sorry that for a time I am obliged to suspend my interesting experience. I am sure your method makes only for good, and I look forward to an opportunity of meeting you again. With all good wishes.[21]

F.M. later claimed that he had 'kept a nightly vigil in the prompt box to ensure Sir Henry used himself properly'.[22] This would presumably have been between April and June 1905, when Irving gave his last London performances, playing Becket at the Drury Lane Theatre. From what F.M. told Carrington, Irving took a considerable liking to F.M. and asked him to stay on in his dressing room after lessons, sometimes talking to him for hours on end, and dispensing wisdom that F.M. remembered for the rest of his life. 'Once I used to send my young people to watch the great artists, but I have given that up now for they only copy their mistakes . . .'[23]

On 2 October 1905, now a desperately sick man, Irving resumed his provincial tour; following a performance of *Becket* at Bradford on the 13th, he collapsed and died. Although F.M. had lost his greatest hero, he had aquired another grateful pupil in the form of Sir Henry's son H. B. Irving (1870–1919), himself a celebrated actor: in February 1906, H.B. wrote to F.M. that 'You have made a new man of me.' While there is little to corroborate the existence of the friendly relationship F.M. claimed briefly to have had with Sir Henry (there is no mention of him in Irving's accessible papers for those months), we must assume that the relationship did exist, for H.B. would have known the truth of the matter, and he never ceased to be a supporter of F.M.: in October 1909, for example, he wrote to the editor of the *Pall Mall Gazette* urging that advantage be taken of an offer made by F.M. 'to give the nation his services in the matter of the physical education of children'.[24]

Before moving to the Adelphi in 1904, the Asches had been members of Beerbohm Tree's company at His Majesty's (where they would take over the management a few years later); so it was inevitable that F.M. should come to the notice of Tree before long. It was Tree's actress daughter Viola (1884–1938) who first became F.M.'s pupil; in a letter of January 1907, she praised his method 'because it entails no effort and is entirely natural' and hoped it would 'be put into general use – in the theatrical world and in all worlds'. On the same day, Tree himself wrote a line to F.M. for him to use in his publicity: 'I have great pleasure in saying that I have received assurances from several members of my profession to the effect that they have benefited most surprisingly from your treatment.'[25] Tree founded London's Academy of Dramatic Art (later RADA) in 1904–5; and while is is not certain that he took lessons himself, he is said to have shown interest in F.M.'s experiences of training actors in Sydney in 1901–3. F.M. also achieved success with two celebrated young actors who were protégés of Tree (as well as friends of the Asches) – Constance Collier (1878–1955) and Matheson Lang (1879–1948). Miss Collier was grateful for his help when she came down during rehearsals with 'a heavy bronchial cold'. (In her later years, she became Hollywood's leading voice coach, and one wonders if she made use of the Alexander Technique.) In his memoirs, Lang describes how he lost his voice playing Hamlet at the Lyceum in 1908 and appealed to F.M., who helped him 'enormously, coming night after night to the theatre to see me safely through the performance'. He adds that they became lifelong friends.[26]

F.M.'s interest in the stage, and ministrations to actors, were not limited to classical theatre. He loved music hall and gave lessons to many performers in that genre, mostly female singers. He also saved the career of the comedian James Welch, a patient of Dr Jakins, after he had collapsed on the opening night of *When Knights Were Bold* at Wyndham's Theatre in 1906. Welch later wrote to F.M. jocularly protesting 'that with the additional inch and a quarter you have put on to my height, and the two and a half inches on my chest, none of my old clothes fit me'.[27]

As with all aspects of F.M.'s life in Edwardian London, one longs to know more about his involvement with the theatrical world. How did he rate the actors and actresses he saw on the stage and taught in their dressing rooms? How well did he get to know them? What was the outcome of his discussions with Tree on the training of actors? How far was he tempted to return to the stage himself? It is significant that, in his attitude to the theatre (as in his approach to dress), F.M. always remained an Edwardian at heart. It was the mannered style of acting associated with Irving and Tree that he loved; he never came to appreciate the more naturalistic style which succeeded it. When he himself mounted student productions of Shakespeare plays at London theatres in the 1930s, featuring himself in the leading roles, critics were struck by the curious old-fashionedness of his interpretations.

* * *

In his Australian article of December 1903, F.M. had expressed his intention of publishing a book during 1904 to 'explain' his method; and arriving in London, he still seems to have planned to produce some such book in the near future. Writing from Sydney, however, Young urged him not to do so until his work had become established, otherwise he risked both giving away his discoveries and having them misunderstood;[28] and he was relieved to hear during the autumn of 1904 that F.M. had given the book up for the time being.[29] Indeed, so busy was he during his first years in London, fostering his contacts and establishing his practice, that the production of a substantial literary work was scarcely a practical possibility. Nevertheless, he clearly yearned to express himself in writing; and during the next five years he wrote a series of pamphlets of varying length and character, along with several letters to the press, in which he attempted to explain his discoveries. These make somewhat arduous reading, for it is notoriously difficult to put the Alexander Technique into words, and F.M., while evidently a persuasive talker, possessed little natural talent as a writer: his style is plodding and repetitious, he tends to make a series of random points rather than develop a case, and he pads out what he has to say with frequent (and sometimes doubtfully relevant) quotations from other writers.* Nevertheless, these articles (now collected by Jean Fischer with an excellent commentary) are important in the life of Alexander and the history of his Technique, for they show how F.M.'s methods and theories developed during these years, and how he gradually evolved a language in which to convey them.

The first pamphlet, entitled *A Respiratory Method*, was in the nature of a circular for advertising purposes, and appeared early in 1905.[30] Like his Australian newspaper

---

* He also had a curious predilection for quoting at length from his own previous writings.

advertising, it is orotund in style and uses the third person. 'In consequence of the success that attended Mr Alexander's efforts in Australia, the members of the medical profession ... urged the founder to introduce his methods in London ... Leading members of the medical profession in London, before whom the method has been demonstrated, consider that it is the *most effective* that has been brought to their attention ...' There follows a long list of claims for the method, which 'restores control over the true thoracic mechanism, prevents "sniffing" and "gasping", ensures perfect dilation of nasal passages, removes all strain in respiration and vocalisation from the region of the throat ...' As in his *Daily Express* interview, F.M. stresses the importance of nasal breathing: he goes so far as to claim that his method 'makes nasal respiration possible at all times and under all reasonable circumstances'. He also quotes from Spicer's Oxford lecture on the subject of nasal breathing (though the passage quoted is so technical that few readers can have had any idea what it meant).

The next pamphlet, *Mr F. Matthias Alexander's New Method of Respiratory and Vocal Re-Education*, appeared in January 1906 and describes some of his successful cases during his first year in London, including the leading doctor (Spicer) relieved of his tendency to colds, the tubercular lady restored to health, and the leading actress (Lily Brayton) cured of her laryngitis.[31] F.M. also describes his success with a 'leading lady vocalist' prostrated by hay fever, two young boys suffering from spinal curvature and bronchial attacks, a titled lady whose progress was 'beyond the most sanguine expectations', and a gentleman who consulted him reluctantly but had to admit to a 'quite remarkable' improvement after four weeks. F.M. goes on to formulate some basic principles of his work, and in so doing first enunciates the idea of 'conscious control': 're-education' is necessary for 'adequate control and development of the respiratory mechanism', and this involves 'conscious employment of the mechanism governing the respiratory act'. He promises another pamphlet shortly to explain this concept further.

The promised sequel appeared later that year under the similar title *Introduction to a New Method of Respiratory Vocal Re-Education.*[32] It begins with a statement indicating how busy F.M. found himself after two years in London. He has hitherto hesitated to write about the details of his method and so 'run the risk of being misunderstood', and has preferred to make those details 'known to doctors by means of personal demonstration'; but 'the impossibility of continuing these demonstrations in consequence of the number of pupils studying under my direction forces me to attempt now this written explanation of my method'. The piece is directed at students of singing. F.M. states that singers are often unaware of breathing defects which make their studies 'a struggle with the impossible', and that the overcoming of these defects is not just a technical problem but involves 'a correct mental attitude'. But yet again, he feels obliged to postpone explanation of such matters. 'In a future work I hope to deal more fully with the scientific aspect of practical respiratory re-education. At present I simply state the great principle to be antagonistic action, perfect employment of which is the forerunner of that control which ensures the correct use of the muscular system of the thorax in its fullest sense as the primary motive power in the respiratory act . . .' F.M. does not elucidate what he means by 'antagonistic action'.* The main significance of this article is that it introduces a new procedure in Alexander's teaching – the

---

* The concept of 'antagonistic action' is well known to modern practitioners of the Alexander Technique, and refers to the 'stretching pull' created as the head goes 'forward and up' and the back 'lengthens and widens'. F.M.'s attempt to explain it, however, in the 1910 edition of *Man's Supreme Inheritance*, was not a great success: 'In the process of *creating* a co-ordination one psycho-physical factor provides a position of rigidity by means of which the moving parts are held to the mode in which their function is carried on. This psycho-physical factor also constitutes a steady and firm condition which enables the Directive Agent of the sphere of

so-called 'whispered "ah"', the acid test of correct breathing. 'The breath control necessary in the whisper tone is much greater than during the use of the ordinary speaking or singing one; consequently the student who is taught from the very beginning of his respiratory re-education to convert the air exhaled into whispered tones . . . will have learnt what should always be one of the simplest forms of vocal effort, but is, in effect, one of the most difficult . . .'

In the next piece, *The Theory and Practice of a New Method of Respiratory Re-Education*, a sixteen-page booklet published in March 1907, price one shilling, F.M. leaves behind the singing voice and returns to general human health.[33] The bad habits which cause inadequate breathing affect the whole 'symmetry of the body', and by impairing circulation and thus elimination they lead to disease. These endemic bad habits can be prevented by the education of infants and eradicated by the 're-education' of adults. However, re-education 'will not prove successful unless the mind of the pupil is thoroughly imbued with the true principles . . . In other words *it is essential to have a proper mental attitude*' so that 'each and every respiratory act is the direct result of volition'. But though he goes into some detail about incorrect use, he again gives no explanation of what he means by 'proper mental attitude', except to say that 'the tendency unduly to expand . . . any part of the thorax . . . is prevented by the detailed personal instruction given in connection with each exercise in its application to the individual defects of the pupil . . .' Scattered through the pamphlet is some new phraseology indicating aspects of F.M.'s developing thought. He writes about 'positions of mechanical

---

consciousness to discriminate the action of the kinaesthetic and motion agents which it must maintain without any interference or discontinuity. The whole condition which thus obtains is herein termed "antagonistic action" . . .' (Included in the Mouritz edition, 1996, as Appendix A(ii).) What this is supposed to mean is anyone's guess, and the passage was dropped from later editions of the book.

advantage'; states that 'anything that makes for good may be rendered harmful in its effects by . . . improper use'; and enunciates the 'chief principle' that 'where the human machinery is concerned Nature does not work in parts, but treats everything as a whole'.

Unusually, this pamphlet was favoured with an unsigned review in one of the principal daily newspapers, the *Morning Post*.[34] This makes the valid point (applicable to all F.M.'s writings up to this time) that 'from start to finish the reader expects a revelation and receives only dark hints', that Alexander says much about the benefits of his method but leaves the reader little the wiser as to the substance of it. 'It leaves the critic wondering whether the victim of his criticism is (1) a quack with a true method which he keeps secret, (2) a quack with a false method which cannot be explained, (3) a genius with a true method which he has not the literary power to make clear, or (4) a genius with a true method which none but a like genius could understand from the printed page, but which is well understood after actual treatment by actors such as Messers Beerbohm Tree, H. B. Irving and Oscar Asche, and by actresses such as Mesdames Lily Brayton, Constance Collier and Viola Tree.' (The point was frequently made down the years that F.M., however valuable his discoveries, had many of the attributes of a quack. Lulie Westfeldt relates that, in America during the First World War, he was known as 'the confidence man who really did have the gold brick'.[35] And Leonard Woolf, who had lessons in 1937 to rid himself of a tremor, wrote in his memoirs: 'I feel sure he [F.M.] had hit upon a very important truth . . . and that his methods could cure a number of disorders . . . What was fascinating about him was that, though fundamentally honest, he was at the same time fundamentally a quack. The quackery was in his mind and came out in the inevitable patter and his claim to have discovered a panacea.'[36] As we shall see, the last decade of F.M.'s life was to be dominated by a libel action which he brought against another writer who had described him as a 'quack'.)

F.M. may have taken the *Morning Post* criticism to heart;* for his next pamphlet, *Why 'Deep Breathing' and Physical Culture Exercises do more Harm than Good* (July 1908), contains for the first time a practical description of his work.[37] He has long believed that 'in our schools and in the Army human beings are actually being developed into deformities by breathing and physical exercises',† and this belief has recently been reinforced by a visit to 'one of the first public schools of England'. All manuals of these exercises instruct the pupil to do four things:

 a. to assume a proper standing position . . .
 b. to draw in a 'deep breath'
 c. to hold the breath for a certain time . . .
 d. to expel the air retained by forcing in some part of the chest or abdominal wall.

The first instruction is wrong because the correct standing position is different for every individual. The notion of drawing in breath is wrong, because this is something which ought to happen naturally. 'As a matter of fact, if one wishes to correct a pupil's errors in breathing, the first thing to do is to tell him *not to breathe*, simply because his mental conception of breathing is sucking in air . . . Tell him, therefore, *not to breathe*, but enable him to obtain those mechanical advantages which give atmospheric pressure its opportunity, *i.e.*, such relaxation of certain parts, tensing the muscles of others, and ordering the head upwards as will cause the spine to

---

* He certainly never forgot it, and seems to have been rather proud of it. As he wrote to Mungo Douglas on 25 September 1952: 'A rare fine fellow who wrote that, one ready to admit that he couldn't come to grips with the matter . . . I take my hat off to him.'
† F.M. had expressed this belief in a letter to the *Pall Mall Gazette* four months earlier.

assume a more normal position. He will then breathe as perfectly as his condition permits . . .' The third and fourth injunctions place harmful strain on the throat and the chest, and ignore the fact that correct breathing does not require force but happens by itself. Finally, F.M. states for the first time a precept which will become central to his teaching – that the perceptions and sensations of every person needing respiratory and physical re-education are quite unreliable . . .'

This precept lies at the heart of F.M.'s next pamphlet, which appeared in December 1908.[38] Despite its monstrous title, *Re-Education of the Kinaesthetic Systems Concerned with the Development of Robust Physical Well-Being*, it is so much better written than anything else produced by F.M. at this period that one wonders what assistance he may have had with it. It opens with a summary of the whole nature and purpose of his work in two complex sentences:

> By this process of re-education an effective installation is made of the reflex muscular systems involved through the creation of an intelligent directive power on the part of the individual, thus removing a crude and useless *kinaesthesia* [defined by F.M. as 'sensory appreciation of muscular movement'] which must be regarded as either debauched or deformed, and establishing one of valid and unfailing function.
>
> By use [in lessons] of a preliminary and temporary employment of a group of exercises of ideo-motor nature an induction is gradually assured of an automatic sensori-motor activity, by which correct and healthy bodily movements and poses are always certain without further attention on the part of the individual, except such as a very brief daily exercise may demand.

F.M. then sets out clearly the principles underlying his work. As a result of poor co-ordination, 'all conscious effort exerted in attempts at physical action causes, in the great majority of the people of today, such tension of the muscular system concerned as to lead to exaggeration rather than eradication of the defects already present'. A pupil cannot overcome such defects by his own conscious effort because 'he relies upon *his own faulty sensations for guidance* . . .' For progress to be possible, a teacher 'must . . . place the pupil in a position of mechanical advantage, from which the pupil, by the mere mental rehearsal of orders which the teacher will dictate, can *ensure the posture specifically correct for himself* . . .' Such orders must above all be directed to '*the inhibition* of incorrect and unconsciously performed acts*' – hence orders 'concerning what is *not* to be done' must 'precede all positive commands'. The pupil must concentrate his thoughts on the '*means whereby* he is to gain what he requires, and not . . . upon the end sought . . .'

'The inhibition of incorrect and unconsciously performed acts'; concentration on the 'means whereby' rather than 'the end sought' – here at last we have a description of the Alexander Technique in the terms with which we are familiar today. It was some sixteen years since F.M., the young reciter in Melbourne, had started examining himself in mirrors to recover his lost voice. Had the formulation of his method, the process of discovery outlined in *The Use of the Self*, really taken him all that time? Or had he spent those years hesitating to give away his secrets, and struggling to put into satisfactory words what he all along knew and understood? Given his remarkable proven achievements throughout those years, one must incline to the latter view – with the proviso that F.M. was constantly developing and refining his work, and may only gradually have come to realise that what he eventually called 'inhibition', certainly present from the beginning, was in fact the central element.

*   *   *

* This is the first mention of 'inhibition' in Alexander's writings. It must be stressed that he always uses the word to convey the idea of consciously refraining from some activity, never in the 'Freudian' sense implying psychological repression.

What else is known about F.M.'s life in Edwardian London between 1904 and 1910 – his 'beautiful years', as he later liked to call them?[39]

It is clear that, within a short time, he achieved considerable material success. There is no reason to disbelieve his comment in his 1906 booklet that he was so busy with pupils that he no longer had time to demonstrate his work to doctors. And his standard fee during these years was the same as that charged by fashionable Harley Street consultants – four guineas for a consultation lasting up to an hour. As F.M. was a man of laborious days who would have thought nothing of working fifty or more hours a week, this would have given him potential earnings of two hundred guineas a week or more than £10,000 a year – fantastic sums at a time when an annual income of £1000 (the equivalent, taking income tax into account, of about £100,000 today) put one among the highly prosperous. Of course, it is unlikely that F.M.'s actual earnings were ever anything like so high: not everyone would have been charged the full rate; and there would have been periods when the work either fell off (notably from August to October, when the fashionable left town), or F.M. (given his absorbing interest in the stage, the turf, and literary composition) took time off. Also, income tax (then assessed at 5 per cent) had to be paid; his professional expenses (notably the rental of his smart rooms) had to be disbursed; and much of his earnings during these years would presumably have been remitted to Australia for the maintenance of his mother and sisters and the repayment of his many creditors there.

Still, he seems to have had enough left over to enable him to lead a fairly opulent life. We know that he dined regularly at some of London's best restaurants – Rules, Simpson's, the Café Royal – where he would later be remembered as one of their oldest customers. He acquired a taste for, and knowledge of, the best food, wine and cigars. He kept a horse, and engaged in the fashionable pursuit of taking a morning ride in 'the Row',* his riding companion for many years being his pupil the Reverend William Pennyman, rector of the prestigious Grosvenor Chapel in Mayfair. As in Australia, F.M. showed the keenest interest in racing, a pastime which may have accounted for a substantial proportion of his income, becoming familiar with all the principal courses and their fixtures. (His mentor in the racing world was his pupil Hugo Cunliffe-Owen [1870–1947], an engineer who combined a successful business career with being one of England's best-known racehorse trainers.) He also hunted periodically with the Devon and Somerset Staghounds. And he made a point of being properly and indeed beautifully dressed for all these activities, suggesting the expenditure of not a little time and money at a good tailor. (F.M., who adored quoting from *Hamlet*, seems to have taken to heart Polonius' advice to Laertes: 'Costly thy habit as thy purse can buy . . . For the apparel oft proclaims the man.')

How much did he travel? The Australian letters of 1904–5 mention visits to castles to give lessons to aristocratic pupils, though once his practice had become established he expected even the richest and grandest to come to him. Occasionally he went to stay with friends outside London, though he may not have been a universally popular guest as he expressed himself candidly on any subject which aroused his disapproval. There is a story of his staying with the Dean of Christ Church (head of the grandest of the Oxford colleges), and remarking on the 'decadence' of the languid undergraduates; another tells of his visiting an admiral at Portsmouth to inspect a new type of battleship, and observing that the naval ratings in their exercises were unable to 'get length'.[40] F.M. came to love the English countryside and seaside, but did not care for 'abroad'; indeed, travels on the Continent in 1905–6 seem to have put him off the experience for life, and

* Rotten Row, on the south side of Hyde Park.

confirmed his insular prejudices. As he wrote to his former assistant Irene Tasker in 1941:

As the song goes, 'There's always something fishy about the French . . .' I think you know of my impressions of those people when I visited there in 1905/6. I never visited again. Seemed to me to be all wrong. All rotten in fact. Was little more impressed with the Italians on that trip, and the hordes of Germans I ran into in different places I visited served to confirm my earlier opinion of those lowly evolved people.[41]

What was F.M. like to meet in those days? On the one hand, he possessed (as the Sydney newspaper editor put it) 'strong magnetic power'; on the other, his professional manner could be intimidating. McKay had warned him against his tendency to 'frighten the b——y inside out of a patient'; there are stories of his bullying pupils by shouting at them or threatening them in some way if they used themselves badly;* and John Skinner, his secretary during his last years, told Edward Owen that F.M. (at least until suffering his stroke in 1947) had always possessed 'terrific force of personality, dynamism, even ferocity'. (Soon after his death in 1955, Skinner gave lessons to an old lady who had been F.M.'s pupil fifty years earlier, who remembered him as 'terrifying, like no one she had ever met'.[42]) One must remember, however, that F.M. had arrived in London unknown and knowing nobody; he had to make his way in a world of total strangers; and this 'force of personality', with its mixture of charm and brusqueness, was probably what was needed to win friends and get on.

And how friendly was he with his friends? The parting

---

* For example, he is said to have threatened actor pupils – even Irving – with throwing the book at them from the prompt box if they pulled themselves down during performance. (Frank Pierce Jones, *Freedom to Change*, Chapter 3.)

advice he had received from his mother was not to trust strangers: 'I know you are careful, and that is the right thing to be.' All his life, F.M. was an extremely private individual; and this must have been especially the case during his first years in London, when he operated in an unfamiliar world and was anxious that no one should find out much about his background. Although he enjoyed the social company of such associates as Spicer and Asche, he is unlikely to have opened his heart to them: he was acting a part, and could not afford to let the mask slip. Indeed, like many men who are principally interested in their own ideas, F.M. tended to have supporters and disciples rather than intimate friends, and was basically a 'loner'. He always refused to join a club; he was not a party-goer; and it went against the grain for him to join any kind of society or association, or even buy a season ticket to a racecourse. Similarly, despite his simple patriotism, he had little interest in politics: humanity did not interest him *en masse*, only as individuals.

F.M. often felt lonely during his first years in London, and sorely missed his mother and siblings and Robert Young (as he told them in his letters);[43] and it was his declared intention to 'bring them over' after a few years, once he felt financially, professionally and socially secure. Meanwhile, he probably saw only one person who belonged to his old life and with whom, so to speak, he could 'be himself' – and that was Edith Young, who followed him to England, arriving in September 1904. As we have seen, she had been his mistress for some years; and she joined him with the encouragement of her ailing husband, who made F.M. promise both to look after her and 'be true' to her. For F.M., the presence of Edith was not an unmixed blessing. She was uninterested in and even scornful about his work. (When he heard she was joining him, F.M. hoped 'she would be able to take the 10/6* pupils';

---

* That is, ten shillings and sixpence, or half a guinea – presumably F.M.'s minimum rate.

but he was disabused by his mother, who wrote to him that Edith had declared 'she would not teach for she hated the sight of teaching . . .'[44]) On the other hand, she longed to establish herself on the London stage, and F.M. had the unenviable task of helping her find work in that sphere. Although she did manage to get a small part in a chorus soon after her arrival, it cannot have been easy to satisfy her theatrical ambitions, which were much in excess of her slender talent; nor can her vanity have been comforted by the fact that she had once been a beauty, but was now getting on in years. (Four years older than F.M., she reached forty in 1905, and was in indifferent health.) It may be significant that he did not invite her to live with him in Westminster, but found rooms for her in the remote suburb of Streatham, five miles distant: aside from considerations of respectability, he may have been anxious to keep her apart from his everyday London life, and from his new associates before whom she might give away details of his past and origins. Yet for some years she may have been the one person before whom he never had to pretend, with whom he was able to reminisce about his old life and friends in Australia, and who offered him intimate comforts. And F.M. did not forget his vows to his best friend, either during Robert's lifetime or after his untimely death in September 1910, aged fifty-four.

During 1908 and 1909, two things happened which had important implications for F.M. and his work. He received an unexpected accolade from an official quarter. And he had a bitter and unresolved quarrel with his first London friend and patron, Scanes Spicer.

Dr Alexander Leeper (1848–1934) was a distinguished classical scholar who served from 1876 as Principal of Trinity College, Melbourne. He also served on several public bodies of the State of Victoria; and when he took leave in England in 1908, one of these, the Teachers and Schools Registration Board, asked him to compile a report on 'physical culture' in

English schools. In the Report[45] he presented to the Board on
8 March 1909, Leeper began by discussing the roles of games,
military drill and swimming in the English educational system,
and then came to 'breathing exercises and correct voice production', a subject which 'is coming to be recognised alike by
doctors, singing teachers and elecutionists as a prime necessity in physical training'. In this area, Leeper

> should, without hesitation, give the first place to the system
> associated with the name of F. Matthias Alexander, who,
> it will interest the Board to know, is a Victorian by birth
> and education.* He taught in Melbourne for some
> years. He has now settled in London, and has further devel-
> oped, and, as he thinks, perfected his method of what he
> calls respiratory re-education. He has secured very remark-
> able results. It would take too long, and in any case it
> would be difficult merely by oral explanation, to make
> clear to the Board the rationale of his method. More than
> that, I am inclined to think that it is not possible to give
> a really satisfactory scientific elucidation of it. I believe that
> his method is as yet largely empirical, and that there is
> some element of chance in the discoveries on which he has
> lighted.

To satisfy himself, Leeper had not only taken a course of
lessons with F.M. but got in touch with some of the actors
and doctors who recommended him. The actors included
H. B. Irving and Beerbohm Tree, both of whom were loud
in his praise; the doctors included not only Spicer and Jakins
but one of the Royal Physicians, Sir Alfred Fripp, who
admitted that he had been 'much impressed with the good

---

* F.M. was not, of course, a Victorian but a Tasmanian – but he was
generally evasive about his background and may well have claimed to be
a native of Victoria when questioned about his origins.

results I have seen accomplished by Mr Alexander's methods'. In the conclusions of his Report, Leeper recommended 'that what is known as the Alexander method . . . is deserving of the Board's special attention', adding that F.M.'s brother (A.R.) was carrying on his work in Melbourne and would be happy to give a demonstration to the Board.

Leeper is also said to have discussed informally with F.M. the possibility of the latter returning to Australia himself to introduce his work to schools – though one may doubt whether F.M. would seriously have wished to abandon the successful practice and brilliant life he was enjoying in London, even temporarily. In any case, the call never came. Whereas most of Leeper's other recommendations were eventually implemented by the Victorian authorities, his suggestion that Alexander's method be incorporated into the educational system was ignored. This appears to have been at least partly due to opposition from the powerful socialist federal politician Billy Hughes (1862–1952), later Prime Minister of Australia from 1915 to 1923. By a curious irony, Hughes took lessons from F.M. in London in the late 1920s, was impressed by the results, and confessed to F.M. that he may have been instrumental, twenty years earlier, in denying official recognition to his work, which he now believed ought indeed to be taught in all schools.

In his Report, Leeper quotes from a letter he had received from Spicer praising F.M. 'The results, not only in the production of the voice, but also in deportment, appearance, and general health, surpass anything I have hitherto met with . . . The complete scientific explanation of the subject is not yet possible, but the results are in the greatest degree beneficial.' So in 1908, four years after they had met, Spicer continued (with a minor qualification) to support F.M. Not long afterwards, however, an element of mutual disenchantment seems to have entered into their relationship. While one cannot be certain as to the cause, each had doubtless come to feel that his contribution to their 'partnership' was insufficiently appreciated by the other. Spicer evidently believed that F.M., who for all his insights lacked medical knowledge or training, was becoming too big for his boots,* while F.M. was becoming obsessed with the thought that Spicer was 'stealing' his work. At a meeting of the British Medical Association in July 1909, Spicer read a paper entitled 'Some Points in the Mechanics of Respiration', in which he (controversially) argued that faulty breathing might be a contributory cause of throat cancer. He incidentally referred to 'the correct use of the postural and respiratory mechanism', adding that the methods employed to obtain such use were 'too grave to be left in the hands of untrained amateurs and ignorant quacks'. Not surprisingly, F.M. took umbrage; and in a letter to the *Pall Mall Gazette* in October 1909, followed by a pamphlet issued the following month, he suggested that Spicer had not only 'borrowed' his ideas without acknowledgement, but described them wrongly.[46] Spicer made no direct reply; but in another lecture he delivered in January 1910, he again referred to methods such as F.M.'s, this time adding that they ought only to be taught by medical men and not 'exploited by some irregular hypnotists, suggestion healers, physical and vocal trainers *et hoc genus omne*'. Again, F.M. responded with a pamphlet – *A Protest against certain Assumptions contained in a Lecture delivered by Dr R. H. Scanes Spicer, BSc, MD (London)* – accusing him, this time in direct and sarcastic terms, of plagiarism and distortion.[47]

How justified was F.M. in these accusations? On the one hand, Spicer had both benefited from taking lessons with F.M. and learned much from his work; his descriptions of the means to secure correct breathing certainly owe something to

---

* It should be borne in mind that there was much debate at this time, in the medical and also the general press, as to whether doctors ought to associate with unqualified practitioners: in 1911, an anaesthetist was even struck off the Register for assisting the bone-setter Herbert Barker (1869–1950), who would later be knighted for his help to wounded servicemen during the First World War.

F.M.; and he never saw fit to reply to F.M.'s attacks. On the other hand, F.M. did not possess a monopoly of wisdom on the subject; Spicer had (as he had told the *Daily Express* in 1904) 'been working for many years along the same lines' as F.M., and had (as Jean Fischer points out[48]) made a number of independent observations similar to those of F.M.; and his remarks on the mechanics of breathing were couched in terms at once more technical and more hypothetical than anything contained in the writings of F.M. Whatever the merits of F.M.'s case, the trading of accusations appears to have been not so much the cause as the consequence of the breakdown of his relations with Spicer. Spicer's gratuitous swipe at 'untrained amateurs and ignorant quacks', provoked by we do not know exactly what, seems to have been an obvious insult directed at F.M., who was not one to take an insult lying down.

One result of his break with Spicer, the oblique attack on his competence and the belief that he had been plagiarised was that F.M. decided the time had finally come to produce his long-contemplated book. He approached the respected publishing firm of Methuen, who were at first unwilling to associate themselves with the venture, even though F.M. offered to pay the costs of production; but they changed their minds after getting a favourable opinion of his writings from Professor Frank Granger of Nottingham University. At first, F.M. sought the assistance of a professional writer: this was provided by the novelist J. D. Beresford (1873–1947), soon to be famous for his science fiction classic, *The Hampdenshire Wonder* (1911). However, Beresford's contribution to the early chapters caused Alexander to doubt whether he fully understood his ideas, and so he wrote most of the book by himself. Such was his haste to get it into print that it was published in three consecutive parts: a short volume entitled *Man's Supreme Inheritance* appeared in October 1910; forty-eight pages of *Addenda* followed in March 1911; another short volume, *Conscious Control*, came out in October 1912. (The print run was two thousand copies in the case of *Man's Supreme Inheritance*, fewer than a thousand in the case of *Conscious Control*,[49] suggesting that the sales of the former had not been sensational.) In 1918 the three publications were incorporated (with many additions and amendments) into a single volume, entitled *Man's Supreme Inheritance: Conscious Guidance and Control in Relation to Human Evolution in Civilisation*. In his preface to the 1910 volume, F.M. admits that it is 'woefully inadequate', but explains that 'the necessity for a certain urgency has been forced on me' – presumably by the fear that Spicer would continue to 'plunder' his discoveries – 'and I have deemed it wiser to outline my subject at once rather than wait for the time when I shall be ready to publish my larger work'.

It must be said that *Man's Supreme Inheritance* is a deeply flawed book. Despite a certain rhetorical force, it lacks coherence. (In F.M.'s libel case in the 1940s, a former President of the Royal Society would describe it as 'a mass of pretentious verbiage'.) The chapters do not form a logical progression: the first deals with the whole development of mankind from apes to modern times; the second concerns the inadequacy of Edwardian physical culture exercises; the third is supposed to explain what F.M. means by 'the subconscious self', but merely tells us what he does not mean by it. F.M. fails to apply his concept of 'inhibition' to the art of writing, and indulges (as was admittedly not unusual in the literature of the period) in much prolixity and repetition. He also frequently spoils his case by exaggeration, a factor which would be used against him in future controversies. He goes so far as to claim 'that by the application of this principle of conscious control there may in time be evolved a complete mastery over the body, which will result in the elimination of all physical defects';[50] for the present, his method can be guaranteed to treat successfully 'any case of incipient appendicitis'.[51]

A further weakness is that F.M., in an attempt to expand his discoveries into a system of universal philosophy, constantly refers to two concepts which were then extremely fashionable, but of which he possesses a muddled understanding. The first is that of 'evolution', which eventually found its way into the book's subtitle; the Edwardians were fascinated by this concept, discussion of which reached a crescendo in 1909, Charles Darwin's centenary year. However, although on the second page of his book F.M. insists that he is referring to evolution in its Darwinian sense of 'the operation of natural selection', it is obvious that he did not understand the theory of Darwin, whose works he had probably never read, and that he had in fact absorbed the unscientific evolutionary theories of the Victorian popular philosopher Herbert Spencer (1820–1903), who believed that the 'higher races' of man were advancing biologically in tandem with the advance of civilisation. F.M. argues that man is moving towards a new stage of development in which all thoughts and actions will be controlled by conscious reason: whether or not one accepts this, it is difficult to connect it in any way with Darwin's theory. In the course of discussing 'evolution', F.M. also advances other unscientific ideas which were then in vogue but which have since become so discredited as to bring his entire book, in the minds of some people, into disrepute: these include the inheritability of acquired characteristics (including the tendency to criminality or debauchery), the proposition that 'savages' are more closely related in their behaviour to animals than to 'civilised' human beings, and the 'science' of eugenics which advocates the improvement of human stock by racial selection.*[52]

The other concept which F.M. mentions frequently but not always satisfactorily is that of the 'subconscious', which he vaguely defines as comprising those elements of our psychophysical make-up – 'a composite of animal instincts

---

* To be fair, F.M. was in two minds about eugenics: he was 'in sympathy with many of its principles' but could not accept it completely because of his belief that each individual 'is capable of rising to a higher potentiality'. (*Conscious Control*, Chapter II.)

and habits acquired below the plane of reason either by repetition or suggestion'[53] – responsible for all behaviour not
controlled by conscious reason. For F.M., the subconscious
is an enemy which needs to be conquered and kept firmly
in its place; his distinction between our conscious and subconscious selves somewhat resembles the Victorian moralistic
distinction between our 'higher' and 'lower' selves (as in Dr
Jekyll and Mr Hyde), especially as he keeps telling us that
'depravity' and 'debauchery' arise from individuals being
'enslaved' to their subconscious. (Needless to say, he regards
'blacks' and 'savages' as entirely controlled by their subconscious.) Although F.M. is unlikely to have heard at this time
of Freud (and when he eventually did hear about him would
claim to disapprove of him), there is a certain link between
the two theorists in that both view what they call 'the subconscious' as a vehicle for unhealthy 'forces' which, largely unbeknown to us, develop down the years and cause us to go
wrong. F.M. concludes rather oddly that 'when we shall have
reached the state of conscious control in civilisation . . . a
new and correct subconsciousness will become established.'[54]

Notwithstanding these limitations, *Man's Supreme Inheritance* contains much that is original and interesting which can
be read with pleasure and profit today. Aside from the
misguided remarks about 'evolution', F.M.'s basic thesis that
civilisation has produced changes faster than man can adapt
to them is a convincing one, forcefully presented. Although
he never gives a satisfactory definition of 'the subconscious',
he does explain by means of numerous instructive examples
what he means by 'conscious control' and 'inhibition'. He
further develops the description of his method contained in
Re-Education of Kinaesthetic Systems,* explaining that 'in
the performance of any action by conscious guidance and

---

* The original edition of *Man's Supreme Inheritance* reproduced the full
text of this pamphlet, omitted in later editions as most of what was in it
had been re-expressed in *Conscious Control*.

control there are four essential stages'.* A chapter on the
training of children shows that F.M. had devoted much
thought to that subject, on which he had some innovative
ideas. Above all, the book conveys a tremendously positive
message – that man has been blessed with the gift of conscious
reason and that, by applying this to the actions of everyday
life, he has the potential to overcome not only the illnesses
and disabilities which afflict him, but the psychological disorders as well. As F.M. writes in the sentence which provides
the book's title, 'man's supreme inheritance . . . is the complete
control of our [*sic*] own potentialities'.[55]

If sales were initially modest, the book seems to have
attracted some notice. In later editions, F.M. quoted
favourable passages from a dozen reviews (some of them in
rather obscure journals, and some, one suspects, written by
grateful pupils) which appeared on publication of the original volume in 1910:[56] these commend its originality, the
plausibility of its main thesis, and the importance of the
chapter on children, which the *Daily Telegraph* thought
'should be read by all parents'. It also provoked a couple of
long letters to the newspapers (one from a famous theatre
critic), which F.M. reproduced in his *Addenda* along with
his equally lengthy replies. For good or ill, he had placed
himself on the literary map; anyone who wanted to know
about his teaching could satisfy his curiosity by visiting a
library or bookshop, and any pupil who had taken a lesson
could, for a modest extra sum, learn something of the ideas
which underlay the beneficial experience he had undergone.

* * *

* These are: '1. the conception of the movement required; 2. the inhibition of erroneous preconceived ideas which subconsciously suggest the
manner in which the movements . . . should be performed; 3. the new and
conscious mental orders which will set in motion the muscular mechanism
essential to the correct performance of the action; 4. the movements . . .
of the muscles which carry out the mental orders.' (*Conscious Control*,
Chapter III.)

The publication of *Man's Supreme Inheritance* coincided with domestic developments in F.M.'s life. He finally issued the long-promised invitation to his mother in Melbourne to visit him in London. King Edward VII had died in May 1910; and Betsy Alexander, accompanied by F.M.'s favourite sister, the still unmarried Amy, timed her visit to coincide with the coronation of the new sovereign George V in June 1911, sailing on the *Afric*, the same boat by which F.M. had travelled. The emotion of the reunion of mother and son after more than seven years (during which they had remained in constant touch by correspondence) may be imagined; Betsy and Amy were thrilled by everything they saw in London, and by the evident success enjoyed by F.M. An indication of his prosperity is that he accommodated them in his old rooms at Army & Navy Mansions while he moved his own residential and teaching rooms to much smarter rented premises not far away at 16 Ashley Place, a spacious apartment (originally created for the politician Henry Labouchère) consisting of the ground floor and base-ment of a stuccoed terrace house near Westminster Cathedral, with its own impressive street entrance: this would remain his professional headquarters for the rest of his life.*[57]

Up to this point, F.M.'s teaching practice had been a one-man band. However, since (as he put it in the preface to *Man's Supreme Inheritance*) it now exceeded the bounds of his capacity, he offered Amy, who had been A.R.'s assistant in Melbourne, the job of teaching some of his female pupils. (There were many at this time, for F.M.'s work was becoming fashionable among ladies of progressive views: these included the Cambridge-educated Elizabeth Glover and Lucy Silcox, both future headmistresses, and the American Esther

---

* The rent was fixed (until the late 1940s) at £600 a year – a high sum for 1912, though it represented good value when the area became fash-ionable after the First World War.

Lawrence, principal of the Froebel Institute for the training of teachers.) As Amy's teaching proved satisfactory, and neither she nor Betsy had much desire to return to Australia, it seems to have been decided, before the end of 1911, that they should remain permanently in England, where the rest of the family would be invited to join them. A.R., his fiancée Grace Nixon, and the unmarried eldest sister Agnes sailed from Melbourne without delay, arriving in 1912; the remaining sister, May, followed in 1913 with her husband Norman Cleland; and Beaumont, F.M.'s scapegrace youngest brother, turned up on the eve of war in 1914.* The family were thus reunited except for the father John, the second son Arthur who had remained with him in Tasmania, and Dick who had emigrated to New Zealand; although John would survive until 1936, outliving his estranged wife by many years, and practising his blacksmith's calling until the end, the family in London never referred to him as a living person, and Betsy pretended (even to her grandchildren) to be a widow.†[58] F.M.'s bachelor existence thus ended and he took on the role of paterfamilias, responsible in varying degrees for the welfare of his three sisters, his two brothers and his mother – not to mention Edith Young, who had become a genuine widow in September 1910, F.M. taking seriously his vow to the dying Robert that he would continue to look after her.

A.R., who married Grace soon after their arrival, became F.M.'s principal assistant at Ashley Place. Amy also continued to work in the practice until her marriage in 1914 to the prosperous ivory merchant George Mechin, while Agnes (who remained unmarried) looked after her mother and carried on her trade as a dressmaker. F.M. gave

* In 1914, Betsy was sixty-seven, F.M. forty-five, Agnes forty-two, A.R. forty, Amy thirty-five, May thirty-three and Beaumont twenty-eight.
† Later on, Amy would tell her children that the family came from Hobart, where in fact none of them, apart from F.M. during a few months of 1894, had ever lived. (Information from Jackie Evans.)

up the lease at Army & Navy Mansions and moved Betsy and Agnes to a more convenient flat in Ashley Gardens, round the corner from Ashley Place. He resumed his former close relationship with his mother, whom he adored and in whose eyes he could do no wrong; when she seriously injured her hand in an accident involving an Army & Navy Stores van, he worked tirelessly (and ultimately successfully) to restore it to full function.[59] His relations with A.R. were also close – people enjoyed hearing them swap Australian reminiscences in dialect – though inevitably certain tensions developed between them, given that A.R. was a rougher character than F.M., in the position of the less favoured younger son, and required to defer to him as his boss and the founder of the work.

The assistance from A.R. and Amy was much needed, for F.M. was inundated with business during the years 1910–14. Eminent pupils included politicians such as Reginald McKenna (Home Secretary from 1911 to 1915), society figures such as Edith, Viscountess Castlereagh (who as Marchioness of Londonderry would become London's leading political hostess), and churchmen such as John Hay, Bishop of Winchester. Waldorf Astor (1848–1919), an American tycoon who had entered British society and would eventually receive a peerage, was a pupil: he owned the *Pall Mall Gazette*, which probably accounts for the fact that F.M. was always able to get a hearing in that newspaper. New pupils from the theatrical world included the dashing actor-manager Robert Loraine (1876–1935). During these years, F.M. made new advances in his teaching. He later explained to Frank Pierce Jones that, by 1914, he was 'just beginning to find a new way of using his hands in teaching. By applying the inhibitory control . . . to the use of his hands he was learning to make changes to a pupil that were different from ordinary manipulation and postural adjustment.'[60] (It was probably during this period that F.M. perfected the directive orders – 'let the neck be free, to let the head to go forward and up, to let the back lengthen and widen' – with which Alexander pupils are familiar today.*)

It has been noted that F.M. possessed considerable magnetism where women were concerned; and a female pupil of this time was destined to become his most devoted assistant. Ethel Webb (1866–1952) was three years older than F.M. and came from a wealthy Unitarian family, her father being a founding partner of the prestigious London firm of manufacturing and retailing silversmiths, Mappin & Webb. She studied music in Germany, taught piano in New York and hoped to become a concert pianist, an ambition frustrated by health problems including a bad back. After reading *Man's Supreme Inheritance*, she took lessons with F.M., which brought her dramatic relief; she became fascinated by his work, and offered to devote her life to helping him. F.M. responded to her offer, and by 1914 had trained her as a teacher of his Technique, the first outside his own family: she took over from Amy, who gave up teaching on her marriage.

Miss Webb also spread the gospel. Early in 1913, she went to study at the Montessori School in Rome, believing that a connection existed between the teachings of F.M. and Dr Maria Montessori. There she befriended two talented young women – the Girton-educated Irene Tasker (1887–1977), a Birmingham clergyman's daughter, and Margaret Naumburg of New York (1890–1983)[61] – whom she persuaded to read F.M.'s book and to take lessons with him in London later that year, lessons which were again miraculously effective, particularly in the case of Miss Tasker who was relieved of a stoop which had been the bane of her life. Like Miss Webb, both these women announced that they wished to be of service to F.M.; Miss Naumburg offered to help him establish his work in New York, where Miss Webb also possessed good

---

* Most of the phraseology is found for the first time in the pamphlets published by Alexander in 1908.

contacts. As it happened, F.M. had long wanted to visit America; and his thoughts were turning seriously in that direction when the First World War broke out in August 1914.

4

America

1914–1924

On the morning of Monday 3 August 1914, Britain waited anxiously to see whether Germany would invade Belgium, the Kaiser's Government having issued an ultimatum demanding the right to send troops through Belgian territory. One of F.M.'s pupils at the time was Sir Archibald Murray, Chief of the Imperial General Staff. F.M. claimed to have been one of the first non-official persons in London to receive news of the invasion, when Murray's sister telephoned to cancel his lesson. The following day, Britain declared war on Germany.[1]

It was clear that, for the duration of hostilities, there would be a reduction in the normal business of the practice; but this is unlikely to have caused undue concern to F.M. August and September, when 'society' left town, were quiet months anyway; and the general expectation was that the war would be over by Christmas. Indeed, the conflict might have presented him with new opportunities in England, as he had been discussing with Murray the possibility of introducing his Technique into military training.[2] However, for almost twenty years, since the idea had first been proposed to him in New Zealand in 1895, he had dreamed of taking his work to the United States. He had even considered going on there soon after arriving in England in 1904.* He had

* 'It is splendid to get a letter from S[picer] to the big man in America,' wrote A.R. (5 January 1905). However, Young (24 October 1904) urged

aroused the enthusiasm of American pupils such as Waldorf
Astor and Esther Lawrence; and the great American philosopher William James (1848–1910), founder of the science of
psychology, had expressed interest in his work, though had
unfortunately died before lessons could be arranged.[3] After
ten years in London, and the recent discovery of new skills
in his hands, F.M. sought 'fresh fields to conquer'; and
Margaret Naumburg's recent suggestion that he come to
New York had fallen on interested ears. As A.R. and Ethel
Webb seemed capable of running the reduced practice at
Ashley Place on their own, F.M. promptly decided to try his
luck in New York, sailing on 12 September on the Cunard
liner *Lusitania* (destined to be sunk nine months later by a
German submarine).

Before departing, he took a step which may have been in
his mind for some time. Since Robert Young's death in
September 1910, he had accepted responsibility for the welfare
of Edith; and before embarking on a potentially perilous
journey, he felt he should make her his wife. They were
married by special licence at Hanover Square Register Office
on 10 August 1914.[4] As they had already been close friends
for some twenty years, it was an event of domestic rather
than emotional significance. Edith moved into 16 Ashley
Place; but she did not accompany him on his visits to America,
and thus was only to see him intermittently over the next
ten years.†

New York was the financial capital of the world's greatest
industrial power, and vied with London for the title of the
world's largest city. Manhattan, with a resident population

F.M. to 'stick to it IN LONDON, never mind New York . . . Of course I
understand you want "fresh fields to conquer" . . . but that should be here-
after when you can look upon it as a well-earned leisure trip . . .'
† For some reason, F.M. informed Ron Brown in 1950 that he had married
his wife in 1920. (Introductory chapter to 'Alexander and the Doctors'.)

several times what it is today, was one of the most crowded places on earth. Its character owed much to the fact that it was the main original destination of the great numbers of European immigrants who, up to the outbreak of war, had flooded into the United States. With its vibrant economy, its incessant building activity, the bustle of its streets, its receptiveness to new people and ideas, the variety of its immigrant cultures and the dazzling range of distractions which it offered, it may somewhat have reminded F.M. of Melbourne when, twenty-five years earlier, he had arrived there at the height of the boom.

Waratah, Melbourne, Sydney, London, New York . . . Never afraid to face change, F.M. was relaunching his career in a new environment for the fifth time in his life. His circumstances were not as critical as when he had landed in London a decade earlier; for if he failed in New York, he could always return to London, where he now had an established (albeit reduced) practice, the presence of his family,* and money in the bank. On the other hand, he arrived in New York, as he had in London, virtually unknown and friendless: though he probably had a few useful introductions from his American pupils, and Ethel Webb who had lived there in the 1890s, he later told Ron Brown that he had originally known only two people in the city.[5]

One of these was Margaret Naumburg, who had been largely responsible for his coming. The granddaughter of German-Jewish immigrants who had been successful in business, she had received an extraordinary education for a woman of her generation: after undergraduate studies at Vassar, America's smartest ladies' college, she had done postgraduate work at New York's Columbia University under the great

---

* F.M.'s financial responsibilities towards his family had been eased by the recent marriage of his sister Amy to the wealthy George Mechin, who (according to his granddaughter Jackie Evans) helped finance F.M.'s first visit to New York.

philosopher and educationist John Dewey, going on to study with Sidney Webb at the London School of Economics, Dr Montessori in Rome and a professor of psychology at Oxford, as well as with F.M. On her return to New York in 1914, a few months before F.M.'s arrival, she founded an experimental school later known as the Walden School: starting with a small infant class, it went on to become a famous institution with several hundred pupils ranging in age from two to eighteen. It was based on the Montessori principles which stressed 'the development of a child's capacities rather than the accumulation of knowledge'; but it was also a pioneering establishment in other respects. Profoundly interested in psychoanalysis, Margaret eventually insisted that her teachers* both be analysed themselves and apply psychoanalytic methods to their teaching, probably the first time this had been done. The pupils were also encouraged to practise 'free drawing': the art teacher was Margaret's elder sister Florence Cane, and the two of them would subsequently develop the concept of 'art therapy' and devote much of their lives to establishing it as a recognised branch of psychological medicine.[6]

Clearly, Margaret also sought to introduce F.M.'s methods into her teaching, and this was one of her motives in inviting him to New York. When, in 1928, she published a book expounding her ideas on education, *The Child and the World*, she devoted a dozen pages to describing and recommending the Alexander Technique, saluting F.M. by name.[7] F.M. for his part, in the American edition of *Man's Supreme Inheritance* which he compiled in 1917, had things to say about both 'special schools' and 'free drawing' which were

* The school's teaching staff eventually included three men who went on to become internationally famous – the American writer Lewis Mumford, the Dutch historian Hendrik van Loon, and the Swiss composer Ernst Bloch. Of these, at least Mumford (1895–1990) seems to have been familiar with Alexander's work, about which he later wrote (with qualified approval) in a number of books, e.g. *The Conduct of Man* (1952).

less complimentary: 'I must confess that I have been shocked to witness the work that has been going on in these schools,' he bluntly writes, opining that children who are encouraged to 'express themselves freely' with a minimum of supervision are particularly likely to fall into bad habits of use.[8] These remarks (which puzzled Dewey, who wrote that the type of school described by F.M. must be rare indeed[9]), coupled with the fact that Margaret's name is rarely mentioned in connection with F.M. after 1917, suggest that their association (as with so many in his life) did not end harmoniously. That F.M. did however teach a number of Walden School pupils with beneficial results is confirmed by Irene Tasker, who was on the school's staff in 1916–17:[10] whether he merely gave private lessons to those pupils whose parents could afford them, or offered general assistance and advice to Margaret in the running of her school, is unclear.

He certainly owed a debt to Margaret; for she was as good as her word in helping him establish his practice in New York. She found him suitable teaching rooms at the Essex Hotel, and negotiated favourable rates with the management. She lined up two pupils for him to teach as soon as he arrived: these were Arthur M. Reis (1883–1947), a prosperous underwear manufacturer (and future Chairman of New York State Chamber of Commerce); and the brilliant and iconoclastic Yale-educated journalist and novelist Waldo Frank (1889–1967), a close friend of Margaret whom she would marry in December 1916 as the first of his three wives. As a result of F.M.'s success with these well-connected figures, and their recommendation of him to their friends, he soon had a flourishing practice. His early pupils came from many walks of American life (though they could all presumably afford the high fees he is said to have charged*): they included the tobacco tycoons James Duke (1856–1925)

---

* According to John Skinner, F.M.'s secretary in his last years and keeper of his (now missing) archives, F.M., whose pre-war standard rate in London

and his brother Benjamin (1855–1929); the widow and daughter of the railway king Edward Harriman (d. 1909); the dramatist John J. Chapman (1862–1933), married to an Astor relative of F.M.'s London pupil Waldorf; the conservationist Amos Pinchot (1865–1946), founder of the Yale Forestry School and brother of a future Governor of Pennsylvania; and the Yorkshire-born preacher Dr J. H. Jowett (1864–1923), then pastor of New York's Fifth Avenue Presbyterian Church.

By the end of 1914, the practice had swelled to such proportions that F.M. could no longer cope on his own: in particular, he was being asked to give constant teaching to the crippled ten-year-old granddaughter of Andrew Carnegie's partner Schoonmaker.[11] Ethel Webb, who had lived in New York twenty years earlier and had many friends there, came out from London to join him, principally to attend to the needs of the infant heiress. Although recently trained, Ethel proved an accomplished teacher; and when, in May 1915, F.M. returned to England for the summer, she remained in New York to keep the practice going.

As with F.M.'s first years in London, frustratingly little information is readily available about his first years in New York. Few personal records seem to have survived from the period; and (with one notable exception) no account of him seems to have been left by his distinguished clientèle. One feels there is scope here for future research, particularly in one area. During the years 1914–24, Margaret Naumburg and her eventual husband Waldo Frank were prominent in a vibrant group of avant-garde writers, artists and intellectuals

---

was four guineas, charged the equivalent of five guineas (about $25) in New York. He worked furiously hard, sometimes taking sixteen pupils a day. His main expense was the suite of rooms at the Essex Hotel, for which he paid £200 (almost $1000) a month. (Edward Owen's interview with Skinner, 13 November 1961.)

based in Greenwich Village. Several other members of this group, including the essayist Randolph Bourne (1886–1918) and the black writer Jean Toomer (1894–1967), are known to have had lessons with F.M., as a result of which his teachings became widely known within the group and incorporated to some extent into its shared philosophy.* This may have contributed to the fact that, in the mid-1920s, much of the group fell under the influence of the Russian mystic G. I. Gurdjieff (?1866–1949), who preached a philosophy of psychophysical 'awareness' which bore some similarity to F.M.'s theory of 'conscious control'.†[12]

What did F.M. make of America? He certainly saw it as a place which offered great opportunities to himself and his work. In some respects, its 'new world' character and wide open spaces may have reminded him nostalgically of Australia (feelings which were certainly to be generated later in his brother A.R.). However, F.M. was British to the core, and deeply conscious of the differences between Britain and America. In the American edition of *Man's Supreme Inheritance*, he describes the United States as 'a great nation . . . in its early childhood'.[13] Although he seems to have meant this in a positive sense – as if to suggest that the nation's very immaturity rendered it less susceptible to 'rigid habits' and more open to 'conscious control' – he was openly critical of various aspects of the American way of life: he complained to Frank Pierce Jones, for example, that 'Americans . . . would eat anything so long as it was sweet enough and could be consumed in a hurry'.[14] It is probably

---

* A primary source is available in the form of Margaret's letters to Waldo in the Frank Collection at the University of Pennsylvania: these are said to contain references to F.M., though the present writer has unfortunately not had an opportunity to examine them.
† According to Walter Carrington, F.M. did show some interest in the teaching of Gurdjieff and his disciple Ouspensky, though considering it of limited value as they had no practical 'technique'. (He is reported as having expressed much the same views about Jesus Christ.)

too much to suggest, as his niece Marjory Barlow does, that 'he really, really hated America';[15] but he never seems to have felt at home there. It must also be remembered that, until April 1917, Britain was at war with Germany, while the United States remained neutral. F.M. never missed an opportunity to promote the allied cause in America;[16] and it must have galled him that many of those he taught (including most of the Greenwich Village group) were resolutely opposed to American involvement in the conflict.

In 1914 and 1915, F.M. established a pattern which he would follow until 1924. After wintering in New York until April or May, he spent the summer in England, returning to America in September or October. In New York, he worked furiously hard and earned large sums; his English summers were in the nature of holidays, during which he rested and spent some of the fortune he was accumulating. He did some teaching at Ashley Place, where A.R. was now the sole permanent teacher. He also devoted time and money to racing in the company of A.R. and others. (It was probably during the summer of 1915 that, attending a race meeting with Oscar Asche, he was shown the lyrics of the musical comedy *Chu Chin Chow*, destined to captivate London audiences from 1916 to 1921.[17]) His home visits, undertaken at some risk as much allied shipping was being sunk by German submarines,* enabled him to maintain contact with English friends, see his beloved mother and sisters, and experience married life with Edith, who during his long absences devoted her energies to redecorating 16 Ashley Place, using an 'Egyptian' colour scheme in black and ochre which had been fashionable some years earlier.

---

* It is said that F.M. was originally booked on the *Lusitania* for its voyage to England in May 1915, when it was torpedoed off the coast of Ireland with the loss of more than 1000 lives – though for some reason he changed his mind and travelled by another boat. (Patrick Macdonald, *The Alexander Technique as I See It* [Rahula Books, 1989], p. 101.)

Given his difficulties with Edith, he may have welcomed the prospect of spending up to eight months of each year in America as a means of escape from her. However, such occasional correspondence between them as has survived suggests that the relationship (to which distance may have lent enchantment) continued to be affectionate. He addresses her as 'My dear little Loved One'; she calls him 'My dear old worker & toiler'. He is touched by her concern for his safety as he prepares to cross the Atlantic.[18] She misses him, and urges him to 'get rich quick' so he can return to her permanently.[19] Apart from exchanging information about their health and the weather, and discussing English racing results (for which he is avid even in America), the letters are mostly filled with domestic details. Soon after first arriving in America, he complains that his valet has forgotten to pack his silk pyjamas, but put his toothbrushes in the same bag as his shaving brushes so that the former taste of soap.[20] She frets about the shortage of coal and other commodities, and the difficulty of finding servants in wartime. In one letter, she writes of selling their surplus furniture (which fetches good prices owing to wartime shortages), though she is 'keeping a few pieces for our country cottage':[21] this appears to be one of several alluring but distant prospects with which he kept her happy during these years.

The war affected them both deeply, as it did everyone. Although none of F.M.'s close relatives was involved in the fighting, he knew many who were, such as his servant William. Edith was anxious for her Tasmanian nephew Owen Vicary, serving on the Western Front; after he married Gladys ('Jack') Johnson in 1915, Edith had her to stay at Ashley Place. In his letters to Edith from America, F.M. expresses a desperate optimism, assuring her that the war cannot go on much longer, that victory must lie around the corner. Apart from the suffering and deprivation, the war shattered F.M.'s conviction (expressed in *Man's Supreme Inheritance* and shared by most of his Edwardian contemporaries) that humanity was set on an ever-upward path of improvement; as he wrote in

1917, 'this conflict in Europe . . . has shaken our boasted advancement in civilisation to its very roots . . .'[22]

The outstanding event of F.M.'s sojourn in New York in 1915–16 was his meeting with John Dewey (1859–1952).

Dewey was fifty-six at this time, some ten years older than F.M., and already beginning to be regarded not just as America's leading intellectual, but a national sage. The son of a Vermont grocer, he had made his reputation at the University of Chicago before being appointed to Columbia in 1904. Since the death of William James in 1910, he had been the leading exponent of the school of philosophy known as pragmatism: broadly speaking, this taught that thinking and the acquisition of knowledge were practical activities which should be considered in relation to other human experiences, and that ideas of whatever nature should be tested according to scientific principles. Having run a pioneering 'laboratory school' at Chicago, Dewey was also a prolific writer on education, attacking traditional methods and advocating a system of 'learning by doing' which took account of children's needs. He was not one to inhabit an ivory tower, and in an incessant stream of articles he expounded his views on the social and political issues of the day, preaching the need for 'intelligent action' and generally championing the causes of the liberal left. Before 1914, Dewey, brought up during the American Civil War which had devastated his family, had expressed strongly pacifist views; but when the First World War broke out, he argued passionately in favour of the allied cause, a stand which alienated colleagues and students and contributed to a personal crisis in his life.

According to Irene Tasker, one of Margaret Naumburg's original motives in seeking to lure F.M. across the Atlantic had been to introduce him to Dewey, her former postgraduate teacher at Columbia: she saw a link between their teachings, and thought it important for them to meet.[23] F.M. had probably never heard of Dewey until Margaret mentioned him; but once she had done so, he is said to have read and been impressed by one of Dewey's books, even remarking that 'this is the man to introduce my work to America'.[24] During F.M.'s first American winter, no meeting had taken place, Dewey being fully occupied by his teaching and polemics. However, a friend of Ethel Webb from her New York piano teaching days, Mary Potter, had married Wendell T. Bush (1866–1941), a wealthy scholar from Michigan who was now a professorial colleague of Dewey in the philosophy faculty at Columbia; and Ethel persuaded the Bushes to have lessons with F.M. when he returned to America in the autumn of 1915. On their recommendation, Dewey's wife Alice and their younger children then came for lessons.* Finally, during the winter of 1916, Dewey himself met F.M. at a dinner party given by the Bushes, and enlisted as a pupil.

Dewey seems to have been on the verge of a nervous breakdown at this time. His marriage was in difficulties; the European war caused him much moral anguish; and his book *German Philosophy and Politics* (1915) had been savaged by the critics as a work of propaganda masquerading as scholarship. All his life he had suffered from stress-related health problems, notably eye strain, back pains and a stiff neck, and these now became acute. Suffice it to say that, after a course of lessons with F.M., he was (in the words of a female friend who saw him in 1918 for the first time in some years) 'a radically changed person'.[25] Thirty years later, in 1947, Dewey told Frank Pierce Jones about his early experiences with the Alexander Technique.

> He [Dewey] said that he had been taken by it at first because
> it provided a demonstration of the unity of mind and body.

* Alice suffered from depression, though F.M. later told his American publisher that she had 'the keenest mind and shrewdest comprehension . . . of any woman [he had] ever had the privilege of meeting'. (John Macrae to Alice Dewey, 3 October 1921; quoted in Jay Martin, *The Education of John Dewey* (2002), p. 346.)

He thought that the demonstration had struck him more forcibly than it might have struck someone who got the sensory experience easily and quickly, because he was such a slow learner. He had always been physically awkward . . . and performed all actions too quickly and impulsively and without thought. 'Thought' in his case was saved for 'mental' activity, which had always been easy for him . . . It was a revelation to discover that thought could be applied with equal advantage to everyday movements.

The greatest benefit he got from lessons, Dewey said, was the ability to stop and think before acting. Physically, he noted an improvement first in his vision and then in breathing. Before he had lessons, his ribs had been very rigid. Now they had a marked elasticity which doctors still commented on, though he was close to eighty-eight.

Intellectually . . . he found it much easier, after he had studied the Technique, to hold a philosophical position calmly once he had taken it or to change it if new evidence came up warranting a change. He contrasted his own attitude with the rigidity of other academic thinkers who adopt a position early in their careers and then use their intellects to defend it indefinitely.[26]

Another friend of Dewey, Max Eastman, recalled him saying soon after his experience with F.M.: 'I used to shuffle and sag; now I hold myself up.' In his early fifties, Dewey had appeared prematurely aged; in his eighties, he gave an impression of amazing youthfulness, 90 per cent of which he attributed to Alexander.[27]

Apart from the practical benefits which he derived from F.M.'s work, Dewey was also fascinated by it intellectually. It is not possible here to go into much detail about Dewey's philosophy, a vast and fluid body of work which was wide-ranging and ever-changing; but it is easy to see that, both as a pragmatist, seeking to find connections between thought and experience, and an educationist, seeking to find more practical and less 'rigid' ways of teaching the young, there was much in F.M.'s work to interest him profoundly. What appealed to him particularly was that Alexander's theories were constantly being tested and validated by a form of scientific experiment – his lessons with his pupils. In a doctoral thesis written shortly after F.M.'s death, the Canadian scholar E. D. McCormack suggests that, around the time Dewey met F.M., his philosophy was undergoing a transformation, and that the new version of his thinking which emerged shortly afterwards contained a strand which definitely owes something to F.M.[28] Certainly in his book *Human Nature and Conduct*, published in 1922 but based on lectures which he gave in California in the spring of 1918, Dewey devotes some fifteen pages to discussing ideas which appear to be strongly based on those of F.M. (whom he mentions twice by name), explaining that in order to overcome habit one must concentrate on means rather than ends – though Dewey devotes much of this space to a philo-sophical examination of the concepts of 'habit', 'means' and 'ends' which F.M. himself would probably have found incom-prehensible.

In Dewey, F.M. found the most influential supporter he had yet been able to win to his cause. From 1916 to 1924 they met frequently: it is sad indeed that none of their corre-spondence seems to have survived, nor any circumstantial accounts of their meetings and discussions. If F.M. influenced Dewey, how far did Dewey influence F.M.? In F.M.'s future writings, one can often glimpse Dewey's hand. For example, a constant theme of Dewey between 1914 and 1917 was that, although the United States ought to support the Allies in the European war, she needed to guard herself against the evils of militarism; and F.M. repeats this injunction in the American edition of *Man's Supreme Inheritance*.[29] And Dewey clearly influenced the scheme of the famous opening chapter of F.M.'s third book *The Use of the Self* (1932), which is presented in the classic form of a Dewey enquiry. On the whole, however, F.M. was not much of a reader, and his basic teachings cannot be said to owe much to other thinkers* (though he often looked to them for corroboration of, or new ways of presenting, his existing ideas): he was a 'loner' who ploughed his own furrow, and learned (in a way that Dewey would have found admirable) from his own experience.

Whatever may have been Dewey's influence upon F.M., his support was certainly invaluable to the Australian. He rarely missed an opportunity to praise or promote F.M.'s work. His approbation of F.M., and the remarkable results F.M. had achieved with him which were visible for all to see, encouraged other leading New York academics to become pupils, and often enrol their families too: these eventually included the theologian Richard Morse Hodge (1864–1928), the economist Wesley Mitchell (1874–1948), the philosopher Horace Kallen (1882–1974) and the historian James Harvey Robinson (1863–1936). (It is perhaps an indication of the universal application of Alexander's method that his most valued supporters were clergymen in Melbourne, actors in London, and academics in New York.) Dewey also urged F.M. to bring out his book in America, a project to which F.M. was already giving thought when he returned to England in the spring of 1916. In London, *Man's Supreme Inheritance* had enjoyed only modest sales and attention; in New York, it was set to receive the praise of some of the brightest minds of the time.

F.M.'s return to England in 1916 coincided with a frightful phase of the war. Following the costly German failure to break through at Verdun, the Allies launched their own disastrous offensive at the Somme on 1 July, sustaining more than

---

* As Margaret Naumburg wrote to McCormack in 1957: 'I never noticed any interest in Alexander . . . about anyone else's books or ideas' (E. D. McCormack, *Frederick Matthias Alexander and John Dewey: A Neglected Influence* [NASTAT, 1992], footnote p. 46).

half a million casualties for little advantage. F.M. must have been either ill-informed or in a state of 'denial'; for on 18 August he wrote to Waldo Frank in New York: 'I know how pleased you will be to see the Allies moving steadily but surely to decisive victory. It is certain now and within a comparatively short space of time.' The increased British output of munitions was 'like a miracle and serves to prove that the best blood which runs in the veins of the people of the old country and the right good sorts in America is the real A1 article' – possibly not the most tactful remark as Frank (like his future wife Margaret) was the grandchild of German Jews, as well as in two minds about American participation in the war. The main purpose of the letter (one of the earliest written by F.M. which the present writer has come across) was to congratulate Frank on his completion of a novel and his editorship of the new literary journal *Seven Arts*;* he concludes by sending 'best wishes to all our mutual friends'.[30]

Back in New York in the autumn of 1916, F.M., still assisted by Ethel Webb, found himself almost overwhelmed by his burgeoning practice. He was, however, able to recruit another potential teacher of his work in the shape of Irene Tasker, the former fellow student of Ethel Webb and Margaret Naumburg at the Montessori School and F.M.'s grateful London pupil of 1913; having recently accepted an invitation from Margaret to teach at the Walden School,† Irene was so impressed by the help F.M. was able to give some of the schoolchildren in private lessons that she offered to become his apprentice. (Like other women, she had fallen under his 'magnetic' spell.) Although it was some time before she was sufficiently trained to give lessons herself, she gained

---

* This became the mouthpiece of the Greenwich Village Group, but only ran to twelve issues, its financial backers withdrawing their support owing to its opposition to the American declaration of war on Germany.
† Irene had previously been working at a teachers' training college in the North of England which had been forced to close owing to the war.

experience in the meantime by working with children and 'getting them to inhibit in the sense of stopping to think out "means" in whatever they were doing'[31] – a useful preparation for the 'little school' she would later run in England.

Irene also assisted F.M. in his extensive revision of *Man's Supreme Inheritance* for American publication. He made various changes and additions to the existing text:[32] in the chapter on the training of children, for example, he incorporated his dismissive views on progressive education referred to above. He also wrote five new chapters. The most interesting of these applies his theories to addictions and obsessions, suggesting that 'all people whose kinaesthetic systems are debauched and delusive develop some form of perversion or abnormality in sensation', and that addicts and obsessives have no hope of reform until they are 'brought back into communication with their reason' through conscious control.[33] The most controversial of the new chapters is entitled 'Evolutionary Standards and their Influence on the Crisis of 1914'. This amounts to a somewhat crude attack on the Germans:

> That any nation or nations should deliberately adopt, as their highest ideals and aims, brute force in all its hideous aspects, desecration of mind, body and soul for the State, justification of criminal instincts and acts if employed on behalf of the State, destruction, rape and plunder, murder and torture to terrify innocent civilians; that they should adopt, in short, the brutal principle that 'might is right' in that special national form in which it has been manifested in the last half century and directed towards what is now known as 'militarism' – all this is surely proof positive that they have progressed but little on the upward evolutionary stage from the state occupied by the brute beast and the savage.

F.M. portrays Germany as an entire country suffering from faulty use, fixed habits, 'self-hypnotism', lack of conscious control and 'debauched kinaesthesia', her authoritarian system of education and military training, as well as her thoughtless use of industrial machinery, having turned the people into mindless automata. Her rigidity of thought, however, would ensure her ultimate defeat, as 'she has lost the power of adaptability in military matters'.[34]

These words were written when the United States was still neutral; but on 6 April 1917 she declared war on Germany. Two days later, F.M. wrote to Edith:

> Well we are also a warlike people here with the flags flying all over the place and the German plotters are being arrested as fast as they can grab them . . . It will mean a great reunion of America & England, a thing so much to be desired from every point of view. The real people here are Anglo-Saxon like ourselves* & so many of them are really splendid. As a matter of fact the real English never change in character no matter where they may be placed in the world. They carry on the good old traditions all the time . . . Friday fortnight I hope to rush safely across to my darling loved one . . .[35]

He added that he had finally found a New York publisher to bring out the new edition of his book. This was the well-known firm of E. P. Dutton, to which he had been introduced by Dewey: the head of the firm, John Macrae, told F.M. that his readers had rejected it, but that he himself had read it and been interested in it.

When the book appeared in January 1918, it opened with an 'Introductory Word' by Dewey, which singled out three elements of F.M.'s teachings for praise. First, the emphasis on

---

* F.M. seems to have been curiously unaware of the strong German influence on the United States: at one point in the nineteenth century, there were estimated to be more German- than English-speakers in the country. And many of the English-speakers (like F.M. himself) had Irish antecedents.

'balance': 'When the organs through which any structure, be it physiological, mental or social, are out of balance, when they are unco-ordinated, specific and limited attempts at cure only exercise the already disordered mechanism.' Secondly, the paramountcy of intelligence: 'Mr Alexander sees the remedy not in a futile abdication of intelligence in order that lower forces may work, but in carrying the power of intelligence further, in making its function one of positive and constructive control.' Thirdly, the practical and scientific nature of the work. '[He] does not stop with a pious recommendation of such conscious control; he possesses and offers a definite method for its realisation, and even a layman can testify, as I am glad to do, to the efficacy of its working in concrete cases.'

The book's success was assured by a deluge of enthusiastic reviews from F.M.'s distinguished pupils, including Waldo Frank, Dr Jowett, Professor Hodge, Professor Kallen and Dewey himself. The most sensational tribute came from the eminent Columbia historian James Harvey Robinson, author of *The New History* (1911). In a long article published in the prestigious *Atlantic Monthly* in April 1919, Robinson wrote that he had been inspired to read *Man's Supreme Inheritance* by the fact that it had been introduced by Dewey, and had gone on to take lessons with F.M., by whose teaching he had been 'redeemed body and soul'. He was not unconscious of the book's flaws:

> I am not inclined to contend that all his ideas are new, or that this book, which clearly reflects the genial exuberance of its author, might not have been better arranged, or that anyone need accept all the philosophic reflections which accompany the exposition of his system. Nevertheless, no one interested in human improvement can afford to pass by his plan without carefully considering its nature and bearings.

Robinson goes on to give what is probably the earliest circumstantial description of what it was like to have a lesson with F.M.

Mr Alexander . . . is patient and gentle, and with the traditions of an actor, each new audience of one comes to him as a fresh opportunity to explain and illustrate his art. He does not have to undress you, or ask you what is the matter with you . . . Your obviously faulty posture and movements immediately strike his keen, experienced eye . . . He invites no violent exercise – indeed, would have you refrain for a time from exercise, since it but serves to reinforce old and vicious habits. He does not force the change of mind and posture, but bids you have good hope that, by projecting the orders he suggests, and reforming your bodily ambitions, and recognizing the vicious nature of your former habits and aspirations, you will, after twenty or thirty daily 'lessons' lasting half an hour each, find yourself, without intermitting your usual daily routine, a new person. But more than that, he promises that you will continue to improve when the lessons are over . . .

Mr Alexander . . . realizes that the psychic and the physical are always interplaying, sometimes obviously, usually unconsciously. One has to inhibit [one's] familiar and quite unconscious muscular routine in order to make way for the new, well-planned, conscious co-ordination. It seems to me to be Mr Alexander's fundamental invention to have hit upon an effective way of doing this. You are first shown your general incompetence to disassociate and control your movements; then you are given certain fundamental orders in regard to the relaxing of the neck, the position of the head, the lengthening of the body and the broadening of the back. There are, however, at first *mere aspirations*, and you are forbidden to make any attempt to carry them out muscularly, for the simple reason that your old habits will not permit to you to do so. As yet you do not know what it is really to relax the neck, lengthen the body, or broaden the back . . .

Mr Alexander then proceeds literally to remodel the patient, first sitting and then in standing posture. He devotes his chief attention to the neck, lower thorax and abdomen, but sees to it that one's legs are properly relaxed. By pressing, pushing, pulling, stretching and readjusting – all quite gently and persuasively – he brings you back into shape, rising now and then to take a look at you from a distance, as a sculptor might view the progress of his work. This process has a double effect, apparently: it gradually increases your muscular discrimination, and at the same time the correct coordinations he makes tend to hold over and ultimately to become habitual. Slowly you realize that the sensations in your back and your consequent control are increasing. You sit and stand with ever greater ease and satisfaction. You learn to discriminate and separate muscular acts . . . to grasp a chair without implicating the muscles of the upper arm or shoulder, to manage your legs without using the abdominal muscles or contracting the neck . . . At last one has learned to 'brace up', and, what is more, to stay up; to prefer the right posture to the wrong . . .[36]

Not all notices were so positive. F.M.'s former pupil Randolph Bourne, a brilliant cripple and a member of the Greenwich Village Group, writing in the *New Republic* in May 1918, accepted that Alexander possessed 'a rare physiological intuition' and had invented an effective technique. 'The body becomes a genuine instrument, and spontaneity, self-expression, become for the first time intelligible terms . . . But is it not a mistake, when you have so valuable a pragmatic intuition and power, to let your enthusiasm wrap the idea up in a cosmic and evolutionary philosophy which could not, in the nature of things, be half so persuasive as the technique itself?' He was puzzled by F.M.'s contention that all mankind was 'evolving' towards a condition of conscious control.

> If the school must wait until every one of its children has learned conscious guidance and control, the next step in evolution will be very long delayed . . . But do we any longer think of evolution as a road along which mankind moves abreast in a solid phalanx onward and upward forever? Isn't mankind, if it is anything, a pitiful and struggling army . . . ? Will it ever be anything else? Is an era of world war, in which statesmen are proving as blind and helpless as the manipulated masses, quite the most convincing time for so far-flung a philosophy of conscious control?
>
> Philosophy is a dangerous quicksand. Professor Dewey's instrumentalism* has held out to Mr Alexander a helping hand, but has scarcely saved him from getting at times beyond his depth . . . But Mr Alexander's empiric idea and practice are too valuable to be wrapped up in a philosophy that is not just as vigorously integrated and intelligently guided as the muscular system which he skilfully directs towards perfect functioning.[37]

Though it stressed the negative aspect, the conclusions of Bourne's article were not much different from Robinson's – that one need not accept the 'evolutionary' philosophy in order to admire and benefit from the practical technique. However, it provoked a furious letter from Dewey to the editor, defending the philosophical implications of F.M.'s book.[38] Indeed, so passionate was Dewey in defence of F.M. that, forgetting his liberal principles, he threatened never to write for the journal again if it carried further contributions by Bourne – a threat which proved unnecessary as poor

* The name Dewey gave to his particular brand of pragmatism.

Bourne was carried off by the influenza epidemic which swept America later that year.[39]

F.M.'s enjoyment of the success of *Man's Supreme Inheritance* in New York in the winter of 1918 was interrupted by bad news from home: riding in Hyde Park, A.R. had been thrown from his horse, sustaining serious injuries. Anxious both for his brother and the now unmanned practice at Ashley Place, F.M. returned to London some weeks earlier than planned. The doctors predicted that A.R. would never walk again, but were proved mistaken: thanks to his knowledge of 'the work', A.R. made extraordinary progress and by June was sufficiently recovered to see his horse run at Newmarket[40] (though for the rest of his life he would walk with a stick, and teach sitting down). Indeed, soon after F.M. returned to New York in the autumn of 1918, A.R. followed him there to help with the ever-growing American practice, so that for several months there was no one to teach the Technique in London, probably for the first time since 1904. Meanwhile the war came to an end when Germany sued for an armistice in November, and the new edition of *Man's Supreme Inheritance* was published in London by Methuen in December.

Thanks to the book's enthusiastic reception, the demand for F.M.'s services in America had become intense; having joined F.M. to help him satisfy this demand during the winter of 1919, A.R. did so again the following year. A postwar boom was under way and the brothers made a good deal of money, which they invested (with expert advice from pupils in the financial world) in the American stock market. By the spring of 1920, the teaching was no longer confined to New York. Two wealthy and socially eminent Boston ladies who had read Robinson's article, Miss Caroline ('Carla') Atkinson and Mrs Ernest Amory Codman, hastened to New York to have lessons with F.M., and were so impressed that they urged him to teach in Boston, where they put their houses at his disposal. They were well placed to help him establish his work in that city,

especially as Mrs Codman, as well as coming from one of
Boston's first families, was the wife of a famous doctor who
had done pioneering research into X-rays. (Although Dr
Codman declined to take lessons himself, he could not ignore
the fact that his wife, who suffered from arthritis, found
herself able to engage in her favourite hobby of moun-
taineering for the first time in years.) From 1920, therefore,
the Alexander brothers taught periodically in Boston, where
whole families flocked to them. Although they caused something of a sensation in both social and academic circles, they
were not afterwards remembered for their tact. As Frank
Pierce Jones writes:

> At a reception which was given for them by the Codmans,
> and to which a large number of prominent doctors and their
> wives were invited, F.M. announced that the practice of
> medicine was much more advanced in England than in
> America. A.R. said that psychoanalysis was cultish and prob-
> ably did more harm than good. At a time when Harvard
> University was the bastion of Freudian orthodoxy, such an
> opinion could not win many friends in Boston. People
> continued to have lessons, however, and to report back
> enthusiastically to their doctors. At the Massachusetts General
> Hospital, the file on the Alexander Technique was said to
> be a foot and a half thick.[41]

When F.M. returned to England in the spring of 1920,
A.R. remained in America, carrying on the teaching in Boston
and New York. When F.M. returned to America that autumn,
A.R. returned to London – and for the next four years, the
brothers crossed over in this way, so that the teaching could
be kept going in both countries. With the restoration of peace
and (reasonable) prosperity, the demand for lessons was
becoming insistent in London too, and F.M. worked hard to
re-establish his practice at Ashley Place, assisted by Ethel Webb
and Irene Tasker who had returned there for good. New English

pupils around this time included the future Archbishop of Canterbury William Temple (1881–1944), then a Canon of Westminster, and the venerable Quaker chocolate manufacturer and philanthropist Joseph Rowntree (1836–1925), who is reputed to have said of the Alexander Technique that it was 'reasoning from the known to the unknown, the known being the wrong and the unknown being the right'.[42]

This period saw changes to the household at 16 Ashley Place. At the end of the war, Edith's younger sister May Piddock, living in London, had been widowed soon after giving birth (in June 1918) to a baby girl, Peggy; as she already had two teenage children, she found it difficult to cope with the new infant, and F.M. and Edith, childless in their fifties, agreed to adopt her. They both adored Peggy, who may have been a factor in keeping their marriage together at a time when it was running into problems. One problem was that Edith and Ethel Webb hated each other – perhaps not surprisingly, as Ethel harboured romantic feelings towards F.M., had seen far more of him in recent years than had Edith, and had made herself indispensable to him. Edith for her part seems to have felt romantic about her dashing but feckless ex-officer nephew Owen Vicary (born 1891), who following demobilisation had moved into the crowded basement flat at Ashley Place together with his wife Jack and their two young children. F.M. gave Vicary financial help to get him started in the road haulage business; but it must have been a relief for him to escape these domestic pressures and leave for America in the autumn of 1920, A.R. returning to take over the work at Ashley Place.[43]

For some time, F.M. had been contemplating a second book, a sequel to *Man's Supreme Inheritance*; in intervals of American teaching during the winter of 1921, he discussed this with Dewey, and back in London that summer, he started work on it. He was encouraged by the fact that, around this time, three British doctors came to him for lessons, were impressed by the Technique, and offered to help him secure recognition for it: these were the London eye surgeon Andrew

Rugg-Gunn (1884–1972) and two Scottish-trained physicians, Peter Macdonald (1870–1960), practising in York, and Andrew Murdoch (1862–1943), practising in Sussex. All three were prolific writers in the medical press, and eventually wrote much about 'the work'; they may also have provided F.M. with the first serious opportunity since his falling-out with Spicer in 1909 for regular discussions with highly qualified and sympathetic medical men. Macdonald in particular was a considerable personality, who was active in politics (he had unsuccessfully stood in 1918 as Labour parliamentary candidate for the Scottish Universities seat), had married the daughter of F.M.'s millionaire pupil Joseph Rowntree, and was to become Chairman of the British Medical Association during the Second World War; he quickly became an important ally, whose help F.M. acknowledged in the preface to his new book; at a BMA meeting in 1923, he described F.M.'s discoveries as 'epoch-making' and suggested that they 'should be incorporated in the education of the young, if only as a matter of preventive medicine'.*[44] Another distinguished FRCS and medical writer, J. E. R. McDonagh (1881–1965), took lessons in 1925 and was not only converted to the cause but also became F.M.'s personal physician (though he possessed some faddish ideas, notably a fervent belief in colonic irrigation). As well as being associated with him in his work, these doctors seem to have become F.M.'s closest social friends during the last thirty years of his life: he often dined *à trois* in London with Rugg-Gunn and McDonagh, who shared his love of good food and wine, while Murdoch, who shared his interest in the turf, became a racing companion.

For some reason, F.M. did not make his annual visit to America during 1921–2: perhaps he needed a period of settled residence to get down to his book, perhaps he simply found

---

* Macdonald also arranged lessons at this period for his young son Patrick (1910–91), later to be a famous teacher of the Alexander Technique.

himself too busy with new pupils in London. Presumably, A.R. (who liked America and Americans more than F.M. ever did) kept the work going across the Atlantic. During 1922, however, F.M. experienced a shock, with the publication in New York of a book entitled *Invisible Exercise* by Gerald Stanley Lee. Lee (1862–1944) was an American Congregational minister and writer of popular works who had taken lessons with F.M. in London in 1919 and 1920. In his next book, *The Ghost in the White House* (1920), he hailed F.M. as a genius and benefactor of humanity, even suggesting that the entire population of the USA should study his method. In *Invisible Exercise*, however, Lee described procedures which were clearly based on F.M.'s without mentioning F.M. at all, claiming that they had come to him in a religious vision. What particularly incensed F.M. was that he had not only stolen his procedures and inadequately described them, but he had gone on to deny what, as far as F.M. was concerned, was their very basis – the notion of mind–body unity (which Lee as a clergyman purported to regard as anathema). F.M. threatened to sue the publishers, which proved awkward as they also happened to be his own (Dutton); he then tried to prevent such a thing recurring by patenting his method, but was advised by lawyers that this was impracticable. It merely remained to finish his own book as quickly as he could and make it as complete a statement of his teachings as possible.[45]

In November 1922, F.M. sailed for New York after an absence of eighteen months, taking with him the draft manuscript of his new book, now entitled *Constructive Conscious Control of the Individual*, which Dewey had offered to read and introduce. Travelling on the same boat was Émile Coué (1857–1926), a fashionable practitioner of 'miracle cures' by hypnosis, often demonstrated before public audiences. When they landed, Coué was mobbed by reporters and journalists, while F.M. slipped quietly ashore unobserved. This prompted Dewey to write an article in the *New Republic* entitled 'A Sick World', suggesting that 'the contrast between the receptions of the two men affords a fair measure of our preference for a cheap and easy way of dealing with symptoms, of our wish to be cured rather than to be well'.[46] This was an apt curtain-raiser for the book, the publication of which was set for May 1923.

F.M. considered *Constructive Conscious Control of the Individual* to be the most important of his four books. In his preface, he writes of it as a companion volume to *Man's Supreme Inheritance*. In fact, it represents a considerable refinement of the ideas expressed in the earlier work: twelve years on, his theories had become far more coherent, and he had jettisoned much of the extraneous baggage with which he had previously encumbered them. Although he again begins with a long digression on 'evolution', he now uses the term in connection with the specific and plausible argument 'that man has been and still is unable to adapt himself quickly enough to the increasingly rapid changes in the plan of life which we call civilisation'.[47] The book is much better written than its predecessor, doubtless a reflection of the assistance provided by his two highly literate amanuenses, Ethel Webb and Irene Tasker, and the advice received from Macdonald in England and Dewey in America.* Dewey again contributes an introduction, making three points. First, that Alexander's argument is difficult to understand for the very reason that makes it so important, namely that it tells the reader that he is suffering from a condition of which he is probably completely unaware; secondly, that Alexander's system differs completely from other remedial systems in that it deals not with cures but with causes; and thirdly, that the validity of his system is constantly being tested by experiment: 'Mr Alexander has demonstrated a new scientific principle with respect to the control of human behaviour as important as any principle which has ever been discovered in the domain of external nature.'

---

* In Boston during the early weeks of 1923, Dewey is said to have gone through the proofs with F.M. line by line, making numerous suggestions.

F.M. states his basic thesis at the outset: that, owing to man's inability to adapt to the rapid changes of civilisation, he has developed a defective sensory appreciation, leading to poor co-ordination of his psychophysical mechanism; that these defects explain most of what goes wrong with him in every department; and that the way for him to restore proper functioning is to focus on the 'means-whereby' rather than the 'end to be gained'. (The emphasis in this book is on 'means-whereby' rather than 'inhibition' – though the two concepts are of course inextricably linked.) Rather oddly placed in the middle of the volume is a detailed description of the procedures used in lessons to guide the pupil towards this goal, which F.M. wished to put on record following Lee's outrageous plagiarism. Otherwise the book consists of a wide-ranging examination of the implications of his thesis and its relevance to all human activity and development, drawing on the accumulated wisdom of thirty years' teaching and study. It abounds with useful observations, such as that a desirable condition of general alertness should not be confused with the stressful state usually thought of as 'concentration,'[48] and that the vast majority of uninstructed humans are simply incapable of performing a whole range of natural actions – such as moving the head without moving the shoulders, or opening the mouth without moving the head.[49]

Much of the early part of the book is devoted to arguing that prevention (through the establishment of reliable sensory appreciation) is better than cure – for all cures are 'end-gaining', addressing specific symptoms rather than general causes. It is true that people come to Alexander hoping to be cured of specific afflictions, and he is often able to help them by raising their general standard of functioning; but 'my reader will understand that I am forced to work in a so-called curative sphere with adults, in the hope that they may help me in my efforts to gain a wide recognition of the necessity . . . for preventive measures for the children'.[50] Among the 'cures' he considers is psychoanalysis. (As Frank Pierce Jones writes, F.M. knew little about this and would probably not have mentioned it but for the fact that several reviewers of *Man's Supreme Inheritance* had compared his work to Freud's:[51] Bourne, for example, had described the Alexander Technique as 'apparently a kind of reversed psychoanalysis, unwinding the psychic knots by getting control of the physical end-organs'.) This too is end-gaining: it might be effective in dealing with specific 'phobias', but these would never take hold in the first place were it not for our old friend 'debauched kinaesthesia, the result of imperfect coordination, imperfect adjustment, and unreliable and delusive sensory appreciation'.[52]

In the latter part of his book, F.M. argues that virtually all the ills of man arise from these factors of misuse. This is the case not only with regard to disease and disability, but also mind-wandering, loss of memory, the inadequate education of children, uncontrolled emotions, fixed prejudices, class-consciousness, and war. (One often feels that 'debauched kinaesthesia' occupies the same role in Alexander's view of the world as sin does in an evangelical Christian view of the world: his prose has something of a preaching tone, and one must remember his staunchly Protestant family background.) In the final chapter, F.M. gives his views on 'happiness'. True happiness, he argues, consists in doing well the things that interest one, and the way to ensure this is 'to make certain of the satisfactory *means whereby* an end may be secured, and thus to command a large percentage of those satisfactory experiences which develop confidence . . .' Most adults, however, are fundamentally unhappy because they are subconsciously controlled malcoordinated end-gainers, who 'seek satisfaction in less normal and less useful activities, and create an undue and harmful demand for specific excitements and stimulations . . .'[53]

Though one may not agree with all of it (and F.M. as usual overstates his case, as well as writing much that reads oddly today on the differences between man in his 'savage' and 'civilised' state), *Constructive Conscious Control of the*

Individual commands admiration for the coherence of its theory, the force of its argument and the eloquence of its narrative. Yet it received less attention and praise in America than F.M.'s earlier, manifestly imperfect book. This may have been partly due to its cumbersome title (for which, however, F.M. offered no apologies, insisting that he had been unable to find any other phrase which more closely reflected its content). His grateful writer-pupils who had praised the first volume five years earlier did not feel able to write again; and Dewey, though his name counted for much, was beginning to attract a certain ridicule for his support of the Technique. Those intellectuals who had not taken lessons found F.M.'s message excessively 'reductionist': he seemed to think that everything in the universe could be explained in terms of his teachings. Perhaps the book's relative failure was a question of timing: *Man's Supreme Inheritance* had come out at a nervous moment of the war, when people were avid for explanations of the failure of the human condition, whereas an account of the present unsatisfactoriness of man was of less interest at a time when the United States was in the midst of the greatest boom in her history.

While in America awaiting publication of his new book, F.M. experienced a great sadness in his life. In February 1923, his beloved mother Betsy Alexander died in London at the age of seventy-five. She was living at the time with her unmarried daughter Agnes (aged fifty) in Little Venice, having moved there from Victoria after the war, possibly because (like most of F.M.'s female relatives) she did not get on with Edith at Ashley Place. F.M. was unable to return immediately, but dedicated his book 'to the Memory of my Mother'. If he was bereft at her loss, Agnes, who had never lived apart from her, was devastated. This and other family problems forced F.M. to return to London in April, missing the book's New York publication in May. (Meanwhile, John Alexander, the father of the family, who was never mentioned or communicated with, lived on in Tasmania, practising his farrier's trade almost to the last, and only dying in September 1936 at the age of ninety-three.)

During F.M.'s months in London in 1923, an extraordinary episode occurred which sheds light on his personality. No doubt as a result of early experiences in the rough world of Australia, he possessed an almost pathological fear of being cheated, and was constantly suspicious and on his guard. (It is paradoxical that this, like his mania for racing, was exactly the kind of 'obsessive' behaviour which he claimed his work enabled one to avoid.) Meals in restaurants which did not come up to his high standards would instantly be sent back; he once refused (and successfully defended his refusal in court) to pay a taxi driver who he claimed had 'bumped up' the fare; and he took on anyone who supplied him with goods or services which he considered inadequate or at a cost which he regarded as extortionate. That summer, he bought a Marman motor car; some weeks after taking possession, he returned it and refused to pay an outstanding bill of some £200 on the grounds that it had not come up to scratch. When the dealer refused to accept the vehicle back, and sued for the debt, F.M. promptly transferred all his assets (which must have been substantial at the time) into the names of trusted friends (notably his brother-in-law George Mechin); he then left for America in October as planned. As a result, he was declared bankrupt in his absence. Subsequently, his friends 'bought' and cancelled the debt, whereupon the main legal restrictions attaching to F.M., such as an inability to pledge credit or run a bank account, were lifted; but F.M. himself always refused to apply for the discharge of his bankruptcy, which would have amounted to an admission of his former liability, and so technically remained bankrupt for the rest of his life.[54] (As a result, he was henceforth unable to join a club, form a partnership, or act as a trustee – which he may have regarded as more of an advantage than a handicap, given his ingrained dislike of all formal associations.)

F.M.'s annual visit to America from the autumn of 1923 to the spring of 1924 proved to be his last. Henceforth he based himself permanently in London, with A.R. as his partner (though A.R. continued to hanker after America, and would return there ten years later). With the exception of a short trip to New York in the autumn of 1929 to attend Dewey's seventieth birthday celebrations, F.M. would not set foot in the United States again until he went there under a certain compulsion in 1940. Americans who wanted lessons with him now had to cross the Atlantic – as a considerable number seem to have done. (In 1951, he told his American pupil Goddard Binkley that, before 1939, he had sometimes had 'as many as sixteen of them here at one time'.[55])

Why did F.M. give up his lucrative American teaching, and incidentally cut himself off from Dewey, his most influential supporter? The main reason seems to have been that his heart was in London, where there was now more than enough work to keep himself and A.R. busy, and that he no longer had such a financial incentive to go to America, having already amassed a comfortable fortune there. He was fifty-five; and although vigorous for his age, he must have found it inconvenient to divide his working life between two continents and three cities. The time had come to settle down and concentrate his efforts in the place where he felt happiest, and where (particularly in view of the support of his new doctor friends) exciting prospects seemed to lie ahead.

But there may have been an additional reason. Following the lukewarm reception of *Constructive Conscious Control of the Individual*, Dewey wanted to institute a scientific investigation of the Alexander Technique with support from a charitable foundation. While F.M. affected to show interest in this idea, it was in fact one which alarmed him, partly because he had little confidence in such an investigation, partly because he feared that it might lead to his work slipping from his control. He therefore began to distance himself from Dewey (who nevertheless continued to seek funding for the proposed enterprise, and with whom F.M. remained on friendly terms until the 1930s).[56] F.M.'s ambivalent attitude towards all proposals for the development of his work was to be a characteristic feature of his life over the next fifteen years.

5

Progress
1924–1939

The five years 1924 to 1929 marked a golden period in F.M.'s life. After a decade of hard work and shrewd investment in America, he was now quite a rich man, completely free of financial anxieties for the first time in his life. During these years he was able to indulge a beloved but expensive hobby, the ownership and training of racehorses.[1] He was happy in the thought that, in *Constructive Conscious Control of the Individual*, he had set down a mature, comprehensive and lucid statement of his beliefs, and that, thanks to the support of his new doctor friends, he was on the way to receiving general recognition from the medical profession. Meanwhile, he and A.R., assisted by Ethel Webb and Irene Tasker, maintained a permanent joint practice at Ashley Place for the first time since 1914, attracting more business than ever. On the domestic front, the adoption of Peggy brought new light into his family life, making tolerable for a time his otherwise difficult marriage with Edith.

The start of this period witnessed three exciting developments.

First, F.M. became the owner of a country house within easy reach of London. This was Penhill, a substantial eighteenth-century farmhouse with nineteenth-century additions at Bexleyheath in Kent, one mile from Sidcup station. It had been valued before the war at £3000. Its twenty acres included gardens, farmland, stables and paddocks. A lodge in the grounds housed a family of retainers inherited from the previous owners: Arthur Rose served as groundsman, his two sons as chauffeur and groom, his wife as cook-housekeeper and his daughter as maid. The purchase of the property (which must have involved complex arrangements, as F.M. technically remained bankrupt) was completed in March 1925. A second home was necessary, for Edith and Peggy could no longer remain at Ashley Place: as busy professional premises, it was unsuitable for the upbringing of a child, and Edith's relations with Ethel Webb continued to be strained. For the rest of the 1920s, F.M. generally spent weekends with Edith and Peggy at Penhill, living during the week in the basement flat at Ashley Place, where he enjoyed the services of an excellent cook, Mrs Tiffin. F.M. took great pride in Penhill, where he played the squire, rode his horse, cultivated his garden and ran a farm providing organic produce for his table.[2]

The second development concerned a new departure at Ashley Place. In 1924, Irene Tasker became guardian to the 'nervous and excitable' eight-year-old son of relations who were serving in India.[3] When she asked F.M. if she might give the boy not just Alexander lessons but general schooling at Ashley Place, he replied that 'this may be just the opportunity we want'[4] – for his ultimate aim, as he had written in *Constructive Conscious Control of the Individual*, was to apply his methods to the general education of children.[5] Soon, other parents were asking to send their children to Ashley Place, where one of the rooms became the schoolroom. During its first years, the 'little school' (as it became known) generally had from six to eight pupils, most of them handicapped or retarded in some way (though as far as F.M. was concerned, there was never anything wrong with them which 'the work' could not put right). Irene, at this time the sole schoolteacher, gave them lessons in the Technique, ensured that they did not 'pull down' during schoolwork, and encouraged them to be patient and never to try to achieve 'ends' until they had thought about 'means'. F.M., who loved children and identified with them in many ways, often looked into the schoolroom to meet and work on the pupils.[6]

The third development was in the realm of theory. In 1924, Rudolf Magnus (1873–1927), a German professor at the University of Utrecht and a protégé of the great English physiologist Sir Charles Sherrington (1857–1952), published his seminal work on the physiology of posture, *Körperstellung*, the main conclusions of which he summarised in English in lectures delivered in London and Edinburgh. In brief, Magnus concluded that the postural mechanism is controlled by a 'central apparatus' located in 'the sub-cortical area of the brain-stem'; that posture is consequently influenced by the position of the head ('where the head leads the body follows'); and that the efficiency of this 'central apparatus' depends on 'the right interpretation of all sensory impressions'.[7] Macdonald and other medical supporters of F.M. were quick to declare that these findings represented a striking scientific affirmation of principles which F.M. had been teaching for almost thirty years* – that the efficient functioning of the human mechanism depends on the correct alignment of the head, neck and upper back, and on accurate sensory appreciation.[8] Since then, the connection between Magnus's discoveries and those of F.M. has been much debated, critics pointing out that Magnus's experiments had been on animals rather than human beings and that his 'central apparatus' referred to the control of involuntary rather than 'conscious' reflexes. Unfortunately Magnus died soon after his book was published, so was unable to pronounce on the matter himself – though his mentor Sherrington lived on for many years and was to mention F.M.'s teachings approvingly in his book

---

* In *The Universal Constant in Living* (1941), F.M. makes the precise claim that his discovery antedated Magnus's publication by twenty-eight years.

The Endeavour of Jean Fernel (1946).* The general view today is that an important connection between the two theories does exist, even though Magnus and F.M. were not describing quite the same things.[9] At the time, Magnus gave an intellectual boost to F.M. and his supporters. F.M. began using the expression 'primary control' to describe the establishment of the head–neck–back relationship which his technique brought about and which he regarded as a precondition of good overall functioning.[10]

Apart from his valuable medical followers, F.M.'s new pupils during the years 1924–9 included three distinguished but very different men who were to become lifelong supporters of his work and who have left interesting testimony of their early experiences with him. These were the statesman Lord Lytton, the writer Anthony Ludovici, and the industrialist Robert Best. Especially interesting is the fact that, on first meeting F.M., none of them particularly liked him; but they all found their lives rapidly transformed by him and came to regard him as one of the geniuses of the age.

A superb-looking aristocrat† who lived in ancestral splendour at Knebworth House, Hertfordshire, and possessed a strong sense of public duty, Victor, 2nd Earl of Lytton (1876–1947), served as a junior minister in Lloyd George's

* 'Mr Alexander has done a service to the subject [will and reflex action in physiology] by insistently treating each act as involving the whole integrated individual, the whole psycho-physical man. To take a step is an affair, not of this or that limb solely, but of the total neuro-muscular activity of the moment – not least of the head and neck.'

† James Lees-Milne gave the following description of him in his diary for 13 June 1942: 'Lord Lytton pompous, courteous in a keep-your-distance manner, patrician and vice-regal. He was wearing rather precious country clothes, a too immaculate tweed suit, a yellow-green shirt of large checks loose at the collar, and a gold chain round his neck. He has truly beautiful blue eyes. If one did not know otherwise one would suppose him what my father calls "effeminate" by the well-cut, yet long silver hair deliberately curled over the nape of his neck.' (*Ancestral Voices.*)

government from 1916 to 1922 and then as Governor of Bengal from 1922 to 1927, a time of unrest in British India. When he returned to England on leave in the summer of 1926, aged fifty, the strain of public life was beginning to tell, and he suffered from headaches, muscular pains and stomach troubles. A friend suggested he consult F.M., whom he met on 5 July and with whom he had a lesson every day for three weeks.* Writing up his diary on 25 September, during the sea voyage back to India, Lytton described his encounter with F.M. as one of the great events of his life.

> I had read his book *Man's Supreme Inheritance* some years ago and had not been very impressed by it. Nor was I very much impressed by the man himself when I first met him. I must admit, however, that he has done for me just what I wanted and I regard him as one of the great benefactors of the world. He has given me a new body and a new philosophy of life . . . He . . . maintains that complete health is only to be found in the perfect co-ordination of mind and body . . . I began to derive benefit from [his] treatment from the very first day and so long as I was living in London I felt better than I have ever been in my life . . . With the added efficiency given me by Alexander I was in tremendous spirits. I could play all games better than before. I could be about all day without feeling tired and awake fresh in the morning . . . I felt that I should return to India with enormously increased energy.[11]

In August, having left London for Knebworth, Lytton briefly fell ill, and also sprained an ankle playing tennis. 'The only consolation I had was that the body which Alexander had given me was more efficient when sick than my old body had

---

* During the 1920s and 1930s, F.M. generally insisted that new pupils take five lessons a week for at least three weeks.

been when well, and the rapidity with which I recovered from my sprained ankle was a great tribute to his treatment.' Reinstalled that autumn at Government House, Calcutta, he wrote to his mother: 'I am wonderfully well & Alexander's work is having permanent results.'[12] 'We are having banquets every night but thanks to Alexander they no longer tire me.'[13] He was pleased that the Dowager Countess was thinking of seeing F.M. herself. 'I am sure he will do you ever so much good. Don't wait to be ill. He can't help you then. He is not a substitute for the doctor. But he will not only help you to keep well through the trying cold months but will enable you to get much more enjoyment out of life.'[14]

When his governorship ended in 1927, and he returned to live in England, Lytton retired from public life to devote himself to good works. He resumed his lessons, and offered to help F.M. bring his work to the attention of a wider public. This represented a great opportunity, for Lytton was a leading member of the traditional British establishment, with contacts and influence at the highest level, as well as being widely respected for his character and learning. Having recommended the Alexander Technique to his friends, Lytton launched a public campaign in support of it with a long letter to the *Times Educational Supplement* dated 19 May 1928:

I am often asked, 'Who and what is Alexander?', and it is difficult to supply the answer in a few words. He is not a doctor, nor a school teacher, nor a physical culturist, yet his work is of assistance to all these professions. He has helped many who are suffering from functional disorders to regain health; he has shown to school teachers how children, considered mentally backward, may be brought up to the standard of the most efficient; he has rebuilt bodies, even of those of advanced age, and given them new efficiency and youth . . . Mr. Alexander's work, however, is primarily educational, since he recognizes that it is both easier and better to prevent functional disorders of mind and body by teaching the young the right use of their natural equipment than to cure such disorders after they have arisen as the result of wrong use. His principles, therefore, should be in force in every school in the country . . . I have had personal experience of the great benefit which he can render to those who consult him for the relief of definite ailments, but I realize that if I had benefited by his teaching in earlier life the ailments which he has relieved might never have occurred. This is my justification for calling attention to his work in that section of *The Times* which deals with education . . .

The remarkably varied career of Anthony M. Ludovici (1882–1971) included being private secretary to the French sculptor Rodin, English translator of the German philosopher Nietzsche, an artist, a book illustrator, a novelist, and an intelligence officer in both world wars. He also penned numerous eccentric works advocating that England should become an aristocratic dictatorship run by the King and the House of Lords, that she should 'purify' herself of 'alien' elements (notably Jews), and that women should be relegated to a purely domestic role. (He has been described as a 'fascist'; but while admiring certain aspects of Mussolini and Hitler, he disapproved of the populist element in fascism.[15]) In a book of memoirs published in 1961, he describes the unusual way in which he was introduced to Alexander's work. In 1923 he published an anti-feminist tract, *Woman: A Vindication*, which inspired fan mail from one Miss Agnes Birrell, who expressed surprise that, 'as a champion of healthy values', he should be unaware of Alexander's teachings. He replied that he was 'too busy to become acquainted with yet another New Way of Life'; but she continued to write him letters attempting to interest him in the Alexander Technique. After a year, hoping to put an end to this tiresome correspondence, he reluctantly consented to accompany her to Ashley Place and observe F.M. giving her a lesson. He was pleasantly surprised to discover that she was not 'the desiccated old spinster' he had imagined but quite an attractive young woman. F.M., however, he instantly took against on account of his showmanship and 'incessant patter' (including declamations from Byron and Shakespeare); and he tactfully informed Miss Birrell that he was unable to take lessons as he could not afford the fees of four guineas for half an hour. To his horror, she responded by paying in advance for him to have a course of several dozen lessons with F.M.[16]

The sceptical Ludovici began his unwanted lessons in February 1925, aged forty-two. At first he felt confirmed in his view that they represented 'a most obvious racket'. After a few weeks, however, he began to notice that he had ceased to suffer from digestive and respiratory troubles which had plagued him for years, that his waistcoats no longer fitted him, and that friends were remarking on a radical improvement in his posture. 'It is impossible fully to describe the benefits both in health and in *joie de vivre* which I owed, and still owe, to this radical alteration in my physique,' he recollected thirty-five years later. 'I was a changed man.'[17] Ludovici proceeded to act with all the fervour of a convert. In his next book, *Man: An Indictment* (1927), an attack on the 'degeneracy' of the modern male (a theme which would no doubt have appealed to F.M.), he devoted many pages to the Alexander Technique, concluding that 'the recovery of one's lost central control is probably one of the most wonderful experiences it is possible to have',[18] and that 'the claim made by Mr Alexander that an enormous amount of our present degeneration is due to a perfectly unconscious, but very wrong, use of self . . . probably constitutes one of the most constructive pieces of diagnosis and criticism that has been given to the world for many scores of years.'[19] A few years later, he devoted a whole book – *Health and*

Education through Self-Mastery (1933) – to Alexander's work.* As well as helping to popularise the Alexander Technique, Ludovici explained why it was so difficult to write about, 'because inasmuch as it is a sensory experience, registered by the muscular sense, it can no more be conveyed in words than can the taste of bacon, or the look of the colour blue, or the sound of middle C of the piano. No phraseology, however skilful, can define a sensation.'[20]

It was through reading *Man: An Indictment* that Robert D. Best (1892–1984) learned about Alexander. He was a successful Birmingham industrialist who inherited an engineering firm founded by his great-grandfather in the 1840s; he was also a man of culture, being a notable patron of Birmingham's art and music colleges; and he had a restless, questioning mind, the result of a partly German education. He met F.M. to discuss lessons in June 1928, but only found time to start a course in April 1929. Between these dates, something occurred which was characteristic of F.M. and cast a shadow over their relations. At their original interview, F.M. offered to reduce his fees in view of the fact that Best's worst problems (a neck tremor and spinal trouble) arose from war injuries; but he subsequently learned that Best was a wealthy man, and so changed his mind and insisted on charging the full rate. Best acquiesced, but pointed out in a rather sharp letter that he had neither misled F.M. as to his circumstances nor asked any favours of him.[21]

Best experienced the usual rapid improvements as a result of his lessons: within a week, he had ceased to suffer from a longstanding limp. (It is interesting that for a long time he was hardly aware of these changes, though his family noticed them, and they were confirmed by his doctor.) Some years

---

* Ludovici is said to have written this at F.M.'s request, in return for a fee or free lessons (Edward Owen's interview of Irene Stewart, 10 October 1961). An odd excursion in the middle of the book attacking one Professor L. P. Jacks, an advocate of 'self-control', was apparently included at the insistence of F.M., who had some kind of grudge against the professor.

later, he wrote of his belief that 'the effect on humanity of Mr Alexander's discovery will eventually be such that history will recognise him as a very great originator, certainly the equal if not the superior of the giants of the nineteenth and twentieth centuries'.[22] During the 1930s, Best lent his support to F.M. in various ways. He sent all three of his children to the little school; and he helped establish the teaching of the Technique in Birmingham, which thus became the first English centre of Alexander's work outside London.*

Best, however, was far from being an uncritical follower of F.M.: indeed, he loved argument, and believed that all theoretical movements require criticism in order to develop. Both in correspondence and personal meetings, he tried to tackle F.M. about what he regarded as inconsistencies in his books and drawbacks in his methods. In particular, he felt that F.M. left his pupils baffled by explaining so little to them during lessons; even if it was difficult to convey in words the sensory experiences involved, F.M. might at least try to explain the things he was doing to affect those experiences. But he always found F.M.'s response unsatisfactory and dismissive. 'What I said to him seemed not to register, and his replies were generally beside the point . . . There was always the implication that it really didn't matter what I thought because in any case my sensory appreciation was relatively unreliable.' He came to believe that there was an element of paranoia about F.M., who expected his followers to accept his precepts unquestioningly, 'like an orthodox Catholic or Communist', and who seemed determined to keep aspects of his work mysterious. He also came to see F.M., for all his genius, as a fundamentally limited man, who was little aware of the spiritual and artistic sides of life, and who seemed to think that he held the answers to all life's questions and that nothing really mattered except

---

* The Birmingham practice lasted from 1936 to 1939, the teachers being recently qualified students of Alexander's first training course – first Erika Schumann and Irene Stewart, later Patrick Macdonald.

'psycho-physical awareness'. Best summarised his criticisms of
F.M. and his teachings in an essay written in 1941 entitled
'Conscious Constructive Criticism of Mr F. M. Alexander's
New Technique' – though he was persuaded not to publish
this lest it 'harm the work'.[23] His personal relations with F.M.
remained good, and he continued to study and support the
Alexander Technique for the rest of his long life.

F.M. turned sixty in January 1929. That year witnessed a
succession of dramatic changes in his circumstances and
fortunes.

First, it saw the effective end of his marriage to Edith.
That marriage, a legacy of his old life in Australia, had
always been difficult; for the decline of her looks, the failure
of her acting career, and her inability either to understand
F.M.'s work or get on with his female relatives and associates had conspired to make her bitter. During the war, their
relationship had been rendered tolerable by F.M.'s absences
in America; and during the 1920s, the adoption of Peggy
and the move to Penhill had at first provided them with
common interests and given them a brief period of relative
domestic content. By 1929, however, Edith was no longer
happy at Penhill and wished to return to London; and such
was her extreme jealousy of F.M.'s work and friendships
(particularly female friendships) that he no longer felt able
to live with her. They agreed to separate, F.M. paying her a
monthly allowance. Edith and Peggy moved to the flat in
Little Venice which had once been occupied by F.M.'s mother.
Peggy attended the little school at Ashley Place (where Edith
was never seen), and continued to spend weekends with F.M.
at Penhill. Edith gradually became an alcoholic recluse.* She
was to die in September 1938, aged seventy-two, of *angina*

---

* It has been said that she was disabled and disfigured by a stroke; but
this has been disputed, and perhaps the story was put about to explain
the fact that she was never seen with him.

pectoris, from the effects of which the Alexander Technique (which she had always scorned) might have saved her.*

The conclusion of F.M.'s *ménage* with Edith coincided with the beginnings of two other close relationships which were to endure for the rest of his life – with 'Jack' Vicary and Margaret Goldie. Jack, the wife of Edith's favourite nephew Owen Vicary, had left her philandering husband in the mid-1920s and moved to a cottage near Penhill, where she ran a small shop. At first she was a welcome companion for Edith, and helped her look after Peggy, having two children of similar age. F.M., however, became increasingly attracted to her; and after Edith's departure they began an affair, leading to the birth of their own child, John Vicary, in June 1931.† Margaret Goldie (1905–1997) was a disturbed young woman, who as a student at the Froebel Institute for the training of teachers in 1927 had been sent to have lessons at Ashley Place by the principal Esther Lawrence, a pre-war pupil and continuing supporter of F.M. By the beginning of 1929, she had largely overcome her problems thanks to her lessons with F.M.;[24] and (like other women before her) she had become infatuated with him and wished to devote herself to his cause. F.M. sent her to work with the children of the little school, as he wanted Irene Tasker to be free to help him with his new book – *The Use of the Self*.

It was probably with a view to discussing this new work with Dewey that F.M. made a brief visit to New York to attend the philosopher's seventieth birthday celebrations in

---

* F.M. often achieved dramatic results with pupils suffering from angina: in Chapter 5 of *The Use of the Self*, he describes the case of a doctor (probably Andrew Murdoch) who had been obliged to give up both his practice and golf because of the illness, but was able to resume both after lessons with F.M.

† For the sake of respectability, Jack went to America to have the child, which she afterwards claimed to have adopted there. (Marjory Barlow, *An Examined Life*, p. 241.)

October 1929. Certainly the book which F.M. proceeded to write (and to which Dewey contributed a glowing introduction) closely follows the 'method of scientific enquiry' advocated by Dewey – first to identify a difficulty and formulate a problem, then to think of possible solutions, finally to test those solutions by means of observation and experiment. Another probable reason for their meeting was that, around this time, Dewey succeeded in securing support from the Rockefeller Foundation for scientific research into the Alexander Technique. F.M. at first seemed delighted by this development, and was still expressing delight in 1931 – though he was to have so many doubts about the project and insist on so many preconditions that it would eventually be abandoned,* and his friendship with Dewey would effectively come to an end.[25]

In the last days of October 1929 – possibly while F.M. was returning from New York – came the Wall Street Crash. This had a number of disastrous consequences for F.M. His fortune was invested in the American stock market, and soon dwindled to a fraction of its former value. In the ensuing climate of economic uncertainty, the number of pupils taking lessons at Ashley Place rapidly fell off. The crash also ruined F.M.'s brother-in-law, the ivory merchant George Mechin, who had shown much past generosity to the Alexander family and whom F.M. felt bound to help. All this happened within a few months of his assuming the financial burden of his separation from Edith.

F.M. acted resolutely to deal with this crisis in his affairs. He sold his racehorses. He instituted drastic economies at Penhill and Ashley Place, relinquishing most of his domestic servants. After a quarter of a century of teaching in London, he reduced his standard fee for a lesson from four guineas

---

* He later wrote disparagingly of proposed investigations into his work 'by academic gentlemen with big names but small brains and psycho-physical make-ups' (F.M. to Walter Carrington, 19 April 1943).

to three. He also came to a decision of vital importance for the future of his work. For years, his supporters had been urging him to train new teachers of his Technique: indeed, if his work was to flourish and spread (and in the long run to survive), a training course producing a flow of such teachers was essential. As he had made clear in *Constructive Conscious Control of the Individual*,[26] he was in principle thoroughly in accord with this goal; yet up to now he had always hesitated to do anything to implement it. Obviously such a course would have to be under his personal supervision, and he had hitherto been far too busy with his lucrative practice to think of devoting time to it. He also doubted whether others would easily learn his methods (the whole idea of a training course was in a sense 'end-gaining'), and he did not altogether relish the thought that his work might in future extend beyond Ashley Place and his personal control. However, now that his practice was languishing, F.M. announced, in a letter of 22 March 1930, addressed from Lord Lytton's seat at Knebworth, that he proposed to start a course 'whereby students can be trained to impart the technique set down in my books'.[27]

The letter was sent to F.M.'s principal supporters, who wrote enthusiastic replies for publication in the course's prospectus. 'You know how anxious I have been that your valuable work for the welfare of mankind should be carried on,' wrote Lytton on 5 April. 'The experience you have gained and the technique you have evolved are far too valuable to be lost. There must be thousands who like myself have benefited from your help, but we can do no more than tell others of our good fortune; we cannot pass on to them the benefits we have received.' Sir Lynden Macassey KC, an eminent lawyer and government adviser, thought that it would 'be a calamity if such arrangements were not to be made'. Three school principals – Esther Lawrence, Lucy Silcox, and Irene Tasker's brother-in-law

A. G. Pite* – wrote of the 'supreme importance' of 'the handing-on of your own technique' which was 'unlike anything we have come across in our educational experience'. A similar joint letter welcoming Alexander's initiative was signed by seven doctors, including Macdonald, Murdoch and Rugg-Gunn.[28]

Apart from pleasing his supporters, the training course offered two further advantages to F.M. It made up for the departure from Ashley Place of most of its former domestic staff – for the students, in the manner of apprentices, would be expected to do 'odd jobs' such as opening the front door to pupils, helping with secretarial work, placing F.M.'s bets and making his morning cocoa and afternoon tea. It also promised to alleviate his financial problems. Apart from the fact that the substantial fees (£500 for a three-year course, £125 payable on registering) would provide useful additional income to the practice, he was able to announce, on 22 July 1930, the setting-up of an educational trust, which had already been offered two 'substantial donations'. Its trustees were Lytton, Macdonald and Macassey; its purposes were to support both the training course and the little school (in effect, to subsidise the expenses of Ashley Place and its staff). Indeed, the two educational enterprises were linked, for it was proposed that the students, after an initial period of training, should help teach the children of the little school as part of their studies. The course was scheduled to open early in 1931.

This may be a convenient point at which to consider F.M.'s third book, *The Use of the Self*, which was begun early in 1929, completed in July 1931 and published by Methuen in January 1932. It is the shortest of his four

---

* Miss Lawrence was head of the Froebel Institute; Miss Silcox was headmistress of St Felix's, a girls' school near Southwold in Suffolk; Pite was headmaster of Weymouth College in Dorset.

books, barely running to forty thousand words. Its long classical sentences testify to the literary skills of Ethel Webb and Irene Tasker, whom he twice thanks in his preface. Although it endlessly repeats the mantras about 'inhibition', 'means-whereby' and 'untrustworthy sensory appreciation', this repetition somehow produces a hypnotic, compelling effect. It opens with Dewey's 'Introduction', which has become celebrated in Alexander literature for two statements: that each lesson is 'a laboratory experimental demonstration'; and that the Alexander Technique 'bears the same relation to education that education bears to all other human activities'.

There follows the famous chapter in which F.M. describes how he purportedly discovered his Technique. As discussed earlier,* there has been some controversy both as to whether this represents a true account and as to the time-scale of the investigative process outlined by F.M. As he writes about 'primary control', which does not seem to have occurred to him as a concept until Magnus published his work in 1924, it might be argued that the process took place over more than thirty years. Possibly his account should be taken symbolically rather than literally, like the story of the Creation in the Bible. However, although F.M. wrote with the benefit of hindsight (and of Dewey's theory of scientific method), there can be no doubt that, during the 1890s, he did make a remarkable discovery to the effect that the correct use of the postural mechanism is a determining factor of efficient overall functioning; that he first observed this principle in himself, and then applied it to the teaching of others; and that, almost from the beginning, he succeeded in bringing about remarkable improvements in his pupils. So it is perhaps unfair to condemn *The Use of the Self*, as one of F.M.'s acolytes is said to have done, as 'a terrible book which falsified and misled'.[29] Whether strictly accurate or not, F.M.'s account is both

* See above, pp.35–6, 78, 132–3.

enlightening and inspiring, and it probably represents the best he could do in putting into words a protracted process which he originally grasped in practical rather than intellectual terms and which was marked throughout by trial and error.*

The book's central section deals with two classic examples of misuse through 'end-gaining' – 'the golfer who cannot keep his eye on the ball' and 'the stutterer'. F.M. describes in some detail the procedures by which these sufferers can be helped to overcome their habits, emphasizing that 'quick cures' solve nothing and that only gradually, by patiently mastering the primary control and learning to 'inhibit', can they acquire the necessary sensory appreciation and 'means-whereby'. The final chapter consists of a plea to incorporate his principles into standard medical training; for 'no diagnosis of a case can be said to be complete unless the medical adviser gives consideration to the influence exerted upon the patient, not only by the immediate cause of the trouble – say, a germ invader – but also by the interference with functioning which is always associated with habitual wrong use of the mechanism and helps to lower the patient's resistance to the point where the germ invader gets its opportunity'.[30] In this chapter, F.M. criticises the celebrated medical statesman and royal physician Lord Dawson of Penn† (1864–1945), who had denounced the 'folly' of attempting 'to treat disease without knowing what is wrong with the body as a whole', while failing to recognise the validity of F.M.'s principles.[31] F.M. concludes by wondering whether, if his Technique 'were to be made the basis of an

* As Alexander Leeper wrote in his report of 1908 (see Chapter 3 above): 'I believe that his method is as yet largely empirical, and that there is some element of chance in the discoveries on which he has lighted.'

† Dawson is best known to history for two things: his successful recommendation in 1918 that a Ministry of Health be established; and the bulletin he issued from George V's deathbed in 1936 that 'the King's life is drawing peacefully towards its close' (whereas in fact Dawson was about to kill the sovereign with a euthanasia injection).

educational plan', it might not 'lead in time to the substitution of reasoning reactions for those instinctive reactions which are manifested as prejudice, racial or otherwise,* herd instinct, undue "self-determination" and rivalry, etc., which . . . have so far brought to nought our efforts to realise goodwill to all men and peace upon earth'.[32]

The Use of the Self attracted good reviews and sales in Britain; but despite Dewey's imprimatur, it aroused little interest in America. This was a disappointment to F.M.;[33] for although it was eight years since he had last taught in the United States, a steady flow of pupils had continued to cross the Atlantic to take lessons with him in London, often at some financial sacrifice. Indeed, of the nine students participating in his training course at the time of the book's publication, three were American women who had been taught by him in the late 1920s and won over to his cause.

The first training course started in February 1931 with eight students, all former pupils of F.M. Six were women: Margaret Goldie, who took time off from her work at the little school; Irene Stewart (1906–90), a schoolfriend of Goldie; Erika Schumann (born 1912), Ethel Webb's German niece, whom F.M. had helped overcome her curvature of the spine; Jean MacInnes, a former pupil at the little school; and two Americans, Marjorie Barstow (1899–1995), a teacher of ballroom dancing, and Lulie Westfeldt (1895–1965), a tiny woman with a biting wit whom F.M. had saved from becoming seriously crippled. The two men were close friends who had recently come down from Cambridge – Gurney MacInnes, Jean's asthmatic brother, and George Trevelyan (1906–1996), a handsome dilettante from a famous political dynasty whose father was then education minister in Ramsay Macdonald's

---

* This seems to indicate that F.M. had shed (or wished it to be thought that he had shed) some of the 'racial' views he had expressed in *Man's Supreme Inheritance*.

Labour government. During the next three years, they were joined on the course by five others: Kitty Merrick (1900–88), an American friend of Lulie, who was accepted by F.M. despite suffering from schizophrenia; Patrick Macdonald (1910–91), a Cambridge boxing blue and son of F.M.'s great medical ally Dr Peter Macdonald; Charles Neil (1917–58), an asthmatic teenager in whom F.M. took a fatherly interest; and two members of F.M.'s own family – his niece Marjory Mechin (born 1915), daughter of his sister Amy, and his nephew Max Alexander (1916–97), son of A.R. The three Americans were in their thirties; the rest were in their twenties or younger, Neil being a mere sixteen when he joined in 1933. Marjorie Barstow, the MacInneses, Macdonald and Trevelyan came from wealthy families; none of the rest was well off, and some had to struggle to pay their fees and make ends meet. Several of them were to leave interesting recollections of their years with F.M.[34]

The method of training was simple. From ten to twelve every morning, five days a week, forty weeks a year, the students would assemble in A.R.'s teaching room at Ashley Place, where each would receive in turn a short lesson from either F.M. or A.R. (or sometimes both together) while the rest watched and listened. During the afternoon, either in a small 'students' room' at the back of Ashley Place or in their own lodgings, they would practise on themselves or each other, using such experience as they had gained. After studying for a year or so, they would also do some work on the children of the little school under the supervision of Irene Tasker. In the evening, F.M. would occasionally take a party of them to the theatre or cinema, commenting on the 'use' of the actors, or invite them to dinner at Penhill, after which he would nostalgically recite either Shakespeare monologues or the Australian ballads of his youth. On the whole, however, he maintained an attitude of detachment, not wishing to hear much about their lives outside the course.

At the outset, the students were fired with tremendous idealism: most of them had already been considerably helped

The Young Reciter, 1894

ı his future wife Edith Page, *c*.1900

In London, 1910

With John Dewey in New York, *c.*1920

ill

his horse, Peter

With his adopted daughter, Peggy

With the children of the Little School

Entertaining training course students at Penhill, *c.*1932. L. to R.: F.M
Kitty Merrick, Ethel Webb, George Trevelyan, A.R., Erika Schumann,
Lulie Westfeldt, Gurney MacInnes, Marjorie Barstow

ey MacInnes and George Trevelyan during the First Training
se, *c.*1934

ck MacDonald teaches
y to box at Penhill, while
ge Trevelyan looks on

Walter Carrington around
the time he joined the
Second Training Course, 1936

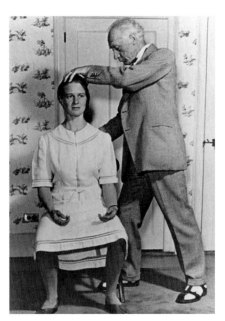

Teaching Margaret Goldie

Teaching John, son of the
Birmingham industrialist
Robert Best

The actor-reciter performing at
Penhill (the spats being part of
his normal attire)

With Lord Lytton, 'the best friend we have ever known in the interests of the work', on F.M.'s 70th birthday, January 1939

…h Sir Stafford …d Dame Isobel …ripps, 'friends …n high places', on F.M.'s …0th birthday, January 1949

At Ashley Place, with 80th birthday portrait by Colin Colahan

Cartoon by Ronald Searle
in the *News Chronicle*,
26 February 1953:
'He Teaches the Way
back to Health...'

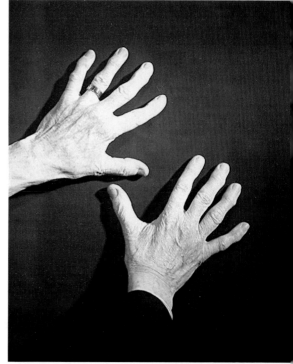

F.M.'s hands, 1941

by F.M., and they regarded themselves as pioneers in a great enterprise. Inevitably, an element of disenchantment set in. By the end of the first year of training, they tended to feel that, while gaining personally from the morning sessions with F.M. and A.R., they had learned little and understood less – a feeling which, if anything, intensified during the second year. Like Robert Best, they were frustrated by the fact that so little was explained to them: although F.M. talked incessantly and indeed fascinatingly during training sessions, often relating anecdotes from his life, his words gave them few real insights as to what was going on. Eventually, they learned to listen less and observe more, and to regard their studies not as an 'end-gaining' exercise but as a process of gradual development. (They were, after all, trying to acquire in less than forty months the skills F.M. had taught himself over forty years.) Only during the third year did they begin to feel that they were at last acquiring some proper understanding of the art.[35]

The attitude of the students towards F.M. varied considerably. At one end of the spectrum, Margaret Goldie worshipped the ground he trod on; at the other, Lulie Westfeldt felt affronted by his lack of personal interest in her. Most came to regard him as a flawed genius. As time passed, the students divided into two rival groups, one led by George Trevelyan, the other by Patrick Macdonald.[36] (These two Cambridge men did not get on, Trevelyan being a tea-drinking 'aesthete', Macdonald a beer-drinking 'hearty'.) Trevelyan's group included the MacInneses, Erika Schumann and Irene Stewart, Macdonald's the three American students and Marjory Mechin. On the whole, the Trevelyan group continued to admire and respect F.M., while the Macdonald group became irritated by his remoteness and inability to explain and preferred the more down-to-earth A.R. Macdonald himself (who had grown up with the Technique, having had lessons since he was ten) saw F.M. as 'a great experimenter and an artist – a Leonardo da Vinci – but a bad teacher', who 'couldn't understand what went on in the minds of others', whereas A.R. was 'much better at expressing himself . . . and had more insight into people's feelings and reactions'.[37] The Trevelyan group, on the other hand, regarded A.R. as a dreadful bully, and even signed a petition in the third year complaining about his behaviour.[38] In any case, A.R. was no longer happy at Ashley Place owing to personal differences with F.M. (which the rivalry of the student groups can have done little to assuage): his wife having died in 1933, he emigrated to the United States the following year, to revive the teaching in Boston.

F.M.'s attitude towards the students was equally ambiguous. He enjoyed having disciples; and though it was in his nature to keep a certain distance, he saw them as a kind of family. The course was inevitably something of an experiment, and as such he regarded it as a challenge. Yet from the beginning, he had doubts about the whole enterprise. He thought that the students ought to be able to find things out for themselves, as he had done, and was irritated by their constant questioning. He foresaw that, when they graduated, some would imagine they could teach, though in fact barely competent to do so, whereas others would leave him and become successful in their own right, possibly perverting his principles in the process. He did not believe that any of them would ever approach his own standard of teaching and understanding. After the course had been going for a year, Lulie Westfeldt sensed that he was becoming bored with it; she heard it said that his heart had never really been in it, that he had begun it merely to keep his supporters happy.[39]

During the third year, F.M. astonished his students by announcing that they would be appearing in public performances of *The Merchant of Venice* which he proposed to produce at two of London's most famous theatres, the Old Vic and Sadler's Wells, both of which were then managed by his old friend and pupil Dame Lilian Baylis (1874–1937). He himself would play Shylock, and he would personally coach the students in the other parts using his methods. The Alexander Trust Fund would advance the expenses of the production, which it was hoped to recoup from ticket sales. This prospect certainly had the effect of reviving F.M.'s enthusiasm: it both enabled him to relive memories of thirty years earlier, when he had produced the play all over New South Wales with the students of his 'Sydney Dramatic and Operatic Conservatorium', and represented the fulfilment of his life-long ambition to appear on the London stage. He threw himself into the project with gusto, giving up much of his afternoon teaching to train the students in their roles.[40]

While the production made a refreshing change to their normal routine, the students were somewhat nonplussed by it. Unlike the Sydney students of yore, none of them had signed up for a drama course; most knew nothing about acting, and some did not care to appear in public. Moreover, F.M. had a totally unrealistic view of his ability to turn them into actors ('he thought all he had to do was to get us to put our heads forward and up,' recalled Macdonald[41]), and after several weeks of rehearsing there were no signs that the production was going to be anything other than a disaster. Reluctantly, F.M. called in a professional director, Reginald Bach, who at first thought the students the worst actors he had ever encountered, though he was amazed at how rapidly they learned and improved thanks to their knowledge of the Alexander Technique. When they finally performed at the two theatres, on charity nights in December 1933, they were adjudged by the critics to acquit themselves creditably. F.M. gave a sympathetic and accomplished (if somewhat old-fashioned) rendering of Shylock, and the students, for all their shortcomings, were brisk and audible and showed no stage fright. The audiences were enthusiastic, consisting as they largely did of F.M.'s friends and supporters: when he came out in front of the curtain at the Old Vic to make a few introductory remarks, so deafening was the applause that it was some minutes before he could say a word.

The original students had now finished their three years; but F.M. pronounced them not yet ready to teach, and invited them to stay on for a fourth year (1934) without extra fees. This they all gratefully agreed to do – though when they heard that F.M. would be using them in another Shakespeare production, this time *Hamlet*, with himself in the epony-mous role, it occurred to some of them that he may have been more interested in having a company of actors at his continued disposal than in perfecting their training. (*Hamlet* was the other play which F.M. had produced with his Sydney students in 1901–3.) During this year, however, most of the students did make the breakthrough which had hitherto eluded them, and at last felt confident to teach. With the benefit of experience, they encountered fewer difficulties in their Shakespeare rehearsals,* and their performances in November 1934 received much praise. The *Daily Telegraph* wrote:

> With the exception of Mr Alexander himself, not one of the cast had any real acting experience, even as an amateur; and in spite of that, the performance was a good one . . . It certainly speaks well for his methods that his pupils were able to bear themselves with such confidence and to speak so clearly that their manifest lack of stage technique was discounted. In the part of Hamlet, Mr Alexander had an advantage over the company. Thirty years ago . . . he was an elocutionist; and the fact was apparent last night. There was balance, rhythm and intelligence in every line he spoke.[42]

Despite all the problems associated with it, Alexander's first training course must be considered a success in that, with a single exception, all the original students stuck to it until the end, were awarded their certificates, and went on to teach, some eventually becoming outstanding teachers.

---

* The students also benefited from the advice of F.M.'s old friend Matheson Lang, now a film star, who had been playing Hamlet at the Lyceum when he had first turned to F.M. for help in 1908.

(The exception was Kitty Merrick, who experienced a serious recurrence of her psychiatric trouble during the course – though even she ended up as an accomplished teacher.) Patrick Macdonald, Marjory Mechin, Erika Schumann and Irene Stewart stayed on as assistant teachers at Ashley Place, where their services were needed after the departures of A.R. and Irene Tasker. George Trevelyan practised on his own in London,* later becoming a master at Gordonstoun. Gurney MacInnes also went to teach at a boarding school, Weymouth College, where the headmaster, Pite, was a supporter of the Technique and introduced it into the curriculum (the only time this was to happen at an established school for many years). Jean MacInnes joined a recent medical supporter of F.M., Dr Mungo Douglas of Bolton, Lancashire, giving lessons (with limited success) to his patients. Marjorie Barstow and Max Alexander went to Boston to become assistants to A.R. Lulie Westfeldt set up her own practice in New York, and was furious to learn that F.M. was telling people that he knew of no one competent to teach his work there. Charles Neil, whom he had treated like a son, did what F.M. had most dreaded – after a short spell of teaching at Ashley Place, he set up on his own in London, eventually teaching what F.M. regarded as a bastardised version of his Technique.

In September 1936, by which time the last arrivals on the first course (apart from Max Alexander) had graduated, F.M. accepted the first of a second intake. This second course eventually grew to have about twenty students: the leading lights (all destined to become famous Alexander teachers) were Walter Carrington (born 1915), a vicar's son whose mother had been

---

* According to Trevelyan's biographer, parental disapproval of his decision to become an Alexander teacher may have led to his disinheritance: in 1937, his father, Sir Charles Trevelyan, Bt, without even informing George, his eldest son and heir, decided to donate the family seat of Wallington in Northumberland to the National Trust (Frances Farrer, *Sir George Trevelyan and the New Spiritual Awakening* [Floris Books, 2002], pp. 35–6, 59–60).

helped by F.M. to overcome an incapacitating illness; Eric de Peyer (1906–90), an Oxford-educated archaeologist; Wilfred ('Bill') Barlow (1915–91), a charismatic Welshman who combined his training with the completion of medical studies at St Thomas's Hospital; Richard ('Dick') Walker (1911–92), a championship golfer inspired by *The Use of the Self*; and Walker's wife Elizabeth (born 1914), formerly a radiologist.[43] F.M. had learned much from the first course – for example, that it was a mistake to allow students to put their hands on others until they had been training for at least a year. The students also benefited from being able to compare experiences with their predecessors who were now assistants at Ashley Place. There were no more theatrical productions: F.M. had got that fantasy out of his system. There were now several dozen teachers, students, doctors and supporters who considered themselves to be actively involved in Alexander's work; and in 1937 the Alexander Society* was founded, with George Trevelyan as its secretary, to enable them to keep in touch.

Though it still consisted of a small class of children with special difficulties, Irene Tasker's little school at Ashley Place had continued to develop and flourish. Parents wrote gratefully that their sons and daughters had become 'different in every way' after a spell there. Dewey, who spent two days observing its work on a visit to London, declared that he wished he had been a pupil there.[44] The involvement of the training course students from 1932 onwards lent a new dimension to the school's activities. At the end of each term, the children produced a magazine called the *Alexander Times* and gave a concert to demonstrate their improved 'use': the concert was originally known as the termly 'Do', until a pupil pointed out that this

---

* This society, whose functions were purely social, effectively ended its brief life with the outbreak of war in 1939, and is not to be confused with the later attempts (described in Chapters 6 and 8) to found a 'society' in the sense of a professional association with regulatory powers.

was hardly appropriate in view of the fact that they were being taught what *not* to do, whereupon it became the 'No-Do'. After attending a No-Do in 1931, F.M. wrote in the *Alexander Times*:

Last Thursday I was present at the No-Do given by the pupils in the little school. I have recollections, pleasing recollections of the 'Do's' previously given by the pupils, but the 'No-Do' has provided me with even more pleasing recollections . . . [I]nstead of the bustle and excitement usually associated with children's performances at end of term, there was a calm and deliberate attitude pervading all that was done. Miss Tasker . . . was sitting in the audience obviously confident they would not fail to be true to the principle of No-Do performance. Even the youngest pupil carried out his parts with the assurance of the trained and experienced performer. When one little girl forgot her lines she was not in the least disturbed. No shuffling of feet or twitching of mouth or fingers. Just placid 'Non-Doing' until 'Memory became once more faithful to his office', and on she went as if nothing had happened . . . It was noticeable that the attitude of calm and confidence was passed on by the young performers to the adults and others in the audience, and we all had an enjoyable and instructive experience . . .[45]

By 1933, it was clear that the school would soon have to move out of Ashley Place: there were now about a dozen school pupils, and with a dozen students also on the training course, the premises were becoming cramped. At this moment, a fairy godmother appeared in the form of Miss Esther Lawrence, the wealthy American who had recently retired as Principal of the Froebel Institute. Since taking lessons before the First World War, she had been a fervent supporter of Alexander; during her years at the Froebel, she had sent him a number of her students, such as Margaret Goldie. She now bought a large Victorian house in Cromwell Road, West London, which she proposed to hand over to F.M. for the establishment of a proper school, at which children of all ages might be taught all subjects according to his principles. She bought furniture for it; she installed a housekeeper; she proposed to bring in some of her most talented Froebel graduates to help with the teaching. F.M. professed to be delighted: he gave a party at Ashley Place to celebrate the news, and asked Ludovici to announce it in his *Health and Education through Self-Mastery*, the publication of which was imminent. However, when the students returned from their summer vacations, it was clear that there had been a row between F.M. and Miss Lawrence, and that the move to Cromwell Road was off. Possibly F.M. had been alarmed to learn that Miss Lawrence envisaged a continuing role for herself and her Froebel teachers in the new school. At all events, she had no more to do with F.M.[46]

What finally happened was that, in 1934, the school became a boarding establishment and moved to Penhill. Much as F.M. loved this property, its upkeep had evidently been a strain since his financial disaster of 1929. He moved out of the big house into the cottage which had formerly been occupied by the Rose family of retainers. The cost of establishing the school at Penhill was met by the Alexander Trust Fund (which presumably paid rent to F.M. as landlord). The reception rooms were turned into classrooms, the bedrooms into dormitories. F.M.'s mistress Jack Vicary ('Aunty Jack' to the children, who adored her) became the matron; the excellent Mrs Tiffin, formerly at Ashley Place, did the cooking. Irene Tasker assumed the title of headmistress, with Margaret Goldie (who had graduated early from the training course) as her deputy. During the week, the students of the training course came down in relays to help teach the children. At weekends, F.M. himself appeared and spent much time with the children, in whose company he always seemed happiest and who seemed to accept him as one of themselves. (Once, when Patrick Macdonald was teaching at the school, a child smacked his backside and then explained, 'Sorry, I thought you were F.M.')

A problem now arose, in that Irene Tasker (aged forty-seven) and Margaret Goldie (aged twenty-nine) found it difficult to live under the same roof: both harboured romantic feelings towards F.M., who had recently paid Goldie the highly sugges- tive compliment of inviting her, in his Shakespeare produc- tions, to play Portia to his Shylock and Ophelia to his Hamlet, as Edith had done thirty years earlier. (Some believed that Goldie, like Jack Vicary, was F.M.'s lover – though others found it hard to imagine this somewhat frigid personality having a physical relationship with F.M. or anyone.) Such was the atmosphere that, after only a few months at Penhill, Irene decided to resign. With F.M.'s encouragement, she went out to establish the work in South Africa: arriving there in 1935, armed with a letter of introduction from Lord Lytton to General Smuts, she quickly built up a successful practice and befriended many eminent people, whom she sent to have lessons with F.M. on their visits to London. Goldie took over as headmistress at Penhill, assisted by the student teachers. Whereas 'Miss Tasker' had been a remarkable teacher of the children, and much loved by them, 'Miss Goldie' was regarded by them as a cold, bossy and unsympathetic woman, though F.M. would never hear a word against her.*

In the mid-1930s, with the return of economic stability, F.M. again found himself busy with his private practice at Ashley Place. His new pupils at this time included three internation- ally famous personalities (all of whom happened to be iden- tified with the left in politics, and causes such as pacifism) who were to become notable supporters of his work – the novelist Aldous Huxley, the playwright George Bernard Shaw, and the lawyer and politician Sir Stafford Cripps.

A grandson of the great Victorian scientist T. H. Huxley who had been Darwin's friend and supporter, Aldous Huxley (1894–1963) rose to fame in the 1920s with a series of

---

* 'Margaret Goldie is a genius as a teacher and such an one [*sic*] must be given a free hand.' (F.M. to Waldo Frank, 5 December 1936.)

brilliant, sceptical novels about contemporary English life, and became recognised as one of the literary giants of his generation with the publication in 1932 of his satirical vision of the future, *Brave New World*. He had always suffered from poor health, notably with regard to posture (he was a stooping giant), eyesight and digestion; and while working on his new novel *Eyeless in Gaza*, which incorporated many traumatic themes from his own life, he found himself racked with insomnia, depression and muscular pains. He was on the verge of a total breakdown when he began a course of lessons with F.M. in November 1935.[47] The results were dramatic: within one month, he was able to overcome shyness and disability to make a public speech for the first time in years; within three months, he was able to finish his long-stalled book. On 21 February 1936, his wife wrote to his American publisher: 'He [Alexander] has certainly made a new & unrecognisable person of Aldous, not physically only but mentally & therefore morally. Or rather, he has brought out, actively, what we, Aldous's best friends, know never came out either in the novels or with strangers.'[48]

Like Dewey, Huxley was not just transformed by the Alexander Technique, but intellectually fascinated by it. In recent years, his philosophical quest had brought him to the conclusion that people only exist as individuals and that all change must ultimately come from within. This was also central to F.M.'s thinking; and Huxley, like F.M., believed in mind–body unity. In completing *Eyeless in Gaza*, Huxley paid F.M. an unusual compliment by including recognisable elements of him in the character of Miller, the charismatic doctor whom the (autobiographical) hero, Anthony Beavis, meets in Mexico and by whom he is 'saved'. Certainly the physical description fits: 'He was an elderly little man, short and spare, but with a fine upright carriage which lent him a certain dignity. The face was curiously proportioned, with a short nose and an upper lip unusually long above a wide, tightly shut mouth. A mouth like an inquisitor's. But the inquisitor had forgotten himself and learned to smile . . .'[49] On first meeting Beavis, Miller makes various Alexander-like observations. 'Slumped down like that – it's awful . . . And when the spine's in that state, what happens to the rest of the machine?' 'You've got to change if you want to go on existing.' 'You're a clever man, that's obvious. But it's equally obvious that you have an unconscious body. An efficient thinking apparatus and a hopelessly stupid set of muscles and bones and viscera.'[50] F.M. is even mentioned in person: when Miller starts to treat Beavis, he employs (amongst other methods) 'training, along F. M. Alexander's lines, in the use of the self, beginning with physical control and achieving through it (since mind and body are one) control of impulses and feelings'.[51] Later, in Beavis's diary, we read a straightforward summary of the Technique, using Alexander's terminology – 'Become conscious, inhibit, cease to be a greedy end-gainer, concentrate on means . . .'[52]

F.M. was delighted by these references, as is clear from a letter he wrote to Waldo Frank in August 1936,[53] a month after the book's publication. He was probably less delighted that 'Miller' combined the Alexander Technique with various ideas from other sources, including a brand of mysticism (from Huxley's friend Gerald Heard), a belief that most disease originates in the intestines (from McDonagh, the doctor shared by Huxley and F.M.), and even the homespun philosophy of a plumber to whom F.M. was giving free lessons at the time, whose witticisms he had shared with Huxley.[54] Much as he admired F.M.'s teachings, Huxley never believed that they constituted a complete system. (This was a view he shared with Robert Best, to whom he wrote in 1942: 'That this art discovered by F.M. can be combined with other arts of physical, mental and spiritual education seems to me obvious; and if it doesn't seem so to dear old F.M., that is because he manifests the defects as well as the merits of a completely one-pointed mind.'[55]) Nevertheless, Huxley, as Frank Pierce Jones remarks, 'did more than any other writer to bring Alexander's work to the attention of the reading public'.[56] In 1937, he published *Ends and Means*, the first of many philosophical works in which he recommended the Technique.

Whereas Huxley was forty-two when he took lessons in 1935, one of the *enfants terribles* of the day, George Bernard Shaw (1856–1950) was eighty when he met F.M. the following year, a grand old man of English letters. He learned about F.M. through his friendship with George Trevelyan's father, the patrician socialist Sir Charles Trevelyan; staying with the Trevelyans at Wallington, their estate in Northumberland, in the summer of 1936, he was intrigued to hear mention of Alexander's work by Lady Trevelyan, and duly signed up for a course of forty lessons. Not only did Shaw obtain relief from his angina and other problems, but he and F.M. struck up a warm friendship based on their common love of music hall: when he came for lessons, Ashley Place would echo with snatches of Edwardian songs emanating from F.M.'s teaching room. The only matter on which they disagreed was Shaw's vegetarianism and teetotalism, which F.M. deplored, assuring the old man that he would benefit from eating a good steak washed down with burgundy.[57] As Jackie Evans has fascinatingly explained in her family history of the Alexanders,[58] Shaw may have been one of the few people in England who knew the truth about F.M.'s background: for Shaw's cousin, another Bernard Shaw, had been a landowner in Northern Tasmania; he had been the employer of an Irish immigrant named William McKenna; McKenna's son Ben had gone on to become the local racehorse trainer; and F.M.'s long-forgotten father John Alexander (who died in September 1936, just as Shaw was taking lessons with F.M.) spent the last twenty-seven years of his long life as Ben McKenna's resident blacksmith.

Shaw continued to have lessons with F.M. for the rest of his life, which he was convinced had been prolonged by the Alexander Technique. Although he did not take the same intellectual interest in F.M.'s teachings as Huxley, he was nevertheless fascinated by them for two reasons. First, he shared F.M.'s cynical view of the medical profession and its concept of 'cure': F.M. must have been familiar with Shaw's play *The Doctor's Dilemma*, first shown in 1906 soon after his arrival in London, and its famous preface alleging that medicine is a racket designed to get people to spend money on 'cures' which are at best unnecessary and at worst harmful. Secondly, he saw F.M.'s theories as a useful stick with which to beat one of his *bêtes noires*, the Russian behaviourist I. P. Pavlov (1849–1936), with his theory of 'conditioned reflexes'. In the preface to a collection of his 1880s music criticism which appeared in 1937, Shaw wrote: 'Alexander has established not only the beginnings of a far-reaching science of the apparently involuntary movements which we call reflexes, but a technique of correction and self-control which forms a substantial addition to our very slender resources in personal education.'[59]

Considered one of the most brilliant minds of his generation, Stafford Cripps (1889–1952) distinguished himself while young both as a chemist and a lawyer, and went on to make a fortune at the patent bar. He was a fervent Christian who entered politics almost by accident in 1930, when he was prevailed upon to take office as Solicitor-General (carrying a knighthood) in a Labour administration which included his father Lord Parmoor, his uncle Sidney Webb, and Sir Charles Trevelyan. (Cripps was not even an MP at the time, though elected soon afterwards at a by-election in a safe Labour seat.) As the 1930s progressed, he adopted extreme socialist views, which often put him at odds with the Labour Party. Like Huxley, he suffered from poor health (both men were considered unfit for service during the First World War), not helped in his case by the fact that he was a workaholic who tortured himself over moral questions. Like Shaw, he was a vegetarian and a teetotaller – though in other respects, despite his later identification with socialist 'austerity', he enjoyed his considerable wealth and lived well.

Cripps and his wife Isobel became aware of F.M. through their friendship with Waldo Frank, F.M.'s New York pupil of 1914 and now a prominent figure in the international socialist movement. During the 1920s, Frank had been divorced by Margaret Naumburg and married Alma Magoon, a child psychologist. In 1937, Alma came to London to join Alexander's second training course, staying with the Crippses. Lady Cripps had long suffered from headaches and exhaustion which no doctor could diagnose or cure; and Alma persuaded her that the Alexander Technique might be the answer to her problems. As Isobel later wrote: 'I did a course of three weeks' lessons with Alexander and . . . felt a definite relief from pressure and felt more sure than ever that I had stumbled upon some truth. He has the most wonderful hands . . . After my three weeks . . . I got Stafford to go and CANNOT be grateful enough for what it has done for us both . . .'[60] So transformed did Cripps feel that, after his original course, he sought a lesson from F.M. before making any important speech. F.M. did not generally have a high opinion of politicians, but he admired Cripps for his intelligence, independence of mind and high principles: although Cripps was 'in the wilderness' when he first came to F.M. early in 1938, he was to hold high office throughout the 1940s,* and render many useful services to F.M. and his work. Cripps was to say of the Alexander Technique: 'The extraordinary thing is that, when you experience it, you become perfectly convinced it is right.'†[61]

With the establishment of his school and training course, the publication of another book, the approval of some prominent doctors, the support of men such as Lytton and Huxley, and (apart from the lull of the early 1930s) the steady

---

* Ambassador to the USSR, 1940–2; Lord Privy Seal, Leader of the House of Commons, and Churchill's envoy to India, 1942; Minister for Aircraft Production, 1942–5; President of the Board of Trade, 1945–7; Minister for Economic Affairs, 1947; Chancellor of the Exchequer, 1947–9.

† Other well-known pupils of F.M. during the 1930s included the novelist Maurice Baring, the writer and publisher Leonard Woolf, the actress Marie Ney, the actors Robert Donat and Leslie Howard, the conductor Sir Adrian Boult (who also sent his stepson to the school at Penhill), the poet Robert Nicholls and the artist Paul Nash.

expansion of his practice, F.M.'s work made important progress during the fifteen years covered by this chapter. Had he died at the beginning of the period, the work would probably have died with him; by 1939, it had a chance of survival. Yet the great breakthrough did not occur. He still received no official recognition from any quarter. The enthusiasm he aroused among some eminent people was matched by equal scepticism among others.* The school and the training course marked steps in the right direction; but with only a handful of pupils and students, they represented small beginnings.

It is difficult to avoid the conclusion that F.M. was himself partly responsible for the fact that his work did not progress as far and as fast as it might have done. He seems to have been perpetually torn between two conflicting desires, to see his discoveries sweep the world, and to keep them firmly under his personal control; and the latter generally prevailed over the former. Thus it repeatedly happened that, when his supporters tried to help him, he at first welcomed their help, but finally rejected it. Two striking examples occurred in the early 1930s – Dewey's attempt to institute scientific research into the Alexander Technique, and Miss Lawrence's offer of a house for the school. Both episodes were witnessed by the students of his first training course, who were invited in each case to a celebratory party, only to hear later that the cause for celebration had been abandoned. Lulie Westfeldt speculated as to why F.M. should have behaved in this way. 'An opportunity presented itself, and he welcomed it as it increased his prestige and importance. Then gradually he commenced to sense where it would lead. It would lead to the necessity for co-operation and give-and-take with other people; other people might even criticise him; he might be forced to adopt some of their ways; he would no longer be monarch of all

---

* For an unflattering depiction of him in the literature of this period, see H. G. Wells's novel *Apropos of Dolores* (1938), in which he is satirised in the character of Bunnington.

he surveyed, no longer accountable to no one. As this picture took shape in F.M.'s mind, F.M. must have felt that the opportunity would have to be killed.'[62] Dewey similarly concluded that F.M. refused to proceed with the research project 'because of obstinate early prejudices – whose formation or persistence is readily understandable on any theory except his own'.[63]

To be fair to F.M., it was not just a jealous and possessive nature which led him to take this view. His work was subtle, rigorous, and difficult to understand, and he was constantly fearful that, if it escaped from his control, various 'popular' versions of it would become established, and the essence would be lost. He had some reason to hold these fears: for he had (as he saw it) been outrageously plagiarised (by Spicer in 1909, and by Lee in 1922); and by 1939, some of his former students who had set up on their own (notably Charles Neil) were already starting to 'adapt' his teachings. But F.M.'s habit of biting the hands that fed him did his cause no good. Dewey and Miss Lawrence had been among his most passionate supporters; neither wanted much more to do with him once they understood that their efforts on his behalf had been wasted. Other supporters, such as Best, were constantly exasperated by F.M., putting up with him reluctantly because of their belief in his work. It is possible that F.M. was inspired to start his training course (which he seems to have done with some doubt and hesitation) by hints from crucial supporters such as Lytton and Macdonald that they might otherwise abandon him.

Another factor which held F.M. back was that he suffered to some degree from an inferiority complex as a result of his humble origins, lack of formal education and limited powers of self-expression. He may well have been apprehensive that he would be 'shown up' by clever research scientists in America, or clever Froebel teachers in Cromwell Road. His refusal to be drawn by men such as Robert Best into a discussion of his work was probably rooted in a lack of intellectual self-confidence. For similar reasons, he was reluctant to spread his message by such means as lecturing or giving public demonstrations.* Another pupil who tried to help him was John Hilton (1880–1943), Professor of Industrial Relations at the University of Cambridge; he recommended the Alexander Technique in a speech to the Institute of Labour Management in 1936,[64] but felt frustrated by F.M.'s attitude when he attempted to discuss with him other ways of publicising his work. Hilton wrote to Best: 'On the one hand, he wants to make his theory and his practice widely known with a real desire to see mankind improve along his lines, but on the other he very much wants to retain the proprietary rights in his technique, which he fears might pass from him if he "gave his methods away".'[65] On the whole, F.M. was adept at winning adherents to his cause, but inept in his long-term dealings with them: as Patrick Macdonald told Edward Owen, 'he could "read" people from the viewpoint of "use" but didn't understand what made them tick otherwise'.

One category of supporters which F.M. warmly encouraged were the doctors who believed in his work. Throughout the 1920s and 1930s, Macdonald, Murdoch and Rugg-Gunn published a steady stream of learned papers in his support. (Of particular interest is Murdoch's *The Function of the Sub-Occipital Muscles: The Key to Posture, Use and Functioning* [1936], which attempted to provide a physiological explanation for the Alexander Technique.[66]) McDonagh also praised F.M. in a multi-volume work which he brought out during these years, *The Nature of Disease*.[67] F.M. seemed immensely pleased when, on 29 May 1937, a letter appeared in the *British Medical Journal* signed by nineteen doctors, claiming that he had much to offer the medical profession, suggesting that his teachings ought eventually to be included in the medical curriculum, and urging that 'as soon as possible steps should be taken for an investigation of Alexander's work', adding that

* A rare example of F.M.'s performance in both genres was his lecture-cum-demonstration at Bedford Physical Training College in August 1934: the proceedings survive, and do not give the impression that the audience was greatly inspired by F.M. (Fischer (ed.), *Articles and Lectures*, XXIV.)

F.M. had 'given us an assurance that he is ready and willing to give us the benefit of his experience for the carrying out of any plan which those concerned may suggest, provided that in his opinion [*sic*] the plan is one that would make it possible for him to help us to the desired end'. The signatories included eminent physicians who had known him in Edwardian days, such as Percy Jakins and Bruce Porter; the faithful quartet of Macdonald, McDonagh, Murdoch and Rugg-Gunn (along with all Murdoch's partners at his group practice in Sussex); and newer supporters such as Dr Mungo Douglas of Bolton (who would resign from the British Medical Association in 1945 in protest at its failure to take more interest in Alexander's work).[68] However, the pleas of the nineteen fell on deaf ears (had they not done so, their attempts to promote 'investigation' might well have suffered the same fate as those instigated by Dewey); and F.M. did himself no favours by his frequent and some-times intemperate attacks on the medical profession, and such influential figures within it as Lord Dawson. As his coming libel case was to show, he had acquired a bad reputation among the leading lights of British medicine, though few of them had much acquaintance with his work.

The 1930s brought F.M. both sadness and responsibility as head of his extended family of brothers and sisters. In 1932, his eldest sister Agnes died, never having got over the death of their mother nine years earlier. In 1933, his brother-in-law and friend George Mechin died, having been ruined by the economic crisis: F.M. looked after his widowed sister Amy, and took a fatherly interest in her two daughters, accepting Marjory on his training course and employing Joan in various capacities at Penhill and Ashley Place. The same year also saw the death of A.R.'s wife Grace, followed by A.R.'s departure for America, F.M. keeping an avuncular eye on his son Max during his years on the training course (1934–7). F.M.'s greatest worry, however, was Beaumont (1886–1982), the youngest of the family and his junior by eighteen years, a charming conman who frequently turned to F.M. for help when on the run: though sorely tried by him, F.M. seems to have retained a special affection and even a sneaking admiration for 'young Monty'.

F.M. continued to support his wife Edith and visit her at the flat in Little Venice where she led her reclusive life. All who knew of the relationship considered his behaviour towards her a model of patience and 'conscious control'. When she became ill in the summer of 1938, he had her moved to a nursing home in South London – though after her death there in September he characteristically refused to settle a bill for some extra comforts to relieve her sufferings, ordered by her nephew Owen Vicary but not approved personally by himself.[69] With Peggy, during her adolescence, he enjoyed (according to Lulie Westfeldt, who frequently saw them together at Ashley Place) 'a relationship of deep trust and love. She called him "Daddy" and he called her "Pet". She went away with him on his holiday every year.* This relationship . . . brought out a tenderness and affection in him which was not often seen.'[70] When Peggy grew up, however, Lulie detected that the relationship had become notably less harmonious, confirming her in her suspicion that F.M. only found it easy to have satisfactory friendships with children.[71] He gave a dance to celebrate Peggy's twenty-first birthday in June 1939 – attended by the students of his training course, who observed that he waltzed beautifully. It was John Vicary, F.M.'s eight-year-old son by Jack, who now accompanied him on his holidays, and had probably supplanted her in his affections.

F.M. was seventy on 20 January 1939. The Alexander Society gave a dinner in his honour at the Carlton Hotel, chaired by Lord Lytton. Though not given to sentiment, he was touched by the large turnout, the warm expressions of affection and the family atmosphere of the occasion. On the same day

---

* F.M. generally spent his holidays at Elmer in Sussex, where he owned a small seaside villa.

another celebration took place in Boston, where the work had now been firmly re-established, organised by A.R. with the assistance of Marjorie Barstow and attended by Carla Atkinson and other old pupils of F.M. from the early 1920s.

He was a sprightly septuagenarian, considered by his doctor McDonagh to be in remarkable health for his age.[72] Meeting him in 1940, Frank Pierce Jones observed: 'He was shorter than I expected, but had an easy, upright carriage . . . His face was alert, with a bright, quizzical look in the eyes and a slight ironic twist to the mouth . . .* His hair was white but he did not wear glasses, and in voice, manner and movement he seemed much younger than I knew him to be.'[73] He was well groomed and dapper, cultivating an appearance which seemed distinctly old-fashioned: with his monocle, silver-topped cane and spats, he resembled a survival from the Edwardian age, or a stage character. He continued to enjoy (and insist upon) the best food, wine and cigars, and was a well-known figure at the Café Royal and other fashionable restaurants which he had frequented since his early days in London. (The dinner at the Carlton Hotel consisted of turtle soup, sole, chicken, two different puddings and a savoury, washed down with the best vintages of Pouilly Fuissé, Château Margaux, Krug Champagne and Graham's Port.) He still worked a long day, breaking only for morning cocoa, a light lunch, and tea. (Tea was a ritual at Ashley Place, F.M. claiming to be a connoisseur from his days working for a Melbourne tea merchant.) He devoted an hour, usually in the afternoon, to his training course; otherwise he concentrated on his private practice. He had made new advances in his teaching, and claimed that he could now get the 'primary control' going without any co-operation from the pupil.[74] For many years now, he had been absorbed in his work to the virtual exclusion of all other interests: it pervaded his conversation, his correspondence and such social life as he had, his only regular dining companions being McDonagh and

---

* Characteristics shared with Miller in *Eyeless in Gaza.*

Rugg-Gunn. He had no small talk; he was rarely seen to read for pleasure; his perusal of the newspapers was usually confined to the racing and horoscope pages; he no longer showed much interest in the arts, even the theatre, unless a pupil happened to be involved.

Apart from his work his only serious interest was racing, which indeed amounted to an obsession: he followed odds and placed bets throughout the working day. When, in 1933, he offered his niece Marjory Mechin a free place on his training course in return for assistance at Ashley Place, she discovered that her principal duties were in connection with the turf. 'I was on the go all day long, doing all his messages [communications with tipsters], putting on all his bets for the races, rushing down ten minutes after the race to find out who had won, and then back to get my instructions for the next one . . .'[75] He spent the brief intervals between lessons receiving information and giving instructions in this way, like a general keeping in touch with the front. Sometimes he listened to racing commentary on the wireless: to those who listened with him, it was always clear which horse he had backed. On Saturdays he often attended race meetings near London, setting out from Penhill in a chauffeur-driven car, resplendent in morning dress and topper, a carnation in his buttonhole and binoculars swinging from his shoulder.

Age had not greatly mellowed him; he could still be fierce, and sometimes fly into rages. (These were largely 'controlled': he might shout at a pupil in his teaching room, briefly emerge to ask someone calmly to place a bet for him on the 2.30, and then return to resume the shouting.[76]) Stories circulated testifying to his vigour and hot temper in old age. Once, when his woman driver found herself in an altercation with a lorry driver, F.M. got out and knocked the man down.[77] On another occasion, he arrived at Sidcup station to find passengers standing in the rain as there was no official to open the gate: F.M. forced it open, remarking angrily to those who followed him on to the platform, 'Yes, you had to wait for an old man to do it. In Australia, we'd have charged that gate and broken through.'[78] As ever, he was constantly on guard lest he be cheated or given a poor run for his money. He once visited Erika Schumann and Irene Stewart in Birmingham where they were teaching, and took them to an expensive restaurant. They were living on a shoestring and looking forward to their first good meal in weeks, when F.M. to their dismay returned their main course owing to some shortcoming.

During 1939, as for some years previously, F.M. was absorbed in producing a new book. Walter Carrington, the training course student who acted as his private secretary, has recalled the somewhat unusual manner in which this work took shape. In the course of his teaching, various points would occur to F.M. which he felt he had not yet expressed in print. During weekends at Penhill, he would jot these down, handing several pages of notes to Carrington on Monday morning for typing. At intervals, F.M. would sit down with Ethel Webb and Carrington to consider the accumulated notes; together, they would discuss and revise them, and the reworked notes would be filed under the subjects which would eventually become the chapters of the book. As Carrington recalled, 'It was more like the meticulous drafting of a legal document than writing a chronicle of thoughts and experiences.'[79] (He might have added that it did not make for a coherent work of literature.) The task of transforming the notes into chapters was entrusted to Anthony Ludovici, who, F.M. wrote to Irene Tasker in May 1939, was being 'most careful not to miss meaning in any endeavour to improve the manner of expression with a view to easier reading for the general public . . .'

An unexpected development now occurred which had important implications for Alexander's work and offered to give the new book an added dimension. During the 1920s and 1930s, George Ellett Coghill (1872–1941), an American professor of anatomy, had achieved international fame in scientific circles through his pioneering investigations into the relationship between the behaviour of living creatures and the development (both structural and functional) of their nervous systems. Coghill's painstaking researches concentrated on a species of American newt, the ablystoma, though he believed that his conclusions were generally applicable to all vertebrates. In essence, those conclusions were that behaviour depended on a 'total pattern of integration' in the mechanism which proceeded from the head downwards. The functioning of each part was related to the functioning of every other part. So long as the functionings of the various parts were 'integrated' with each other, all would be well; but if some parts started functioning 'individually', without reference to other parts, problems would arise in behaviour. As Coghill put it in his presidential address to the American Association of Anatomists in 1933,

. . . the processes of integration and individuation of parts are antagonistic to each other in the development of behaviour. The mechanism of total integration tends to maintain absolute unity and solidarity of the behaviour pattern. The development of localised mechanisms tends to disrupt unity and solidarity and to produce independent partial patterns of behaviour. In the interests of the welfare of the organism as a whole, partial patterns must not attain complete independence of action; they must be held under control by the mechanism of total integration. Parts become integrated with each other because they are integral factors of a primarily integrated whole, and they remain integrated, and their behaviour is normal, so long as this wholeness is maintained. But the wholeness may be lost through the decline of the mechanism of total integration or through the hypertrophy of mechanisms of partial patterns. This, I believe, is the biological basis of that conflict in behaviour which expresses itself widely in the field of psycho-pathology . . .[80]

The connections with Alexander's teachings are obvious: he too believed in the 'wholeness' of the organism, and mind–body unity (which was implicit in Coghill's theory); he had endlessly written about the human body as a complex machine in which all parts were interdependent and needed to operate in correct relationship to one another; and he had always argued that faults in functioning, and consequent health problems, resulted from a breakdown of this integrated relationship. It is perhaps surprising that only in April 1939 was the link between the two theories first mentioned in print when the New York journalist Arthur Busch, a pupil of A.R., devoted an editorial to the subject in the *Brooklyn Citizen*. This led to a vigorous correspondence in that newspaper, as a result of which Coghill, then a sick man living in retirement in Gainesville, Florida, began studying the writings of F.M., of whom he had not previously heard. On 4 June, he wrote to F.M. that he was reading his works 'with a great deal of interest and profit, amazed to see how you, years ago, discovered in human psychology and physiology the same principles which I worked out in the behaviour of the lower vertebrates. Yet until now we have never come into personal touch. Possibly this is because we are technically laymen as far as the medical profession is concerned. I am glad to see that the British profession is now recognising your accomplishments and that you are getting the credit and the hearing which you so richly deserve . . .'[81]

F.M. was overjoyed to receive this letter. He did not know of Coghill (though his students Walter Carrington and Alma Frank had heard of his work), and he probably found it difficult to understand a word of his highly technical writings, but it meant much to him to have this striking affirmation of his guiding principles from an expert source. 'According to Alma Frank he is "somebody" in the scientific world over there,' he wrote to Irene Tasker. 'Amazing, isn't it?'[82] Armed with this testimonial, he could 'now talk to the supposed scientific lads on a bit higher platform to theirs'.[83] He immediately invited Coghill to come to London for a free course of lessons, but regretfully Coghill had to decline: he was 'very restricted' by a heart condition, and dared not leave his Florida home with its private laboratory, where he was still able to work intermittently but feared he had all too little time to complete his researches.[84] F.M. had thought of bringing out his new book before the end of the year, but held it up as he wished to find some way of mentioning the link with Coghill.

Although F.M. generally took little interest in politics and world affairs, he was naturally preoccupied by the international news during 1938 and 1939. He was a firm supporter of Neville Chamberlain's policy of appeasing the dictators, and had little time for Winston Churchill, whom he regarded as a dangerous adventurer. (His attitude may have owed something to the fact that Churchill's wife Clementine had once taken lessons with him, and kept them secret from her husband who, as she told F.M., would greatly have disapproved of them.[85]) His letters to Irene Tasker during the first months of 1939 show him to have been incurably optimistic and extraordinarily naïve. He wrote that Hitler and Mussolini had ruined their countries,[86] that Britain alone was more than a match for them both,[87] and that they would never go to war for fear of incurring the enmity of America.[88] But on Friday 1 September, Germany invaded Poland; and on Sunday 3 September, Britain declared war on Germany. F.M. wrote to Irene from Penhill: 'Well, we are at war with Germany. That devil-maniac has had his evil way and plunged the world into darkness and misery . . . The consolation is . . . that the Nazi creed will be shattered in the dust and Hitler will go down to history as the greatest arch-enemy of mankind ever known. On this I shall have something to say in the new book.'[89]

6

War

1939–1946

The outbreak of war in September 1939 inevitably caused some disruption to F.M.'s work. Several of his assistant teachers, training course students and pupils left for the armed services, or took up war jobs outside London. As it was considered unsafe for the children to return to Penhill owing to its proximity to the Kent airfields, the school was evacuated to Conock Manor in Wiltshire, whose owner, the pioneer military aviator Colonel Robert Smith Barry, had been helped by F.M. to overcome war injuries.[1] Jack Vicary stayed behind to look after Penhill and Irene Stewart replaced her as school matron, further depleting the staff at Ashley Place.

Nevertheless, until the spring of 1940, things carried on much as before. F.M., still assisted by Marjory Mechin and Walter Carrington, continued teaching at Ashley Place, as well as training those students (including Wilfred Barlow) who remained on the course. The practice was soon busy again, as the stresses of war brought a new wave of interesting pupils: these included Squadron Leader Norris of the Air Ministry, Major Mahoney of the Irish Guards, Sir Richard Rees of the Red Cross, and Canon Shirley, Headmaster of King's School, Canterbury.[2] In other respects, life remained surprisingly unchanged. F.M. went racing as usual at Newmarket that autumn,[3] and had no trouble with the blackout thanks to his 'bushman's eyes'.[4]

Before the First World War, F.M. had discussed the possibility of introducing his methods into army training with his pupil General Murray – though these discussions were not followed up, doubtless in part owing to F.M.'s absence from England after 1914. During the early months of the Second World War, his supporter John Hilton, now Director of Home Publicity at the Ministry of Information, urged Colonel Wand-Tetley, Inspector of Physical Training at the War Office, to take note of Alexander's work, as a result of which some changes to the training regimen seem to have been made just before the Battle of Britain – though F.M. later considered these to have been of limited value, since 'although there may have been some appreciation by the Army authorities that the head-neck relationship should not be interfered with, they have relied on direct instruction [rather than inhibition] to attain this end'.[5]

The uncertainties of war resulted in a spate of hurriedly arranged marriages, several of which touched F.M. He had mixed feelings when Peggy, with whom his recent relations had been strained, announced that she had fallen in love with an NCO some years older than herself. 'I hope it is all right,' he wrote to Irene Tasker. 'Peggy is determined to marry him and there it is.'[*6] It was with greater pleasure that he reported the engagement of his assistant teacher and favourite niece Marjory Mechin to his training course student Wilfred Barlow, who had just completed his medical studies: F.M. believed the union would 'be of great value to the work in future, he being a doctor'.[7] Soon afterwards, Walter Carrington got engaged to Dilys Jones, a pupil of F.M. who did secretarial work at Ashley Place. Carrington had thought of becoming a Jesuit after completing his training in the summer of 1939, but was prevailed upon to stay on at Ashley Place by F.M., who found

* 'You know what I think about marriages these days,' he wrote to Irene on 22 April 1942, 'when people's sensory impressions, including those of selection, are so liable to lead to misunderstanding and too often to mild tragedy.'

him indispensable: F.M. helped secure the deferment of his military service by accompanying him to an exemption tribunal and demonstrating the Technique to the astonished tribunal members, grabbing them in turn by the neck.[8]

On 10 May 1940 the Germans invaded France and the Low Countries, and Churchill replaced Chamberlain as premier. During the next two weeks came the dreadful news that the main allied force had been routed by German armour. 'We are in the throes of great uncertainty and danger,' wrote F.M. to Irene Tasker, 'chiefly because of treachery and stupidity on the part of the French.'[9] He continued to be optimistic, however, drawing comfort from American support of Britain. Mussolini's entry into the war did not worry him, as 'the Dago never was a fighter and I think he will be shown to be on a lower standard now that he is under fascist rule'.[10] His great-nephew by marriage Peter Vicary, Jack's elder son, was captured fighting in France and later died in captivity.

By mid-June, France was about to capitulate and the invasion of Britain loomed. Friends of F.M., including Stafford Cripps, urged him to leave for America, as he was likely to have been 'blacklisted' by the Germans after what he had written about their barbarity and 'rigid habits' in *Man's Supreme Inheritance*.[11] F.M. was loath to go, but prepared for departure. The easiest solution was for him to leave together with his school, as there were official plans at the time (later abandoned) for the mass evacuation of British schoolchildren to Canada and the United States.* It was complicated to make arrangements at so critical a juncture, but F.M. had influential allies in the form of Cripps, Norris of the Air Ministry, even the Foreign Secretary Lord Halifax, whose niece Mrs Dundas had a daughter at the school. After a chaotic week of preparations and a turbulent journey north, F.M.'s party sailed

---

* By the time the scheme was discontinued as impractical in September 1940, only about 3000 of 200,000 child applicants had been evacuated, many of them lost when their ships were sunk.

from Glasgow on 8 July on the *Monarch of Bermuda*, a former cruise liner bound for Canada with British schoolchildren, German prisoners-of-war, and (unbeknown to the passengers) a large part of Britain's gold reserves. The party consisted of F.M. (carrying the manuscript of his new book) and his ever-faithful Ethel Webb; Margaret Goldie and Irene Stewart in their capacities as headmistress and matron of the school; a wealthy supporter, Mary McNair Scott, daughter of the newspaper tycoon Lord Camrose, together with her four children (two of whom were at the school) and their nanny; and six other Alexander schoolchildren (another six following by a later boat). 'I'm on the Wallaby track once more because of the German dogs, and I resent it,' he wrote to Irene Tasker. One consolation was that he would have an opportunity to meet the ailing Coghill and give him some lessons which might save his life. 'If I succeed with him, I shall probably ask him to do a foreword to the new book.'[12]

Yet again, and this time in his seventy-second year, F.M. found himself having to make a new start in life. The journey on which he and his party had embarked was a hazardous one, and they were fortunate in that, owing to the gold consignment, it had the unusual protection of two battleships, two destroyers, two cruisers and an aeroplane: as it was, a German submarine was sighted, and attacked with depth charges.[13] After their safe arrival in Canada, they faced the problem that, owing to exchange control regulations, they had been able to take very little money with them. (F.M. hoped eventually to have the funds of his educational trust at his disposal; but getting these sent over, as with everything else, was a long and complicated business.) Fortunately, they found themselves surrounded by well-wishers ready to offer them hospitality and help them in every way.

F.M. planned to re-establish his teaching practice, his school and his training course in the United States; but it would take time to make suitable arrangements, and meanwhile only

F.M. himself and Ethel Webb were able to obtain American visas. Accordingly, the children and their guardians embarked on an extended vacation in Canada, while F.M. and Ethel crossed the border to spend the summer at a cottage offered to them by Alice Fowler, Ethel's New York friend from the 1890s, at Southwest Harbor, Maine – 'quite one of the most beautiful places I have seen,' F.M. wrote to Carrington.[14] There, by a lake in a pine forest, he did most of the remaining work on his book. A.R. came from Boston to visit him, and they discussed how to organise the teaching and where to set up the school. Though still awaiting his American work permit, F.M. was able to do some unofficial teaching, as several of his old pupils were holidaying on Mount Desert Island nearby. He also took on two interesting new pupils. One was an eight-year-old boy, the heir to a fortune, who had never spoken, but managed to utter a few words after a week's lessons with F.M.[15] The other was Frank Pierce Jones (1905–75), a professor of classics at Brown University, Rhode Island, who had been taking lessons with A.R. in Boston since 1938: these had so transformed both his health and his outlook that he was thinking of devoting himself to the Alexander Technique, and on learning that F.M. had arrived in the USA, he made a pilgrimage to meet and take a lesson with him.[16]

During August and September the fate of Britain hung in the balance, as the RAF and Luftwaffe battled for control of the skies. F.M. must have followed the news anxiously, though his letters were suffused with the usual blithe optimism. On 7 September, a bomb fell on Ashley Place: although No. 16 escaped serious damage, the windows were blown out, and a newly delivered consignment of coke was scattered over the building, rendering it temporarily uninhabitable. Since F.M.'s departure, the teaching had been carried on there by Marjory Barlow (as she now was) and Walter Carrington; they now decided to close the house, Marjory subsequently joining her husband in Oxford, Carrington training as an RAF pilot. A bomb also fell on the warehouse of Fred Watts – a publisher pupil of F.M. who had taken over the publication of his books from Methuen during the 1930s – destroying much of the stock of F.M.'s previous three titles just as the fourth was nearing completion.

In October, F.M. obtained his American work permit. Henceforth, he and A.R. practised alternately in New York and Boston, where they based themselves in hotels, the Blackstone in New York, the Braemore in Boston. 'The prospects here are splendid,' he wrote to Carrington, 'and we will have a big season.'[17] By December, visas had been obtained for the children, who at first stayed in Connecticut with Mary Olcott, a wealthy and longstanding supporter of the work. It had not yet been decided where to locate the school, when F.M. was approached in the new year by Dr Dexter, Director of the Unitarian Association of America, offering him a former home for retired clergymen, the Whitney Homestead at Stow, consisting of two neoclassical mansions (one dating from before the Revolution) set in 129 acres of grounds some twenty miles west of Boston. The Unitarians were interested in the work, recognising (as F.M. wrote to Irene Tasker) that 'the first principle in religion must be to do something concrete in psycho-physical development'; and the terms of their offer were generous.[18] At the end of January 1941, thirteen children, accompanied by Margaret Goldie, Irene Stewart, Mary McNair Scott and F.M.'s former training course student Alma Frank, moved into the Homestead, which would serve as F.M.'s headquarters until September 1942.

Meanwhile, he had fulfilled his ambition to meet and teach Coghill, whom he visited in Florida the weekend before Christmas 1940. As he wrote to Carrington: 'I arrived at his home at 1.30 Friday and worked with him right on until Monday at 1.15. My longest lesson. It was all most interesting . . . I met a very ill man dragging one leg and foot badly. Not so when I left.'[19] F.M. later described Coghill as 'one of the best pupils he ever had, for he seized on the significance of what was being done immediately'. During the three-day lesson, Coghill reflected paradoxically 'that he, as a healthy young man, had devoted his life to science and had, by poring over a microscope, discovered these principles and yet been ruined in health, whereas F.M., as an ailing youth, had looked in the mirror and discovered these same principles and used them to become what he is today'.[20] F.M. was convinced that, had Coghill managed to come to New York for further lessons, he could have given him a new lease of life;[21] but Coghill could not afford to make the journey,* and died in July 1941. Before his final illness, he did, however, succeed in writing an 'Appreciation' of F.M.'s work to serve as a preface to the new book.

In this piece, written in the language of a scientist, Coghill made four main points. First, that F.M.'s work was founded on the same general principles regarding the integrated functioning of the organism that he himself had established during his forty years of research into the lower vertebrates. Secondly, that F.M. was 'pre-eminently an educator. He seeks to restore the functions of the body through their natural uses.' His methods were 'original and unique', and although it was almost impossible to describe them, their results were 'marvellous'. Thirdly, Coghill explained in somewhat technical terms his own beneficial experience. 'He [F.M.] enabled me to prevent misdirection of the muscles of my neck and back and to bring about a use of these muscles that determine the relative position of my head and neck to my body and so on to my limbs . . . This led to changes in the muscular and other conditions throughout my body and limbs associated with a pattern of behaviour more natural . . . for the act of

---

* Coghill had been dismissed from the Wister Institute in Philadelphia following a quarrel in 1935, since when he had been struggling to carry on his research privately in Gainesville, Florida. F.M. did not charge Coghill for lessons, but the scientist could not afford the cost of a month's visit to New York. F.M. managed to raise funds from his friends for this purpose, but too late: Coghill had suffered a stroke, and died soon afterwards. (See Carrington, *A Time to Remember*, pp. 48–50.)

getting on my feet. The whole procedure was calculated to occupy my brain with the projection of directive messages that would enable me to acquire conscious control of the proprioceptive component of the reflex mechanism involved.' Fourthly, Coghill recognised that F.M., 'by relieving this conflict between the total pattern which is hereditary and innate, and the reflex mechanisms which are individually cultivated, conserves the energies of the nervous system and by so doing corrects not only natural difficulties but also many other pathological conditions that are not ordinarily recognised as postural'.[22] He concluded that Alexander 'lays hold of the individual as a whole, as a self-vitalising agent. He re-conditions and re-educates the reflex mechanisms, and brings their habits into normal relations with the functions of the organism as a whole. I regard his methods as thoroughly scientific and educationally sound.'

Coghill did not live to see the book he had thus prefaced, which was published by Dutton in New York in September 1941 and Chaterson (Fred Watts's company) in London in February 1942. After agonising for more than a year over what to call it, F.M. finally decided on *The Universal Constant in Living* – a title which provoked criticism, though he insisted that he had been unable to find any other which more closely reflected the subject matter. He dedicated it grandiloquently 'To the Peoples of the British Empire, Whose Understanding of, and Faith in, the Principles of Liberty and Loyalty, and Whose Confidence in their Own Strength as Defenders of the Faith, Enabled Them, Alone and Unaided, to Check the Mad Onrush of Mechanized Means of Destruction which, if Unchecked, Would Have Made it Possible for Evil Forces to Overrun the Whole World and to Enslave the Peoples Living in it.' This was certainly a brave thing to write in the summer of 1941, when the British had just been defeated in Greece and North Africa, and Nazi Germany effectively held sway over the entire European continent apart from the Soviet

Union, through whose territory her armies then appeared to be slicing like a knife through butter.

From the literary point of view, *The Universal Constant in Living* is inferior to F.M.'s previous two books, probably reflecting the fact that he no longer enjoyed the collaboration of Dewey and Irene Tasker. The piecemeal way in which it was put together is all too apparent: as Jones remarks, it 'has very little organisation and can only be considered as a long, disconnected appendix to the earlier books'.[23] F.M.'s fondness for quotation has got somewhat out of hand: if one includes the series of essays praising his work which he tacks on as appendices, about one-quarter of the entire content consists of the words of others. Jean Fischer notes that all this quotation goes to show 'that his technique has the support of many educated and distinguished people';[24] but the impression made on the educated reader is that F.M. had inadequate confidence in his own powers of expression, and that, even in old age, he was still at heart the Australian huckster, using 'testimonials' to peddle his wares.

Some of the outside contributions are very interesting – apart from Coghill's 'Appreciation', they include Murdoch and Douglas on the physiological basis of the Technique, Hilton on its importance in industry, and a new piece by Aldous Huxley (incongruously, in view of his pacifism) on its application to military training – and F.M. might have done better to present the book as an annotated miscellany of writings about his work. As it is, those parts written by himself, while incorporating his latest reflections, do not contain much that is likely to be either unfamiliar to those who have read his previous books or easily comprehensible to those who have not read them. If *The Use of the Self*, written under Dewey's influence, concentrates on the 'scientific' basis of the Technique, *The Universal Constant in Living*, written (in its later stages) under Coghill's influence, concentrates on the concept of 'wholeness' – the integral nature of the human mechanism, and the unity of mind, body and spirit. Another unifying theme (as implied in the title) is that of the 'universality' of F.M.'s principles, which (as he argues) can be applied to any kind of change sought by human beings, not just in the spheres of health and education. There is a slight change in terminology, in that F.M. now refers to 'manner of use' rather than 'use'. As before, he attempts to explain his work through illustration: in particular, the second chapter describes various medical cases he has helped, going into some detail regarding one case with a view to showing how his work enables sufferers to deal with their problems without either constituting 'treatment' or effecting 'cure'. If one were to ask what aspects of the book are truly original, the answer would probably be that he lays greater emphasis than before on the concepts of inhibition and prevention, and that the best passages show a level of philosophical profundity which is never quite attained in his previous works. To quote the last sentence:

> My teaching experience has shown me that a person who has accepted the idea of freedom of thought and action, and has consistently advocated it in daily life, is not on this account any more capable of commanding freedom *in* thought and action when trying to keep to a well-considered decision to employ procedures which demand, for their successful carrying-out, a use of the self which is not his habitual reaction in thought and action.

The book was quite widely reviewed on both sides of the Atlantic. As might have been expected, those reviewers who had experienced F.M.'s work, such as Frank Pierce Jones in America and Mungo Douglas in England, were enthusiastic, while those who had not generally expressed a degree of puzzlement or scepticism. Luckily for F.M., something of a sensation was created by Aldous Huxley's long notice in the *Saturday Review of Literature*, in which he declared that only two solutions had ever been found to bridge the gap between the ideal and the practical. 'The first, which is very ancient, is the mystic's technique of transcending personality . . . The second, which is very recent, was discovered some fifty years ago by F. M. Alexander . . .' Thanks to the latter, it was

> now possible to conceive of a totally new type of education affecting the entire range of human activity, from the physiological, through the intellectual, moral and practical, to the spiritual – an education which, by teaching them the proper use of the self, would preserve children and adults from most of the diseases and evil habits that now afflict them; an education whose training in inhibition and conscious control would provide men and women with the psycho-physical means for behaving rationally and morally; an education which, in its upper reaches, would make possible the experience of ultimate reality . . .'[25]

During 1941 and 1942, F.M.'s life in America was not very different from that which he had led there during the First World War. As before, he was assisted by the invaluable Ethel Webb. From October to April, he based himself at his New York hotel, immersing himself in his private teaching. 'I am very busy here,' he wrote to Carrington in January 1942, 'and ere long it looks as if one will be overwhelmed again as in the old days. The people now coming are the best lot I have had in this country.'[26] During these months, he made regular visits to Stow, supervising the work of the school (and presumably pursuing his relationship – of whatever it consisted – with Margaret Goldie). From May to September (previously the months of his annual return to England), he based himself at Stow, where pupils could visit him for extended periods, there being plenty of room for them to stay: one such pupil was the Speaker of the Massachusetts legislature. A.R. continued to base himself in Boston, though he often taught in New York when F.M. was at Stow and at Stow when F.M. was in New York. As in England, the main recreation of both brothers was racing: they tried to organise their teaching so as to attend meetings at Suffolk Downs, the principal course near Boston.

The school's situation was idyllic, and the original evacuees were joined by several children of F.M.'s American pupils, who found it a very 'British' experience. Margaret Goldie was not popular with the children owing to her authoritarian attitude: Robert Best's son John, who was eventually withdrawn from the school, later expressed the view[27] that whatever benefits they gained from the Technique tended to be cancelled out by the fact that she constantly made them feel guilty. On the other hand, the children loved and looked forward to the visits of F.M., who (as one of them recalled) 'gave Stow a dynamic atmosphere. His eyes twinkled with spirit and enthusiasm.' He gave group lessons, moving rapidly from one child to another while keeping them entertained with a stream of amusing talk (though woe betide any child who stopped 'thinking' and 'pulled down'). He also joined them for Shakespeare readings, and recited poetry to them after dinner. During the summer of 1941, F.M. resurrected his training course at Stow. Originally it consisted of just one student, Frank Pierce Jones; he was subsequently joined by his wife Helen, Mary McNair Scott and three others, while former students such as Alma Frank and Lulie Westfeldt came down for 'refresher' courses.[28]

The decision to train had been a difficult one for Jones, involving as it did the sacrifice of his academic career. As Dewey's introductions to F.M.'s books had originally inspired him to have lessons with A.R., he wrote to Dewey seeking his advice; Dewey wrote back assuring Jones that he still subscribed to the opinions expressed in the introductions, and applauding his intention to train in the work.[29] Dewey (who since 1934 had been taking lessons with A.R.) was in fact resuming something of his old friendship with F.M., taking lessons with him in New York and sending him new academic pupils.[30] In the autumn of 1941, he was responsible for getting him to address the Dutch Treat Club, a gathering of three hundred professional, literary and scientific men whom F.M. found 'more interested than any group I have ever talked to'.[31] Yet F.M's failure to take advantage of the research opportunities Dewey had obtained for him continued to rankle with the philosopher; and their relations were not as before. Dewey neither contributed to nor reviewed the new book.

Apart from the seclusion of the Homestead, F.M. did not enjoy being in America. He complained to Irene Tasker that 'the standard of everything had gone down since we were here in the past',[32] and that he no longer liked New York, 'a foreign city filled with foreign people'.[33] In conversation, he spoke of the superiority of everything British to everything American, which cannot have endeared him to all.[34] He was nevertheless grateful for the haven provided to him and his work by the United States, and recognised her as Britain's friend in need. 'The great majority of people in this country are with us,' he wrote to Carrington in October 1940, 'and will see to it that we have more planes and all the other needs for war.'[35] After Pearl Harbor, his satisfaction at American participation in the conflict was tempered by the reflection that life would cease to be so comfortable:[36] in particular, it became difficult to obtain the fuel oil needed to heat the spacious buildings at Stow.[37]

In correspondence, F.M. expressed his longing to return to 'the old country', as well as his perennial confidence that he would soon be able to do so thanks to allied victory: even at the grimmest moments, he found some reason to believe in the imminent defeat of Germany and Japan. He tried to keep in touch with friends and supporters in England, though letters often failed to arrive owing to shipping losses in the Atlantic. All male teachers of the Technique had now been called up. In the intervals of childbearing, Marjory

Barlow kept the teaching alive, and she and Jack Vicary did their best to look after F.M.'s interests in England. Both Ashley Place and Penhill suffered further bomb damage, while remaining structurally intact (unlike F.M.'s seaside villa at Elmer, which was requisitioned and pulled down by the army). F.M. concentrated on the good news. Early in 1942, he was excited to learn that one of his old pupils, William Temple, had been appointed Archbishop of Canterbury, while another, Stafford Cripps, had become a minister in Churchill's War Cabinet. 'It means much for the work in the future,' he wrote to Irene Tasker, venturing to predict that the new Lord President of the Council would be the next Prime Minister.[38]

During the summer of 1942, the Unitarians sold the Homestead, requiring F.M. and his school to leave by the end of September. Thus ended twenty months during which he had been able to carry on his activities in an enchanted private setting. It did not prove possible to find an alternative location for the school, whose pupils (who had in any case recently declined in numbers) dispersed to various other schools. The six training course students continued their work under A.R. at the Braemore Hotel in Boston. Margaret Goldie and Irene Stewart accompanied F.M. to New York in October, at first assisting him in his practice. During the autumn, however, a community of Quakers in Pennsylvania, under the patronage of Esther Duke, became interested in Alexander's work, as a result of which Goldie and Stewart began spending much of their time in Philadelphia, Goldie teaching a class at the Media Friends School, Stewart giving private lessons. This new centre of the Alexander Technique proved so successful that, a year later, A.R. would be persuaded to move there from Boston with his practice and training course, and Media would briefly acquire the mantle of the Alexander school.

In New York, F.M. found himself busier than ever during the winter season of 1942–3; but he was now desperate to return to England. Deprived of the comfort and seclusion of the Homestead, he found it hard to bear America, 'where all is muddle, strife and trouble, and the underworld is as much in power as during those awful days of Prohibition'.[39] He heard from his English medical supporters – Wilfred Barlow, Mungo Douglas, Rugg-Gunn – that a significant and on the whole constructive debate about his work was developing, and this contributed to his homesickness. 'Everything seems to be coming our way, so far as I can find, and it is very, very interesting,' he wrote to Douglas. 'I want to be home with you all so that we can all take part in the chase, although I don't expect to find the "kill" for some time to come.'[40] He was excited by the news that his friend Peter Macdonald had been elected Chairman of the British Medical Association, and seems to have had a somewhat exaggerated idea of what he described as 'strong support in high places when I get home again'.[41] But Cripps and other friends with influence were at least able to arrange a priority sea passage for him; and in July 1943, exactly three years after they had left, he and his three female teachers returned to England on the troopship *Capetown Castle*.

England had changed almost out of recognition during F.M.'s absence. It had been battered by three years of heavy bombing (with the terror and destruction of the flying bombs still to come); a huge Anglo-American military establishment was being created for the invasion of Europe; and civilian life was dominated by shortages, rationing and queuing. F.M., however, was filled with patriotic ardour, convinced that his work was needed as never before. 'We will do our bit for the principle of simplicity and wholeness as against separation and complexity and we will win,' he wrote to Douglas.[42] Despite bomb damage, he lost no time in re-establishing his home at Penhill and his practice at Ashley Place. On 4 August 1943, less than a month after his return, he wrote that he was already 'full up with pupils'; in November, he reported that he, Goldie and Stewart were all so busy that they were having to turn people away.[43] Irene Tasker, who returned to England from South Africa early in 1944, helped with the overworked practice. F.M.'s new pupils included numerous servicemen, as well as another doctor, the gynaecologist Dorothy Drew (1908–88), who was so impressed by her improved functioning that she sent her children too, and expressed a desire to train in the work.[44] Meanwhile, Wilfred Barlow, now an army doctor, secured a posting to London so he could complete his training with F.M.[45]

The war resulted in a mania for reading, especially books and articles which claimed to offer solutions to the world's ills. F.M.'s new book was selling well, and there was a renewed demand for his other works which proved difficult to satisfy owing to paper rationing. Of his medical supporters, Murdoch had died and Macdonald was preoccupied by his BMA work (contributing to the creation of the future National Health Service); but Barlow, Douglas and Rugg-Gunn continued to be active on his behalf, publishing articles in learned journals and writing letters to the press. This exposure of his work naturally pleased F.M.; but it also gave him an altogether disproportionate idea of the extent to which his teachings were becoming accepted by professional medical opinion. ('The future of the work is assured in this country,' he wrote jubilantly to Jones in October 1944, reporting the publication of another supportive contribution in a medical journal, this time by Dr Drew.[46]) Whenever F.M. encountered anything that did not fit in with his theories, his reaction was dismissive. When the myopic Huxley, who had given him so much support over *The Universal Constant*, became a propagandist for the Bates method of eye exercises, F.M., who regarded such exercises as 'end-gaining', concluded that Huxley must have gone off his head. And he was scornful when Barlow showed him copies of some correspondence between Robert

Best and John Hilton which was mildly critical of him. 'What do these people think they know?'*[47]

Things had gone well for F.M. during his first year back in England. His physician McDonagh gave him his best bill of health in fifteen years, so he hoped 'to go on with the work for many a day to come'.[48] The summer of 1944, however, brought a series of unsettling blows. He fractured his ankle stumbling on the stairs at Ashley Place, and retired to convalesce at Penhill in time for the worst 'doodlebug' raids of the war, which shook the house to its foundations and tested his nerves to the limit. He was dismayed when Walter Carrington, his favourite student and devoted amanuensis, was reported missing in action, his RAF bomber having been shot down over Hungary. (Happily Carrington survived, was helped by Jesuit priests to escape from the military hospital in which he was detained, and was back in England by the end of the year, recovering from serious injuries.) In her delayed mail from South Africa, Irene Tasker received the March issue of the official journal *Manpower*, which contained a long, scurrilous editorial attacking F.M. This was to cast a long shadow over his life; but although he read it with indignation, it did not unduly worry him at the time, as until 1946 he was confident of obtaining a retraction and an apology. Of far greater concern was the news that A.R. had suffered a disabling stroke in Pennsylvania (where he had moved a year earlier to join the new Quaker supporters of the work). It had been 'sheer suicide for him to attempt to do the amount of work he was doing,' wrote F.M. to Jones, 'but my brother is somewhat obstinate and too often

---

* F.M. would have been infinitely more shocked had he read Best's essay 'Conscious Constructive Criticism of Mr F. M. Alexander's New Technique' (see Chapter 5), written in a moment of pique in 1941 after his son John had asked to be removed from the school at Stow. Best had sent copies of this work to all F.M.'s supporters in England; while admitting that it contained some justice, they persuaded him that it would not be a good idea either to publish it or show it to F.M.

determined in a foolhardy way'.[49] It was difficult to see what future the work had in America, where F.M. now had confidence in two teachers only, Jones, who had just qualified, and Alma Frank, who was far from well.

The end of the European war in May 1945 found F.M. riding in North Wales,* enjoying what he described as his first real holiday for years.[50] His admiration of Cripps and detestation of Churchill, along with the spirit of common sacrifice which pervaded the nation during the conflict, had conspired to give the formerly rather conservative F.M. something of a left-leaning outlook; and he welcomed Labour's landslide election victory that July. 'I voted Labour for the first time in my life and I had sound reasons for doing so,' he wrote to Douglas. 'Churchill, Beaverbrook and the Rothermere-Camrose gang† will now know what the mass of the country think of them.'[51] Cripps joined the new Labour Government as President of the Board of Trade and was the minister most trusted by the public, having kept outside party politics for some years. F.M. seems to have hoped that all his problems would now be solved thanks to the patronage of Cripps, who had already helped his publisher Fred Watts obtain an extra paper allocation for the reprinting of his books. In fact, Cripps was a man of such obsessive probity that he would probably never have considered using his official position to confer serious favours on anyone with whom he was privately associated or whom he regarded as a friend.

On the other hand, ever since F.M.'s return to England, Cripps and his wife Isobel, along with Lytton and Macdonald, had, in their private capacities, been pressing him to make some permanent arrangements for the future of his work;

---

* The horse he kept at Penhill, Peter, had died while he was in America.
† Beaverbrook controlled the *Express* group of newspapers, Rothermere the *Mail* group, Camrose the *Telegraph* group (all supporting the Conservative Party).

for F.M., who turned seventy-five in January 1944, could not live for ever. On 5 December 1944, he wrote to Jones:

> We are in the throes of prospective big doings in connection with the work which will mean another place in conjunction with Ashley Place [for] the training course, a nursery school and a place for students, teachers and private pupils . . . [to] meet and discuss matters related to the work. A magazine is to be put into being. Powerful people have approached me in regard to this and it can be a big thing but it must be put on a sound working basis before I will give my consent.

Soon afterwards, he announced a 'meeting of the clans' at Ashley Place on 15 February 1945, 'when Lytton, the Crippses and leading medical men will be present to take their part in the attempt to arrive at a sound working basis'.[52] The meeting discussed detailed proposals for vesting the teaching practice and the copyright in the books in a self-governing 'Alexander Institute';[53] but the discussions led to nothing – always F.M. found some excuse to delay the 'prospective big doings'. Once again, he had fallen prey to the fear and doubt which, during the 1930s, had led him to reject Dewey's attempts to promote scientific research into the Technique, Miss Lawrence's offer of a house for the school, and Hilton's proposals for generating further publicity. Even when the war ended, the only significant development he would countenance was the revival of the training course, which recommenced in September 1945 with nine new students (including Dorothy Drew) and a few old ones whose training had been interrupted by the war (such as the Walkers). 'The evolving of the best way to our end of the new organisation goes on,' he wrote to Jones on 6 October, 'but nothing complete has resulted. I will not allow this to be hurried.' His hesitations were reinforced during 1946 when Philomene Dailey, a former student of A.R.'s American training course, set up an

'Alexander Foundation' in Philadelphia to train new teachers, a task for which she was doubtfully qualified. (The ailing A.R., before returning to England in July 1945, had sanctioned the creation of a foundation, though he was still somewhat confused at the time, and believed that it would only be used to sponsor publications and help impecunious pupils with their fees.) 'It is a sad, sad experience for me at my age to find this,' wrote F.M. to Jones, 'after the way I have protected the interests, present and future, of the work in your country and elsewhere.'[54]

In February 1946, Watts published a new edition of *The Universal Constant in Living*. In his preface, F.M. expressed satisfaction that, since the original edition, he had received many appreciative letters from correspondents at home and abroad, while 'authorities in many fields' had published writings showing 'a clearer understanding and fuller acceptance of the means-whereby of my technique'. As well as revising the text (suitably altering the references to the war, and also modifying some of his medical claims in view of his impending libel case), F.M. contributed a new chapter, entitled 'Knowing How to Stop'. He wrote that, in the atomic bomb, a monster had been created which was a potential danger to all, but which might prove a blessing in disguise as the consequences of mishandling the monster were so terrifying that man was at last forced to stop and think about what he was doing. This, it was to be hoped, might lead him to learn how to master himself as he had learned to master nature, by acquiring knowledge 'of means whereby human reactions can be changed, controlled and gradually improved', the lack of such knowledge having contributed to the outbreak of two world wars. In modern civilisation, 'man's craze is for speed and the short view'; in order to survive in future, he required 'the employment of a technique which makes possible the gaining of experience in KNOWING HOW TO STOP (prevention – inhibition) when dominated by the influence of impulsive uncontrolled reaction'. Although he sometimes spoke of

producing another book,* this chapter was the last significant new writing to appear under F.M.'s name in his lifetime.

In March 1946, Walter Carrington was discharged from the
RAF and returned to Ashley Place, spending several weeks on
the training course to refresh his skills before resuming his
place as an assistant teacher, and also taking over the secretarial work of the practice. For eight months he kept a diary,[55]
giving a vivid glimpse of F.M.'s world at that time. Carrington
joined a team consisting of his old colleagues Marjory Barlow,
Patrick Macdonald and Irene Stewart, joined later in the year
by Max Alexander and Richard Walker.† As qualified doctors,
Wilfred Barlow and Dorothy Drew were also regarded as
members of the team, though the latter had not yet completed
her training with F.M. and it was not professionally possible
for either of them to do paid teaching. Another teacher visiting
that March was Alma Frank, who brought disturbing news
of the chaotic state of the work in America.[56] Ethel Webb,
now eighty and in uncertain health, no longer played an active
role in the practice. Irene Tasker, though still in London, was
also little seen at Ashley Place. Margaret Goldie was effectively living with F.M. as his domestic partner; soon after
Carrington arrived, they moved their common residence from
the Ashley Place basement to a nearby flat in Evelyn Mansions,
and Goldie taught there rather than at Ashley Place. A.R.,
who had made a partial recovery from his stroke, occasionally
turned up to help with the student training, and enjoyed a
close brotherly relationship with F.M.

---

* On 21 May 1942, F.M. had written to Irene Tasker of a new book in
which he hoped to solve 'the age long problem of the coming together of
science, religion and the rest'. It is not known how much of it he ever
wrote, and no manuscript seems to survive.
† F.M. paid his assistants a salary of £5 a week, with a bonus based on
the numbers of lessons given. Pupils were charged one guinea for a lesson
with an assistant teacher. The full fee for a lesson with F.M. remained
three guineas as before – though much 'flexibility' was shown in view of
difficult economic times.

On his first day back, Carrington wrote that F.M.'s teaching was 'better than ever', while the assistants had 'improved beyond all knowledge since before the war'. On his second day he noted that 'F.M. can now get what he wants with the hands with the barest touch. The others are good and can get it but tend to "do" too much . . .' Carrington's descriptions of the training course make it clear that, after fifteen years, F.M. had mastered the art of student training. He talked the whole time with great verve, holding the attention of his listeners with a mixture of aphoristic reflections on his work and anecdotes from his past life. Despite rationing, his love of good food was undiminished. So was his passion for racing: training sessions often had to be moved from the afternoon to the morning to enable him to attend Ascot or Newmarket. His socialist enthusiasms, however, were new: Carrington, one of nature's Tories, was surprised to hear him praise Attlee's 'dull and insipid' speech.[57]

Carrington noted F.M.'s naïve excitement whenever anything happened which appeared to give a boost to the work. 'Some official recognition at last!' was his characteristic reaction when he received a casual enquiry from the Ministry of Labour about the training course.[58] The appearance of Sherrington's book *The Endeavour of Jean Fernel*, with its praising reference to F.M.,* made him 'tremendously excited'; and when he subsequently received a flattering personal letter from Sherrington, his joy knew no bounds.[59] He was similarly pleased to receive approval in print from Professor Raymond Dart of Witwatersrand University, an Australian-born anatomist of international fame who was a pupil of Irene Tasker.[60] He had high hopes of a book of writings about the Technique by divers hands, published that June by Fred Watts under the title *Knowing How to Stop* and prefaced by F.M.'s chapter of that name – though Watts confided to Carrington that it was proving difficult to get it either

* See pp. 132–3

advertised or reviewed owing to the misconception that it was about cures for masturbation.[61]

Like F.M.'s external supporters, his assistants, including Carrington, were anxious that he should do something to safeguard the future of his work. The Barlows seemed 'very important' in this connection, given Marjory's family link and Wilfred's medical status.[62] On 16 May 1946, Carrington dined with F.M. and asked him frankly about the situation, to receive the bland reply that 'we should discuss ways and means of forming a partnership to include all the present teachers . . . These would then inherit the work and employ others on a similar basis to that on which we are now employed. He [F.M.] said that, apart from this, the future was safeguarded to a reasonable extent with his executors, but I did not press for details.' However, Irene Tasker, who knew F.M. all too well, warned Carrington that no satisfactory arrangements were likely to be made in F.M.'s lifetime. She added that she would probably be returning to resume her practice in South Africa, and he was welcome to join her there if he ever felt the need to escape from Ashley Place.[63]

Exactly six months before Carrington's return, F.M. had issued a libel writ against the editors of the South African official journal *Manpower* which had carried the hostile article; but the diary contains surprisingly few references to that affair. Encouraged by his lawyers, F.M. took a relaxed view of the case during the spring and summer of 1946, believing that he was certain of a quick and easy victory.[64] However, the last entry in Carrington's diary, dated 15 November 1946, reports the ominous news 'that the President of the Royal College of Surgeons . . . is willing to give evidence that he considers F.M. a "quack" on the grounds that his books might lead people to attempt non-recognised forms of treatment where medical advice is required'. For the next two and a half years, preoccupation with the case was to overshadow F.M.'s life and disrupt the routine of Ashley Place.

7

Trial

1944–1948

The libel action which would prove the great drama of F.M.'s later years had its origins in Irene Tasker's decision to teach his work in South Africa.[1] A venture into the unknown, this had been crowned with success. Arriving in Johannesburg in 1935, she had been approached by a former London pupil of F.M., now headmistress of a fashionable preparatory school, who arranged for her to address the annual conference of the Transvaal Teachers Association. Of the three hundred attending this gathering, no less than eighty expressed interest in the work. Apart from teachers, other eminent South Africans became her pupils and supporters, including the barrister Norman Coaker, the solicitor Vernon Berrangé, the anatomist Raymond Dart (famous for his research into the origins of man), and the agriculturist Thomas Hall. (In his presidential address to the South African Chemical Institute in 1938, Hall predicted that F.M. would 'one day be among the immortals along with Pasteur'.[2]) She also set up a small school along the lines of the one she had run at Ashley Place: originally this was for children with 'special difficulties', but they were eventually joined by 'normal' children whose parents had become enthusiastic about the work.[3]

By 1942, Miss Tasker had become a respected figure in South African educational circles; and that year her work attracted the attention of Dr Ernst Jokl, the South African Government's recently appointed Director of Physical

Education. Jokl (1907–97) was born in Breslau, Germany, where he studied medicine and achieved some note as an athlete; when Hitler came to power in 1933, he emigrated to South Africa on account of his Jewish ancestry. He was a prolific writer on the physiology of exercise, who would later become celebrated in the United States as 'the father of sports medicine'. In June 1942, he asked Miss Tasker to demonstrate her work to him and give him a course of lessons. She agreed to a brief demonstration, which took place before witnesses; but she declined to give him lessons (though she judged that he had need of them) as he appeared to believe in 'the separation of mind and body' and thus rejected the philosophy on which Alexander's work was based. If he wanted to pursue the matter, she suggested he go to London to see F.M. himself – hardly practical advice during the war when civilian passages (as Miss Tasker would herself soon discover) were hard to come by. She suspected, however, that Jokl was not motivated by friendly interest; and indeed, although he wrote to her that he considered her work 'a highly important contribution in the field of education in its widest sense', he later wrote to a medical colleague that he wished 'to expose the Alexander Technique and attack the racket', and was considering a book to counter 'the interest which a certain type of pseudo-intellectuals [*sic*] are taking in this peculiar semi-religious movement'.[4] On the other hand, his subsequent hostility may have been partly due to an element of 'sour grapes' at having been refused lessons.

In April 1943, Mr I. G. Griffiths, President of the Transvaal Teachers Association, praised F.M.'s work in his address to the Association's annual conference, adding: 'Even a very small acquaintance with the Alexander Technique causes serious doubts concerning the wisdom of teaching physical training to our children. In this subject we make the children perform movements and exercises completely unrelated to anything they do in school or at any other time.'[5] The address was published in *Transvaal Educational News*. Jokl felt he must respond to this attack on his profession. In June 1943, he read a paper to the South African Association for the Advancement of Science (which Miss Tasker had addressed the previous year) entitled 'The Relationship between Health and Efficiency', which turned out to be an attack on the Alexander Technique. Contrary to convention, he had not submitted an advance copy of the paper to the secretary of the Association, which refused to publish it in its *Journal*. Jokl then submitted it to *Transvaal Educational News*, which did publish it, along with a reply defending Alexander's work signed by Coaker, Griffiths, Hall and the head of a university college.

Jokl had a further outlet for his views. In September 1942, under the auspices of the National Advisory Council on Physical Education, he and Dr Eustace Culver, Director of the South African Institute for Medical Research, had founded the biannual journal *Manpower*, 'devoted to the publication of such scientific matter, original and otherwise, as may assist in improving the standards of health, efficiency and happiness of the people by systematically increasing their labour capacity'. It was published by the Government Publisher in Pretoria on behalf of the Union Department of Education: like all official publications, it was printed in both English and Afrikaans (*Volkskragte* being its Afrikaans title). The fourth issue, which appeared in March 1944, opened with a lengthy editorial, consisting of forty-three pages of double columns (one for each language), lavishly illustrated with pictures and tables, entitled 'Quackery versus Physical Education'* and amounting to a vehement attack on F.M. and his work. It was unsigned, but written by Jokl and 'edited' by Culver.

As Jokl had been refused lessons, his article was based on a reading of F.M.'s books; and much of what he wrote may be regarded as fair comment. The books were 'amateurish',

---

* The title, it emerged during the case, had been inspired by a passage in *Man's Supreme Inheritance* suggesting that physical education was a form of 'quackery'.

containing claims which, from the medical standpoint, had to be regarded as dubious, exaggerated or nonsensical. F.M. produced no 'evidence' for his theories in the form of detailed case studies or scientific explanations. The only 'support' he adduced was the writings of others about his Technique; but the writers in question were either (in the case of Dewey and Huxley) professionally unqualified to discuss the workings of the human body, or (in the case of doctors and scientists such as Macdonald and Coghill) only able to give an opinion on the value of his work rather than a scientific explanation of it (and those who attempted such explanations, such as Murdoch and Douglas, were merely putting forward speculative hypotheses). Jokl strenuously denied that F.M. had made the same discovery as Magnus, as F.M. and his supporters claimed. F.M. contended that human health was deteriorating, whereas statistics suggested that, in countries like the United States, it was steadily improving – no doubt partly due to 'the young science of physical education', though physical educationists made far more modest claims for what they could achieve in the realms of human health than F.M.

These were reasonable criticisms; and Jokl would have no difficulty in getting leading experts to agree with them. It is obvious from the article that Jokl completely misunderstood the nature and purpose of the Alexander Technique, which he described as 'a system of postural gymnastics'. He did not mention the concepts of 'reliable sensory appreciation' and 'inhibition of response to stimulus' which (as constantly reiterated in the books) are central to it. He assumed that, as used by Alexander, the terms 'conscious control' and 'primary control' meant the same thing, whereas the first is a process, the second an entity. He ignored the fact that, throughout his books, F.M. stresses that the purpose of his work is educative, not curative. However, the books are not easy to understand, and F.M. had himself stated on numerous occasions that his work could not really be explained or described but had to be experienced; so Jokl (who had requested and been denied the experience) cannot be altogether blamed for his misunderstandings.

Where he strayed into the realms of libel was in suggesting that the Alexander Technique represented 'a dangerous and irresponsible form of quackery'. It was 'quackery' in that F.M., while aware that it amounted to little, used it to extract large sums of money from his credulous followers. It was 'dangerous and irresponsible', if not 'criminal', in that it encouraged people who ought to be seeking proper medical advice to rely on its worthless methods. Jokl wrote of both F.M. and his followers in scornful terms. He derisively referred to F.M. as 'the Australian actor' not once but twenty times, though F.M. had neither lived in Australia nor been a professional actor for forty years. As for the followers, he inferred that Huxley was deranged and Dewey was senile; and he characterised the whole 'movement' as

a typical instance of group hystero-neurosis . . . There is the irrational nature of the new faith and the unwillingness of its adherents to accept any fact which does not agree with the substance of their prejudices . . . There is the emotional atmosphere pervading the entire literature written by believers in the cult; and the revealing attempts made by Mr Alexander's pupils to elevate the Australian actor to an almost supernatural position. Finally there is the intense hate displayed towards everybody who . . . endangers the stability of their paranoiac ideas.

The article ended with a coarse jibe: many of Magnus's famous experiments had been performed on animals whose brains had been removed, and the only true connection between Magnus and F.M. was that the latter also experimented on subjects which appeared to be 'decerebrate'.

* * *

Though the offending issue of the journal appeared in March 1944, F.M. did not see it until August, when Irene Tasker, then staying with her mother in Cheltenham, received a copy from her friends in South Africa and sent it on to him. Wilfred Barlow, who was with him at Ashley Place when he received and read it, recalled that 'his reaction was one of shock and astonishment'.[6] What incensed him particularly was that, in the middle of the war, he should be traduced by a German. He assumed, however, that he would be able without trouble 'to humble that Nazi rascal'.[7] For did not his allies include two British statesmen of international stature, Sir Stafford Cripps and the Earl of Lytton, of whom the first was a member of the British War Cabinet, the second an old friend of the South African premier Smuts? Cripps and Lytton duly approached the South African High Commissioner in London, expressing their astonishment that such an article (in which they were both unflatteringly named) should appear in an official publication and their hope that the South African Government would issue a public withdrawal and apology. The High Commissioner agreed that the tone and content of the article were unacceptable, and was confident that the desired remedial steps would be forthcoming. With a view to securing them, he asked F.M. to provide him with a document setting out his objections and requests: this was sent to Pretoria at the end of the year, F.M. hoping that it would 'prove an unwelcome Christmas present for Jokl'.[8]

However, by the summer of 1945, F.M. had not yet received any satisfactory reply;* he had also learned that, under South African law, a plaintiff suing for libel had to institute proceedings within a year of reading the allegedly defamatory material. In August 1945, therefore, he issued a writ against Jokl and his co-editors of *Manpower* in the

---

* Things may have been held up by a change of High Commissioner, the reassuring Colonel Reitz being replaced by Mr Heaton Nicholls.

Rand Division of the South African Supreme Court, claiming libel damages of £5000: he did not imagine the case would come to court, but believed that notice of proceedings would encourage the South African authorities to get on with issuing their apology. To his dismay, however, they announced their intention of defending the action on behalf of Jokl and his colleagues (whose case was to be handled at every stage by the Government Attorney at the expense of the taxpayer). Friends of F.M. (including Irene Tasker) were appalled that he had got himself into this position, believing that it would have been 'wiser and more in keeping with the means-whereby principle to ignore the attack'.[9] In December 1945, Cripps and Lytton again approached the High Commissioner, suggesting that it was inappropriate that his Government should be a party to such proceedings and urging that it take steps to settle the matter;[10] but these efforts were unavailing, and by March 1946 (when Carrington began his diary) it was clear that F.M. would have to fight the case.

To clarify the background to the case, something must be said about the political situation in South Africa. From 1910, when Britain created the Union of South Africa, to 1961, when South Africa became a republic, two rival movements – both exclusively 'white' and intent on excluding non-whites from the political process – competed for control. One, personified by the philosopher-statesman Jan Christian Smuts, stood for equality between the English-speaking and Afrikaner traditions, a continuance of links with Britain and the Commonwealth, and (at least in theory) the social betterment of the disenfranchised majority. On the other side were the 'nationalists', who believed that South Africa 'belonged' to the Afrikaans-speaking Boer nation, wanted to end British links, and sought to perpetuate the inferior condition of the blacks through segregation. From September 1939 to May 1948, Smuts was Prime Minister, heading a government which (by a narrow parliamentary majority) had brought South Africa into the war alongside Britain. However, from

1924 to 1939, the nationalists had been in power, and had installed many of their supporters in key positions. Thus the state education system was dominated by nationalists. On the other hand, Irene Tasker's grateful pupils who espoused F.M.'s educational ideas were mostly English-speaking and 'liberal' in outlook. Even before the world war ended, the nationalists (many of whom sympathised with the Nazis) launched a propaganda war against the anglophile establishment (which eventually resulted, at the elections of May 1948, in the replacement of the Smuts Government by an extreme nationalist regime which instituted the 'apartheid' system). It is in this context that one must view the attack on the Alexander Technique by Jokl and his colleagues, and the refusal of the South African education ministry, the publishers of *Manpower*, either to apologise for or retract Jokl's article.

These political divisions were reflected in the legal representation of the two sides. F.M. was advised by two devoted supporters of Irene Tasker, the solicitor Vernon Berrangé (1900–83), a former communist, and the brilliant Oxford-educated Norman Coaker KC, a pillar of the English-speaking establishment. To represent Jokl, the Government retained Coaker's great professional rival Oswald Pirow KC (1890–1959), an ultra-nationalist who had served as justice minister in the early 1930s, subsequently becoming an admirer of Hitler and founder of the Nazi-style New Order Party. As Coaker wished to appear as a witness in the case, and confront Pirow in cross-examination, F.M. was eventually represented in court by Harold Hanson KC and Bram Fischer, both of whom would achieve international renown during the 1950s for their defence of Nelson Mandela and other black activists accused of treason and sabotage by the apartheid regime.

At first, F.M. believed he would win quickly and easily – a view in which he seems to have been encouraged by Berrangé, who visited him in London in the summer of

1946.* At the time, three events gave some grounds for optimism. First, as F.M. was outside the South African jurisdiction, the defence were entitled to ask him to pay a sum into court lest he lose: they requested a surety of £4000, but the judge reduced this to a mere £1000, with another £1000 to be paid at the time of the trial. Secondly, it was discovered that the Ling Physical Exercise Association, whose system of 'Swedish' exercises had been used in both British schools and the British army for some years, had published a shortened version of Jokl's article in their *Journal* during 1945: approached by F.M.'s lawyers, they promptly issued the retraction and apology which he had failed to get from *Manpower*. Thirdly, there was the commendation of F.M. by Sherrington, the greatest living physiologist, first in print, then in a flattering letter.[11] During the autumn of 1946, however, the skies darkened. It became known that the defence would be calling some of the most eminent medical names in London as witnesses, including two Nobel Prizewinners and the President of the Royal College of Surgeons. It also became apparent that the strategy of the defence, who had the resources of the South African state behind them, was to drag out the proceedings for as long as possible in the hope of wearing F.M. down. As most witnesses on both sides were British residents who would find it impractical to go to South Africa, it was decided that their evidence should be given before a commission sitting in London; this was originally due to happen in October 1946,[12] but the defence secured several delays and the

---

* Berrangé was described by Carrington as 'excellent . . . like Lawrence of Arabia to look at', but 'way to the Left in politics – disturbing in a way, for we do not want the work to have a leftist bias' (*A Time to Remember*, pp. 40, 45–6). He evidently got on extremely well with F.M. In August 1946, F.M. and the Barlows accompanied him and his wife Yolande on holiday to France: this was F.M.'s only journey outside England after 1943, and memorable for the fact that, towards the end of their visit, he lost all their remaining money in a casino.

commission did not finally sit until July 1947, almost two years after F.M. had issued his writ.

As the months passed, F.M., while expressing his usual optimism, became increasingly anxious. The steadily mounting costs were a drain on his resources; there was no telling how long the whole affair would last; and in view of the eminence of the defence witnesses, victory no longer seemed assured. April 1947 also witnessed a great sadness in his life – the death of his brother A.R. at the age of seventy-three. A.R. had appeared to make a good recovery from his stroke, but then relapsed. He had experienced tensions and differences with F.M. in the past; but since his return to England in the summer of 1945, they had drawn close. As well as feeling emotionally bereft, F.M. lost one of the few confidants with whom he was able to have regular discussions about the progress of the case.

The taking of evidence on commission began on 2 July 1947 before Mr A. H. Ormerod and lasted six weeks, most of the hearings taking place at South Africa House in Trafalgar Square. F.M. was represented by Kenneth Diplock, a junior barrister with a devastating talent for cross-examination who would later become a famous law lord. The defence were represented by Neil Lawson and Frederick Beney, who would go on to make lesser judicial reputations. Both F.M. and Jokl attended all the hearings in person, accompanied by bands of supporters. It was a nerve-racking experience for F.M. His first witness, Duncan Whittaker, a distinguished psychiatrist who had married F.M.'s former student Erika Schumann and was now training under F.M. himself, proved an awkward speaker. Diplock had told his witnesses that, as the South African judge would merely read their testimony, they should take their time; but Whittaker's long hesitations, and propensity for falling into traps set in cross-examination (he agreed that anyone who peddled remedies with the aid of testimonials could be described as 'a quack'), caused agony to F.M.

and his supporters and made them feel that the proceedings had got off to a bad start.

The second witness, F.M.'s old ally Dr Peter Macdonald, insisted that the Alexander Technique 'satisfies the most exact requirements of a scientific method'; that it removed the effects of diseases, without amounting to a 'cure'; that there was a definite link between the teachings of F.M. and Magnus; and 'that the evidence of people as to the value of the Technique, however distinguished they were, was worthless unless they had practical experience of it'. In cross-examination, Macdonald was asked to read from a letter written to Jokl by the celebrated royal physician Lord Horder:

> This [the Alexander Technique] is quackery of the most subtle, therefore worst, form. I always shout when I see the cloven hoof. I think you are doing a public service in exposing this fraud. What can I do to help?

In return, Diplock in re-examination asked him to read from the letter F.M. had received from Sir Charles Sherrington:

> I need not repeat to you that I appreciate the value of your teaching and observations. I was glad to take the occasion to say so in print. I know some of the difficulties which attach to putting your ideas across to those less versed in the study than yourself . . . I am sorry you should be worried by a scurrilous attack . . .

The third witness was Lord Lytton, whose subtle and ironical style of speaking was not ideally suited to the witness box. Asked to describe his first experience with F.M., he said: 'He pulled me about, pulled my head off my shoulders and generally used his hands to put me in the position he wanted. I felt extremely uncomfortable and mis-shapen. I had felt very straight before and I felt very crooked afterwards, and it was altogether rather a surprising experience for me.' He also cheerfully admitted that, on first reading *Man's Supreme Inheritance*, he 'could not make head or tail of it'; he 'did not understand it a bit'. Lytton was adamant, however, that F.M. did not claim to cure. He had originally gone to see him hoping to find relief from a persistent headache, and F.M. had told him frankly that 'if it is a result of your misuse then you will get benefit of more effective use; if not, then it is a matter for your doctor to decide'. The headache turned out to be the result of a chemical imbalance in the blood, and was later successfully treated with drugs – though lessons with F.M. helped in lessening the pain. However, in other respects Lytton had been 'all screwed up' when he encountered F.M., who had effectively straightened him out. 'Alexander does not cure, but enables everyone to get the best out of their equipment.'

F.M.'s fourth witness was Sir Stafford Cripps, who announced that his health had greatly improved since he had become a pupil of F.M.: in particular, he had ceased to suffer from the colitis which had previously plagued him and which his doctors had told him was incurable. He had been sceptical to start with, and he did not find it easy to explain what the Technique was about, but 'the extraordinary thing is that, when you experience it, you become perfectly convinced it is right'. Regarding F.M.'s books, he said that 'once you have got a conception of what Alexander is after, they are easy to understand'. He did not think they would mean anything to someone who had not experienced the work. He admitted that he was an active supporter of F.M., that he had helped him obtain rationed paper for the reprinting of his books, and that he had tried to persuade the South African Government to withdraw Jokl's article, as he considered it regrettable that he, a British cabinet minister, should be 'grossly libelled' in an official publication in the Dominions. True, he had not been traduced by name; but he was mentioned as a prominent supporter of F.M., and the implication of the article was that all such supporters were either knaves or fools.

Next came Jokl's first witness – Edgar (later Lord) Adrian, Nobel Prizewinner in Medicine and Professor of Physiology at Cambridge. From the defence point of view, he proved rather a disappointment. He said that he had found F.M.'s books poorly written, difficult to understand, and full of statements that he was completely unable to accept – though he also disagreed with some statements in Jokl's article, and admitted during his evidence that some remarks of F.M. on which he was asked to comment made slightly more sense than he had originally thought. As with the other physiologists called by the defence, he supported Jokl's argument that the theories of Magnus bore no relation to those of F.M. – for Magnus's discoveries were to do with automatic reflexes, whereas F.M. seemed to be interested in conscious volition. In cross-examination, however, he agreed that Magnus, like F.M., 'described the position of the head and neck as playing an important part in the posture of the rest of the body'. He also agreed that 'bad habits of posture could affect general health, and that general health had a strong impact on disease'. Adrian admitted that he had no experience of F.M.'s work and had merely read his books.

The second defence witness, Sir Henry Dale – another Nobel Prizewinner, a member of the exclusive Order of Merit, and a former President of the Royal Society and Chairman of the Scientific Advisory Committee to the War Cabinet – expressed himself in more robust terms. He had read *Man's Supreme Inheritance*, which as a scientist had struck him as 'a mass of pretentious verbiage'. F.M.'s statement that 'man may in time obtain complete conscious control of every function in the body' was rubbish, and his book indeed represented 'dangerous quackery' as it discouraged readers from seeking medical treatment if anything went wrong with them. Dale had been Magnus's best English friend and he was 'very offended' that Magnus's 'beautiful experimental work' should be compared to F.M.'s. He thought the term 'gymnastics' was an 'unduly favourable' description of the Alexander Technique.

Cross-examined by Diplock, he agreed with F.M.'s statement that the body was in best health when there was the least strain on its parts; but this hardly entitled F.M. to claim that he could deal with cancer and appendicitis. He admitted that he had no experience of F.M.'s work, and did not even know that cases had been referred to him by doctors, but he felt it his duty to appear for the defence, having read his book.

Jokl's next witness was Brigadier T. H. Wand-Tetley, sometime Olympic pentathlon athlete and Inspector of Physical Training in the British army. In October 1940, the late Dr Andrew Murdoch had allegedly been told by him that changes to army training had recently been implemented in line with F.M.'s teachings – news which had been applauded both in a letter by Murdoch published in the *British Medical Journal* that November, and an essay by Huxley published in *The Universal Constant in Living*. Wand-Tetley now denied that he had ever told Murdoch anything of the sort – though in cross-examination, he admitted that some of the file seemed to be missing, that he might have written a letter which gave rise to a misunderstanding, and that he had invited Murdoch to Aldershot in 1942 to give a demonstration of the Alexander Technique. He could not satisfactorily explain why he had failed at the time to write to the *BMJ* denying Murdoch's claim; and Diplock had little difficulty in making him seem evasive and not overly bright.

Jokl's next witness was a leading heart specialist, Dr Paul Wood. He asserted that Jokl was correct in stating that certain things F.M. had written about the functionings of the heart were nonsense. He wondered if F.M. was in reality some sort of hypnotist, and whether the ailments he claimed to be able to eliminate (including his own original throat trouble) were hysterical in origin. Wood had no personal experience of F.M.'s work, had only read *The Universal Constant in Living*, and was surprised to hear that the famous heart surgeon Sir James Mackenzie had referred patients to F.M.

He was followed by Dr Freddie Himmelweit, a bacteri-ologist associated with Fleming in the discovery of penicillin, who adamantly denied the statement of F.M. in *Man's Supreme Inheritance* that 'the science of bacteriology has its uses, but they are of research, not of application'. He did not see how the relationship of the head and neck to the rest of the body could affect the power to resist disease, and thought it 'exceedingly dangerous for . . . any person to rely on Mr Alexander's treatment to protect himself, for example, against . . . typhoid fever or typhus, if he should go into a district which is infested with the agents causing those diseases'. He admitted that he had no experience of F.M.'s work and had read his books only a year ago.

Next came another witness for F.M., Dr Dorothy Drew, who described how, in 1943, F.M. had helped her overcome a host of medical problems which doctors had been unable to diagnose or cure. After this, she 'looked at her patients from an entirely new angle', asking not only medical questions but 'what influence their manner of use could have had in bringing about the things of which they were complaining'. She had assembled case notes of some 150 patients who had taken lessons in the Technique, and proceeded to give details of fifteen of these, whose symptoms included headaches, nausea, general fatigue, shortness of breath, neuritis, lumbago, menstrual problems, thyroid deficiency, depression, anxiety, sterility, difficulties connected with pregnancy, partial blind-ness and suffocation. In almost every case, medical diagnosis had produced little relief, whereas Alexander lessons had considerably helped. She had read F.M.'s books before first going to him but did not really understand them as it was hardly possible to do so unless one had experience of his work.

Jokl's next witness, Sir Alfred (later Lord) Webb-Johnson, President of the Royal College of Surgeons, was scathing with sarcasm. In *Man's Supreme Inheritance*, it was claimed that 'breaking down old habits of mind' could 'dissipate such a morbid condition as cancer'; but he had 'never heard of anyone being cured of cancer by movements of the neck'. Animals in laboratories could be induced to suffer from illnesses whether or not they were suffering from 'erroneous preconceived ideas'. It was indeed 'dangerous quackery' for Alexander to suggest that his methods could prevent appendicitis, where relaxation was merely one factor. Alexander recommended balance and good posture, but this was 'teaching that starts in the nursery and certainly finds a place in medical teaching'. Riders were taught to relax before sustaining a fall, and might think 'that to take lessons from Alexander was an expensive way of learning a simple fact'. He admitted that he had read only one of F.M.'s books, *Man's Supreme Inheritance*, and having done so he felt it was his duty to give evidence and warn the public. He had no experience of F.M.'s work and did not want any, as 'what is obviously an untruth is hardly worth investigating'.

The next witness, Samson Wright, Professor of Physiology at London University and author of famous textbooks, gave the most lengthy as well as the most entertaining evidence of the proceedings. Alone of the defence witnesses, he claimed to have made 'a very conscientious detailed study of Alexander's four books', adding: 'I do not think that Alexander does himself justice in the way he sets out his material. It is rather scattered throughout the books and I think anyone reading through them might not appreciate what his points were.' The main point, as he saw it, was the notion of 'defective sensory appreciation'. Concerning this, he said, to the initial puzzlement of F.M. and his friends:

Alexander's views on the behaviour of the sense organs in ordinary people are quite original, quite novel, and quite revolutionary . . . In his view, most people's sensory appreciation is not reliable, as a result of the evil effects of civilisation, particularly in the last generation or two. Alexander further holds that this widespread defective sensory appreciation has been the cause of a large number of serious illnesses, and that the common view of the causation of disease is fallacious because it has not recognised the overwhelming importance of this factor in the production of disease. Further, in Mr Alexander's opinion, orthodox medical treatment is of limited value, and cannot really produce a thorough-going cure because the medical profession has not appreciated this revolutionary finding of Alexander's and does not when treating patients put right the deceptive sensory appreciation. This doctrine which I have extracted from Alexander's writings, and which he sets out perfectly plainly and clearly in a variety of ways, is one of fundamental importance ... which, if accepted, would revolutionise our whole approach to the subject.

The trouble was that F.M. offered no scientific evidence for his 'revolutionary' thesis. He produced no detailed records of his work. 'If he cannot tell us in detail the methods which he used, I feel that we are not justified in attaching any credence to [his] affirmations.' It was also 'a very curious thing that no one else anywhere in the world has made the same discovery as Alexander. If these extraordinary errors in sensation are as widespread as Alexander suggests, if they are so serious and responsible for so much disease and illness, and if their non-recognition leads to a failure to treat and cure disease, one would have thought that somebody, somewhere, could have made the same discovery.'

There followed a moment of farce. With a view to demonstrating that most people's sensory appreciation was perfectly normal, Wright asked the South African Government Attorney (present for the defence) to volunteer for a simple test by shutting his eyes and raising his hands to what he believed to be the same level, spreading the fingers: were this to be done symmetrically, it would demonstrate satisfactory sensory appreciation. Wright claimed the hands of his volunteer were 'in approximately the same position', whereupon

Diplock riposted: '"Approximately" is the operative word, or is my own kinaesthesia wrong?' Later, in cross-examination, Diplock asserted that, not only were the Attorney's hands at discernibly different levels, but they were pointing in different directions, and also, at the moment he shut his eyes, he had thrown his head back. When Wright asked how this head movement was relevant, Diplock referred to a published study by Wilfred Barlow who, as an army doctor, had observed that only twelve out of fifty-six cadets were aware of the fact that they put their heads back as they sat down, and only seven out of the fifty-six were able to stop themselves doing so after it had been pointed out to them.

Wright agreed with previous witnesses that Magnus's theories had nothing to do with F.M.'s. Asked to comment on Sherrington's encomium of F.M., he replied:

> Mr Alexander has certainly emphasized that one should treat the integrated individual and the whole psycho-physical man, and I imagine that all Sir Charles wanted to say was that it would be useful to the public . . . to be familiar with this notion, which is, of course, a very old and well-established notion, thoroughly familiar to physiologists and clinicians . . . If that were all that Mr Alexander said in his writings it would be a very minor service, but a service. But as this thesis is combined with an immense amount of material which is, in my judgment, entirely untrue and misleading, and probably dangerous, I think, taking his writings as a whole, he has rendered a disservice.

He admitted he had not experienced F.M.'s work, but reiterated that he had made a thorough study of his works and understood his doctrines which, if valid, 'would be a matter of outstanding and quite revolutionary importance'. As it was, those doctrines were 'new and interesting', but 'quite without foundation'.

Jokl's next witness was Lieutenant-Colonel S. J. Parker, Inspector of Physical Education at the Ministry of Education, who said that he had looked at F.M.'s books when they came out, this being part of his job, but found them difficult to understand. He did not agree with F.M.'s claim in *Man's Supreme Inheritance* that 'in our schools . . . human beings are actually being developed into deformities by physical and deep breathing exercises'. He knew Jokl (his South African counterpart) and considered his publications to be 'a valuable contribution to the science of physical education' whereas F.M.'s books made 'no contribution whatever'. He did however admit in cross-examination – the only defence witness to do so – that before giving evidence it would have been useful for him to have had some experience of Alexander's work.

Jokl's final witness was Robert Clark-Turner, Assistant Secretary of the Ministry of Health, who merely stated that, so far as he was aware, his ministry had never given any recognition to the Alexander Technique. Diplock, however, was able to produce a letter signed by a colleague of Clark-Turner to show that, in 1943, the Ministry of Health had recommended to the Ministry of Labour that F.M.'s two assistants, Misses Goldie and Stewart, should be classified as being in 'reserved wartime occupations' owing to the importance of their work.

F.M.'s two best witnesses (who also happened to be his best friends) were the last to appear. His personal physician, J. E. R. McDonagh, FRCS, testified that he had known F.M. since 1925 and found as a doctor that his work was of assistance in studying health and disease. He agreed with Wright that F.M.'s conclusions, if valid, were of revolutionary importance, and he believed that F.M. was quite right in saying that most people's sensory experience was unreliable. He had sent many patients to F.M. and every one had benefited from lessons, 'because they are better able to use themselves and therefore less likely to fall into making the same errors as before'. He agreed with F.M. that the head–neck relationship had to be right 'before other relationships come into proper functioning' – the scientific basis for this was not yet fully understood, but it was true. There was a definite link between F.M. and Magnus, as both 'show that the head and neck have to be in the correct position before the correct expression is given to the reflex that is the basis of the action to be performed' – just as the swan could not get out of the water unless it elongated its neck. He did not see how anyone could comment on F.M.'s work without having experienced it.

The evidence of the final witness, Andrew Rugg-Gunn, FRCS, had a poetic touch. He too insisted that it was impossible to form a judgement of Alexander's work without experiencing it, as what was imparted was 'a sensation' which 'could not be described, only experienced'. He considered it to be 'an empirical discovery of the first importance'. Many factors were in play when it came to illness, but as a rule 'the most you approximate to the normal, the more resistant you are to disease', and the 'short, sagging spine' which the Alexander Technique prevented was responsible for causing or aggravating many conditions. Far from being dangerous, the Technique was 'extremely valuable' and it was difficult to see how anyone could be harmed by it. But 'it is not known; [medicine] has not grasped it yet'. Of F.M., he said:

> Mr Alexander is pre-eminent – none of the others can touch him – in getting the body into this peculiar position which is the right position according to him . . . Amongst everyone who has to do with this, orthopaedic surgeons, masseurs, chiropractors or osteopaths, physical trainers, physical culturists, he is a genius. He has this curious gift, he knows exactly where a part of the body should be, he knows exactly what is wrong, and he puts it right by gentle manipulation, just as a sculptor will take a piece of clay and make a beautiful statue.

Asked in cross-examination about F.M.'s claim to have found a universal guide to living, Rugg-Gunn replied: 'I think it is just an exaggeration. We are all prone to make statements like that in moments of enthusiasm . . . I have already said that Alexander is trying to express the inexpressible. He cannot describe what he does; it is impossible; words fail . . .'

After an uncertain start, the commission proceedings had not gone too badly for F.M. The distinguished defence witnesses had cast doubt on various statements in his books; but none of them had experienced his work, and with the notable exception of Samson Wright, none had even seriously attempted to understand it. They were not, therefore, in a strong position to comment on its practical value, whereas F.M.'s witnesses carried conviction in their insistence on its worth. Yet F.M. had undoubtedly been made to look foolish; a great variety of issues had been raised, some of which reflected less well on him than others; and it remained to be seen what view would be taken by the judge. 'The whole thing has been a "knock" for him,' Ethel Webb wrote to Frank Pierce Jones, 'and he looks older and worn by it.'[13] Certainly there were moments during the proceedings, when his work was being lambasted by the professors or inadequately explained by his own supporters, when he was the picture of anguish. At such moments, he must have rued the day he had issued his writ: his intention had been to teach his ignorant adversaries a lesson, but his life's work was now on trial, and there was no certainty of victory.

It had originally been intended to proceed to trial that autumn; but the defence again secured a delay, this time on the curious grounds that their counsel Pirow had to deal with some criminal charges arising out of his wartime pro-Nazi activities ('hope they hang the swine,' crowed F.M.[14]), and the case was finally set down to be heard in February 1948. F.M. thus faced further anxious months of waiting. He did not relish the prospect of giving evidence in person: 'How I will hate this,' he wrote to Mungo Douglas. 'I can't get any enthusiasm about the idea.'[15] The costs of the case were mounting: including the sureties of £2000 he had been required to give, they already amounted to 'nearly £8,000'.[16] In October, he experienced a further blow with the sudden death of Lord Lytton at the age of seventy. 'He was such a fine humane person and the best friend we have ever known in the interests of the work,' he wrote to Irene Tasker, now back in Johannesburg. 'May he come into all that is best in "the undiscovered country". His mantle will . . . now fall on Stafford [whose] last speech has made him the certain successor to Attlee . . .'* In the same letter, he announced that he would be sailing for South Africa at the end of December, with a stateroom to himself as he recognised the need to rest and avoid strain.[17]

F.M., however, was destined never to see South Africa. Just before Christmas, he suffered a stroke, followed by a second, more serious stroke which left him in a coma for twelve hours and paralysed his left side. For some days, his life seemed to hang in the balance: had he died, the case would have died with him.[18] In the event, he made a remarkable recovery. On 19 January 1948 he wrote in a steady hand to Irene Tasker, thanking her for good wishes on his seventy-ninth birthday. 'Yes, thank you, I am much better. McDonagh says the recovery . . . is the most remarkable he has ever known from such serious trouble. He is also of the opinion that with rest and complete freedom from worry etc. I can in time regain my old condition of well-being.' It was clearly out of the question that he should travel to South Africa to appear as a witness. There was a certain irony in the fact that the case, brought to defend teachings largely based on

---

* Cripps was then Minister for Economic Affairs; he was appointed Chancellor of the Exchequer the following month, in which post he won great prestige through his success in persuading both capital and labour to accept his programme of 'austerity'.

the idea of improving human health by minimising strain, had proved such a strenuous experience for him that it almost killed him, making it impossible for him to attend.

Although it was unprecedented in South African legal history for a plaintiff to win a libel suit without giving evidence in person, the case went ahead. As his 'representative', who would give the crucial evidence explaining and justifying his work, F.M. sent his nephew-in-law Wilfred Barlow, who went out by air at the end of January. Barlow temporarily sacrificed his medical career to play this role, as he was unable to obtain formal leave of absence from his superiors at Middlesex Hospital to go to South Africa, as a result of which his post of registrar was not renewed:* but he had no hesitation in going, seeing himself as the 'crown prince' of F.M., whose days seemed to be numbered. He was accompanied by two other doctors involved in the work, Dorothy Drew and Mungo Douglas – though in the event, Dr Drew merely added further details to the evidence she had already given in London, while Douglas was not called as a witness. 'I am very sorry that I shall not be with you all and much regret that I will not hear the cross-examination of the rascal,' wrote F.M. to Irene Tasker. 'Counsel should be able to slaughter him.'[19]

The case of *Alexander v. Jokl and others* opened in Johannesburg on 14 February 1948 before Mr Justice Clayden (sitting without a jury), and lasted twelve days. Hanson and Fischer appeared for F.M., instructed by Berrangé; Pirow and van Hulsteyn appeared for the defence, instructed by the Government Attorney. Possibly because of the political implications – it was a highly charged time politically, with a general election looming – the case aroused intense interest

---

* This may have been partly due to the influence of Lord Webb-Johnson (as he had now become), who was the leading personality at the Middlesex, and had been the most scathing of the London witnesses giving evidence against F.M.

in South Africa: every day the public gallery was packed, and the proceedings were reported at length in the press. F.M.'s supporters and Jokl's allies followed the daily developments with excitement and anxiety.

Hanson opened the case with a summary of F.M.'s life and work. His books had 'no pretensions to literary skill', though they contained 'all the thoughts and theories which were provoked by [his] observations and which formed . . . his philosophy'. Hanson quoted from Sherrington to show that the conclusions of the great physiologist were similar to those reached by F.M., whom Sherrington had praised in his book. Similarly, Dewey, the 'very famous American philosopher', had been so impressed by F.M.'s philosophy that he had incorporated it into his own. Jokl saw F.M. as a quack curer, but if one read his books properly one would see that he never claimed to cure at all. Jokl had assured Miss Tasker that her work made a 'highly important contribution'; but since then his hostility to the Alexander Technique had been 'unrelenting' – even after his article in *Manpower*, he had launched a further attack in the *Cape Times*. He was clearly out to destroy F.M., who had been compelled to bring the present action. The article was 'cruel, violent and abusive, completely foreign to the type of language to be expected from a scientific journal, and provocative in the extreme'. Only ten lines of it attempted to explain, incoherently and inaccurately, what the Technique consisted of: the remainder was 'libellous and abusive'. Jokl was entitled to criticise F.M. – which he had largely done by quoting him out of context – but not to call him a charlatan. 'Before this libel, the onus was on Mr Alexander to satisfy the scientific world. The . . . defence now have to prove that he is a quack . . .'

Wilfred Barlow then gave evidence for F.M. He had read F.M.'s books while at Oxford, been impressed by what they said about the physical degeneration wrought by civilisation, and decided to go for lessons. Apart from gaining relief from a dislocated shoulder, he saw that one aspect of Alexander's teaching was 'quite new': all other methods took it for granted that 'one's awareness of using oneself' was accurate, whereas F.M. realised that 'a person who had been using himself wrongly for a very long time could not trust his sensory appreciation in carrying out any activity'. As a medical student, Barlow became convinced that F.M. had made 'a most important discovery, which was not being taken into account by the ordinary medical teachers'. He had therefore trained in the work. Other aspects of F.M.'s teachings were by no means foreign to medicine: Barlow read passages from respected medical textbooks which pointed to a strong link between 'faulty body mechanics' and disease. F.M.'s physiology was 'open to criticism', but to dismiss his books on that account was 'scientific snobbery' as they were obviously written by a layman. Pirow cross-examined Barlow fiercely about medical statements in F.M.'s books, but Barlow stood his ground: either he agreed with what F.M. wrote, or he regarded it as a reasonable hypothesis to be tested or a laudable ideal for the future of man's evolution. He was certain that F.M. could help anyone suffering from appendicitis or bronchitis. Questioned about F.M.'s fees, he replied that 'like consultants in medicine, Alexander had a graduated scale in which people who could afford it paid such fees as helped cover the less well-off'. It was not impossible to master the Alexander Technique without having lessons – A.R. had done so, and F.M. had of course taught himself – but it was certain that doctors who knew nothing about it, however distinguished, could not conceivably give a valid opinion on it.

Dorothy Drew gave evidence for a second time, providing further particulars of her medical cases which had been helped by lessons with F.M. Asked by Pirow if she had ever sent F.M. a case which would normally call for a surgeon, she replied that opinion was often divided on the need for surgery, and F.M. never took pupils who were seriously ill. When Pirow suggested that 'the only real way that Mr Alexander has put his ideas across to the public is by means of his books', she riposted: 'The only way he has of putting his ideas across is with his hands.'

Norman Coaker was F.M.'s third witness. He explained that, in 1935, one of his two young sons was severely disabled as a result of an accident, while the other was asthmatic. Having heard about Irene Tasker's school, he decided to send them there; within a few months they had overcome their handicaps. He himself had suffered from a serious kidney ailment, and in 1930 had been given twelve years to live: but he too had taken lessons and was now in perfect health, to the incredulity of his doctors. He had read F.M.'s books and found their philosophy 'striking and convincing'. He had attended the 'demonstration' given by Irene Tasker to Jokl in June 1942, and noticed 'that Dr Jokl had a dropped shoulder, that his head was pulled back, that he had a great roll of fat on the back of his neck, that his hips were forced forward in just the way mine used to be, and that he walked with his feet stuck out like Charlie Chaplin. I was astonished that this was the purveyor of physical culture to the Union of South Africa.' After some 'mild and simple manipulation', Miss Tasker made Jokl look at himself in a mirror, and 'he [Jokl] and everyone present exclaimed at the improvement in his appearance'. Coaker's cross-examination by his arch-rival Pirow was a much-awaited moment: he avoided traps with professional skill, pointing out that almost every question hurled at him was based on erroneous assumptions.

Pirow: Supposing, Mr Coaker, that medical men who represent the very top of the profession . . . are of the opinion that there can be no such thing as the alleged Primary Control, that would not worry you?

Coaker: Well, Mr Pirow, if they came to that conclusion without examining the data at their disposal with regard to the Alexander Technique, they would be perpetrating a piece of unscientific impudence, the giving of an opinion while refusing to examine the evidence . . .

Pirow: Let us try to get to a scientific basis.

Coaker: I am on a scientific basis, Mr Pirow, I assure you. The basis of experimentation, watching results and seeing the connection between the process and results. You are asking me to talk about people who are not on that basis.

Irene Tasker was the last significant witness to appear for F.M. The case had been a nightmare for her: she had been horrified by F.M.'s decision to bring it, yet considered herself responsible for it, as she had refused to give Jokl lessons (which she now recognised as having been a mistake) and had then drawn F.M.'s attention to the offending article. She spoke of her thirty years as a teacher of the Alexander Technique, and recalled her 'demonstration' of it to Jokl in 1942: he had at first seemed appreciative, but then asked why he should not continue with his habitual use, which suggested that he had failed to understand the basis of the work. Seeing her pathetic state, Pirow did not cross-examine her harshly. It was obviously an ordeal for her to give evidence at all: she swayed in the witness box and at one point looked as if she might faint. For the rest of her life, she would refuse to talk about the case: even in an autobiographical lecture she gave in 1967, she made no mention of it.

The next few days of the case were taken up with a reading-out of the evidence given before the commission in London. The defence then called their last witnesses. Dr Culver, Jokl's co-editor and co-defendant, a former professor of physiology and health minister (and sometime pupil of Sherrington), admitted that he was largely responsible for the article which was the subject of the litigation. On hearing about Griffiths's speech to the teachers' association, and knowing nothing about the Alexander Technique, he had read *Constructive Conscious Control of the Individual* and been so shocked by its 'erroneous physiology' that he decided there and then that the Technique 'had to be exposed'. He had approached Jokl, who turned out to know quite a lot about it and to share his views, and persuaded him to write the editorial in *Manpower*. He admitted that he had only glanced at F.M.'s other writings, and knew nothing about his practical work, but he was convinced it must be dangerous as F.M. claimed 'that wonderful clinical results could be obtained from certain tricks with the head and neck'. His 'editing' had consisted of improving Jokl's imperfect English, and he had sent the article to be read by government lawyers, in whose opinion it was not libellous. The language was admittedly strong, but 'it could hardly be too strong to expose this threat'.

The last witness was Jokl himself, who for three days was submitted by Hanson to a pitiless grilling. Reading the report of the cross-examination, it is difficult not to feel sorry for Jokl: his English was not of the best, his dignity had already been dented by Coaker's evidence, and he was easily made to look ridiculous. This German-Jewish émigré, who had perversely fallen in with the nationalists in his adopted country and now found himself defended by 'the South African Quisling',[20] was clearly very touchy. It emerged that he had been hurt by Irene Tasker's refusal to give him lessons, while Griffiths's disparagement of physical education had wounded his professional pride. He objected to being called 'a German' fifteen years after he had left Germany, though he saw nothing wrong in calling Alexander 'an Australian' forty years after he had left Australia. When told that Sherrington's letter to F.M. had concluded with the words

I am sorry you should be worried by a scurrilous attack. A German is of course liable to be violent and rude.

he could not believe that this might refer to him, though it could hardly have applied to anyone else. Hanson got him to make a whole series of damaging admissions: that he had told various persons that he was 'determined to smash the Technique' and 'close it down once and for all'; that he had written to the Medical Council asking that Professor Raymond Dart be struck off the Register on account of his support of the Technique; that he had repeated a rumour that Irene Tasker had been responsible for a cancer patient neglecting medical treatment, which the specialist concerned had confirmed was quite untrue; that he had copied parts of his article from an unfavourable review of *The Universal Constant in Living* which had appeared in the *New Statesman* in 1942. Hanson took him through the article line by line, demanding explanations of every point and frequently getting him to contradict himself. Jokl had some telling points of his own – he had discovered, for example, that F.M., in the reprints of his books which appeared in 1946, had systematically removed the words 'patient' and 'treatment' wherever they appeared and substituted 'pupil' and 'teaching' – but such was his state of confusion that he was rarely able to score them effectively. 'The article was not meant to sneer,' he pleaded. 'It was forcefully written to draw attention to something which I thought was a frightfully serious thing.' Its object had been to show that F.M. had been wrong to describe his technique as 'a scientific procedure', whereas essentially it was 'a faith cult'.

Pirow summed up for the defence. The evidence showed that Alexander was an 'ignorant layman'. His books were worthless both as science and literature, and 'could only be read as advertisements for his technique'. They disparaged all other systems. They claimed that medical diagnosis was valueless, that doctors had inadequate knowledge of the body and its ills, and that physical education was 'quackery'. On the other hand, the claims they made for his own system included everything short of the resurrection of the dead. All his medical claims had 'been completely disposed of by the evidence of medical men of international reputation . . . We must take those claims in their extreme form. If those claims to provide an unfailing preventive to disease – including cancer, appendicitis, tuberculosis and so on – are held to constitute quackery, that . . . disposes of the case.' The fact that he might improve posture or cure headaches was 'beside the point': such benefits were in any case probably in the nature of faith healing, Alexander clearly having a mesmeric personality. The dictionary defined 'quack' as 'an ignorant pretender who boasts that he has knowledge of wonderful remedies' – which would apply to F.M. even if his claims were true.

Hanson summed up for the plaintiff. The article in *Manpower* was a complete misrepresentation of Alexander's teachings, omitting as it did all mention of use, inhibition and sensory appreciation. F.M. had a reputation, built up over half a century, which Jokl set out deliberately to under-mine, claiming he was dishonest, untruthful, fraudulent and in breach of the criminal law. 'Dr Jokl took a lot of hay on his fork when he couched his article in the way he did, and it is for Dr Jokl to convince the Court that what he said about Mr Alexander is the truth . . .' The plaintiff did not ask the judge to set the seal of scientific approval on his claims; but if it had not been proved that his Technique was valueless, then the defendants must fail. The article seethed with malice; it was not written in the restrained language of a scientist, and Dr Jokl had admitted that he had been willing to go to any lengths to 'smash' the Technique. F.M. should therefore be entitled to exemplary damages if he won, and his costs whether he won or not.

The trial concluded on 5 March, the judge reserving judg-ment. F.M., who continued to make an excellent recovery from his stroke, and had been kept closely informed of the proceedings by telegram, newspaper reports and the accounts of his three doctors when they returned to England, thought it had all gone splendidly. 'Of course, we all chuckled . . .

reading Coaker's references to the mal-use of Jokl,' he wrote
to Irene Tasker. 'What a gang the Pirow–Jokl lot are – capable
of doing and saying anything – the real German attitude
and no mistake.'[21] He was awaiting the verdict calmly
'because I cannot conceive of any judgment on the evidence
I have read but full judgment for the plaintiff'. His only
regret was that the press had been cautious about publishing
details of Jokl's humiliation by Hanson; but F.M. would
himself publish everything in the book he intended to produce
about the case. 'Yes, it was a very great disappointment to
me not to have been able to take my place in the trial, but
on the other hand it will add to the importance of the work
that my people could in themselves beat a fellow like J[okl]
and his stupid colleagues.' Although victory was certain, it
would 'take a great load off my shoulders to know of the
end'.[22]

Mr Justice Clayden delivered judgment on 19 April. After
laboriously analysing the evidence, he concluded

> that the defendants have shown that Mr Alexander is a
> quack in the sense that he makes ignorant pretence to medical
> skill . . . they have shown that in its claims to cure the
> system constitutes dangerous quackery. But in these matters
> they misrepresented the views of Mr Alexander and in
> showing how foolish were these views, which he did not
> put forward, they have in the article called him much more
> of a quack than they were entitled to do. In addition they
> have failed in my view to prove that the system cannot bring
> about the results which it does claim in the improvement
> of health and the prevention of disease, and again they have
> made matters worse by overstating the claims made for the
> system.

F.M. was accordingly given judgment and awarded £1000
damages with costs. It was scarcely the ringing endorsement

of his life's work for which he had hoped; but he reacted with overwhelming relief. To Irene Tasker, who had telegraphed the news, he replied with two words: 'TRUTH TRIUMPHANT'.

8

Finale

1948–1955

The case was not yet over bar the shouting.[1] With the encouragement of the South African Government (and within a month of the judgment there was a change of government, Malan's nationalists coming to power with their anti-British and 'apartheid' views), the defendants appealed against both the verdict and the damages, which were the second-highest libel damages ever awarded in South Africa. This involved F.M. in a further year of worry and expense. The appeal was heard by three judges at Bloemfontein in March 1949 and judgment delivered by Watermeyer, Chief Justice of South Africa, on 3 June.* Not only was the appeal dismissed with costs, but the appeal judgment was couched in terms far more favourable to F.M. than had been the original judgment. Watermeyer held that Jokl had completely misrepresented F.M.'s theories, and done so with 'malevolence': his article was 'not a dispassionate scientific analysis . . . of the theories and claims in the books but it directs ridicule and contempt and scorn not only at these theories and claims but . . . at the plaintiff in person'. Alexander's books might display medical ignorance and 'confused thinking', but there was nothing in them to suggest that he was 'dishonest' in

---

* There had been some difficulty putting together a panel to hear the appeal, as several of the appeal judges turned out to have had lessons from Irene Tasker.

the sense that he did not sincerely hold the beliefs he put forward, nor could any such inference be drawn from his personal evidence as he had not given any. True, it was only after Magnus had published his work that F.M. had started using the term 'primary control', but that term amounted to roughly the same as what he had earlier written about the importance of the head–neck relationship. F.M. and his followers may have misunderstood Magnus's findings, but that did not make them dishonest. At the trial, the defence had argued that F.M.'s claims were worthless, they were now arguing that they were exaggerated, and they could not have it both ways. As for the damages, these were held to be reasonable; for although the circulation of *Manpower* was small, the fact that it was an official journal edited by distinguished scientists and sent to important people at home and abroad meant that 'the damaging effect of the defamatory matter was probably far more serious than it would have been if publication had been made casually in a daily newspaper by an unimportant person'.

F.M. was jubilant, writing to Mungo Douglas that he considered the judgment 'such a wonderful recognition of the soundness of the technique'.[2] (It was hardly that.) To Frank Pierce Jones he wrote (with greater justice) that it showed that 'the so-called experts are not always right'.[3] He now wanted a book written about the case. He first approached Anthony Ludovici, always ready to write a book about anything; but Ludovici's flowery prose was ill suited to describing legal proceedings, and even F.M. had to admit that the book he produced was unreadable. He next turned to Ron Brown (1911–55), a journalist pupil working for the Press Association: Brown (who planned to call his book *Alexander and the Doctors*, and to follow it with a biography of F.M.) assembled a mass of material and wrote an introductory chapter, but then fell ill with tuberculosis and lung cancer. F.M. did not seek another author: by this time, he probably accepted that it would be best to draw a line under the whole affair. In retrospect, it had certainly been rash of him to bring the action. Had he lost, it might have killed the practice of his work; as it was, victory had been bought at a heavy price. It had cost him a fortune (even when the South African authorities belatedly paid up in 1950, he found himself several thousand pounds out of pocket); it had for four years distracted him from his normal activities; and worry over it had led to the stroke which had almost killed him.

F.M. had survived, however; and his recovery was remarkable. By the spring of 1948, he had resumed his work with the students of the training course; by the autumn, he was back to his normal routine of teaching. Alarmed at the speed of his recuperation, his physician McDonagh begged him not to over-exert himself, to remain calm at all times, and to moderate his former intake of wine and cigars – advice which F.M. had no difficulty putting into effect thanks to his mastery of 'inhibition'. A year after he had been struck down, there was little to show that he had undergone the experience except for a slight weakness on the left side of his body and face; the main difference noticed by his students was that he no longer gave vent to his famous 'rages'. That autumn, he sat for a portrait by the Australian war artist Colin Colahan (1897–1987), commissioned by his friends in honour of his forthcoming eightieth birthday: this shows an erect, dapper figure with an alert, thoughtful expression, his twisted smile rather more pronounced than before. Some months later, a short amateur film was made of him in his teaching room: this too shows a man unusually upright and vigorous for his years (as well as full of humour), still able to perform a favourite trick of passing a leg over the back of his teaching chair without touching it. His retreat from the grave was an impressive tribute to his mastery of his own principles.

Apart from having won his case and got over his stroke, F.M. had some cause for satisfaction as he approached his ninth decade. He was content in his private life, continuing after twenty years to enjoy the intimate friendship of Jack Vicary (with whom he spent weekends at Penhill) and Margaret Goldie (with whom he lived during the week at her flat near Ashley Place). They had cared for him devotedly during his illness; they saw to it that he wanted for little in the way of comfort. Despite the expense of the case, his finances were in reasonable order: he continued to indulge his passion for the turf, and to enjoy (albeit in moderation) the best food, drink and tobacco. Although life had its disappointments, these generally occasioned him only mild regret. He had hoped to re-establish the school at Penhill, but this proved impracticable: the property had been extensively damaged by flying bombs; by the time it was repaired, he was too preoccupied by the case and his illness to make the necessary arrangements. He had also hoped that John Vicary, his secret son by Jack, would qualify as a teacher of his work: but although John joined the training course in 1947, he showed no great aptitude for it, eventually leaving it to take up a job on Lundy Island, the bird sanctuary in the Bristol Channel.

There was, however, a darker side to the later F.M. All his life, he had tended to be touchy, suspicious, proprietorial, quarrelsome, as well as sometimes ungenerous in money matters; and these tendencies did not diminish with old age and the shock of his stroke. A number of his assistants left him during these years because they found him obstinate, untrusting and autocratic, and felt they were being underpaid. Patrick Macdonald, one of his most gifted teachers and son of his great medical ally Peter, departed after a stormy confrontation in the summer of 1948, setting up his own practice in Cardiff.* The most dramatic break, however, occurred in F.M.'s relations with Wilfred and Marjory Barlow.

---

* There was already some interest in the Technique in Cardiff, where the musician Clifford Lewis was an enthusiastic supporter; Walter Carrington and others had been teaching there periodically with F.M.'s blessing.

Until the summer of 1948, it was widely assumed that the Barlows were F.M.'s chosen 'successors' as guardians and practitioners-in-chief of the work. Marjory was not only his favourite niece, but had looked after his affairs and kept the teaching going during his wartime absence in America. Her husband was the first doctor to train as a teacher of the work; he had become a leading propagandist of the Alexander Technique; and he had given valuable evidence at Johannesburg, going there at some cost to his career. On various occasions, F.M. had intimated that he intended to set up an organisation in which he would recognise Barlow as his deputy; and at a meeting at Ashley Place on 18 June 1948, chaired by Vernon Berrangé, it was agreed to set up a Society of Teachers of the Alexander Technique with F.M. as President and Barlow as Secretary. However, during the following months, F.M. refused to allow any practical steps to be taken to constitute the new Society, and by the end of the year he had disassociated himself from it altogether.* It must be said that Barlow behaved tactlessly, putting it about that F.M., as an undischarged bankrupt, might be ineligible to hold office in the Society. There was also some disagreement between him and F.M. on matters of principle.† F.M.'s withdrawal from the project, however, seems to have been dictated largely by two factors: an ingrained reluctance (which he had frequently demonstrated in the past) to share control of his work, or entrust its future to any kind of institution; and a touch of paranoia in his attitude towards Barlow. Like a Roman emperor, he had come to regard his presumed heir with suspicion; in particular, he had become obsessed by the thought that Barlow, in a Caligula-like way, had tried to 'take over' at the time of his stroke. As he wrote cryptically to

* The Society continued to exist in name, and would be successfully 'revived' by the Barlows in 1960.
† F.M. had been displeased by Barlow's article 'Anxiety and Muscle Tension' (*BMJ*, 1947), which had referred approvingly to Pavlov's theory of conditioned reflexes.

Douglas, he was 'more and more convinced' that 'something happened when I was ill that calls for the breaking of a definite promise in order to change the nature of that something or perhaps get rid of it altogether . . .'[4]

The failure to get the Society off the ground in the autumn of 1948 had unfortunate consequences for F.M. His most prominent supporters were now Sir Stafford and Dame Isobel Cripps: as Chancellor of the Exchequer, Cripps (following his highly publicised evidence in the case) wished to remain in the background, but Dame Isobel continued to involve herself closely and had been present at the meeting which had proposed the creation of the Society. Ever since F.M.'s return to England in 1943, the Crippses had been urging him to make arrangements for the future of his work; and they were disillusioned by his refusal to go along with the proposed Society. They had been intending to use some of their considerable fortune to help further the Technique; but they did not now lavish their philanthropy on F.M. During the early months of 1948, in the aftermath of F.M.'s stroke, they had taken lessons from his former protégé Charles Neil. After the war, Neil had broken away from the main body of teachers and set himself up as a 'kinaestheticist', offering a method which combined elements of the Alexander Technique with physiotherapy; F.M. had disowned him, but Neil, who possessed considerable salesmanship and charm, had had some success with his system. At all events, the Crippses, with whom he ingratiated himself by helping Dame Isobel in her 'Aid to China' campaign, found his teaching effective; and in the late autumn of 1948, despairing that F.M. would ever set up an institution of his own, they gave Neil a substantial benefaction.* He had recently installed his practice in a large villa in Lansdowne Road near Holland Park; he had originally called it 'the Re-Education Centre',

---

* The Crippses had originally offered to help the Barlows, who declined the offer out of a residual sense of loyalty to F.M.

but now proposed to relaunch it, during the winter of 1949, as 'the Dame Isobel Cripps Centre'.

The assistant teachers at Ashley Place, who kept in touch with Neil (while disapproving of what he was doing), were aware of these developments; but they did not dare tell F.M., who knew nothing of them. Around this time, the question arose of how F.M. wished to celebrate his eightieth birthday on 20 January 1949. His seventieth had been marked by a public dinner presided over by Lytton, and F.M. asked that Cripps be invited to preside at a similar dinner. His assistants were horrified, as F.M. was bound soon to discover the Crippses' change of allegiance: but Cripps accepted the invitation, and his speech at the dinner, in which he praised F.M. as 'a great teacher and a great leader in the battle for health and sanity in the world', was widely reported in the press.[5] Within a fortnight, the press were reporting another story, that of the Dame Isobel Cripps Centre. F.M. was stunned by what he regarded as an act of betrayal. He wrote to those newspapers carrying articles about the Centre that he had absolutely nothing to do with it, that it did not teach his work. A year later, when Cripps was forced to retire from public life because of ill health, he wrote again, stressing that Cripps had not been his pupil since 1947 (to which Cripps responded in a generous public statement that he owed F.M. much and that meeting him had been one of the most fortunate events of his life[6]).

This traumatic episode had the effect of re-interesting F.M. in the idea of a society, if only as an instrument with which to 'fight' the rival practice at Lansdowne Road; and he made peace overtures to the Barlows, who had now established themselves in a spacious flat next to the Albert Hall, where Marjory gave lessons and Wilfred ran a medical practice which made use of the Technique. On 16 December 1949, the Barlows attended a general meeting at Ashley Place which was intended to set up a board of trustees to govern what was now described as a 'Teachers' Guild'. The meeting, however, failed to reach agreement and culminated in a shouting match, following which the Barlows stormed out, Marjory in tears. Marjory subsequently wrote to her uncle (whom she never saw again) accusing him of trying to break up her marriage, caring nothing for the future, and 'excommunicating' anyone who did not submit to his will.[7] Soon afterwards, the Barlows started their own training course at Albert Court, which became another rival centre to Ashley Place. There were no further attempts during F.M.'s lifetime to create a body to promote or regulate the teaching of the Alexander Technique, though F.M. assured everyone that he had made suitable arrangements in his will.[8]

When the dust of these events had settled, four teachers continued to be based at Ashley Place – Margaret Goldie, Irene Stewart, Walter Carrington and John Skinner. Goldie taught at the nearby flat which she shared with F.M., first in Evelyn Mansions, later in Carlisle Mansions. Carrington ran the training course, from active involvement in which F.M. gradually withdrew to concentrate on his private teaching. Skinner (1912–92) was an Australian who had heard about the Technique as a Japanese prisoner-of-war through reading Huxley's *Ends and Means*; in 1946, he had used all his savings to travel to London to meet F.M., who had at once put him on the training course, later employing him as his secretary. This was the loyal team which supported F.M. during the last years of his life.* In Goldie's eyes, he could do no wrong; the others sometimes found him difficult, but were nevertheless devoted to him and wished to stay with him to the end.

F.M. continued teaching until a fortnight before his death. Two of those to whom he gave lessons during the 1950s – the American polymath Goddard Binkley and the English journalist Louise Morgan – have left interesting accounts of

---

* Two teachers who qualified during the early 1950s, Peggy Williams and Peter Scott, also did some teaching at Ashley Place.

their experiences, from which it is clear that, as well as finding themselves transformed through improved 'use', they fell strongly under his spell. (Ironically, they were both inspired to go to him after taking lessons with teachers whom he had disowned, Binkley with Philomene Dailey of the 'Alexander Foundation' at Media, Pennsylvania, Morgan with Charles Neil at Lansdowne Road.) Their accounts convey an impression of F.M. as a skilful old actor who managed to hold the attention of his audience to the end.

The son of a Chicago businessman, Goddard Binkley (1920–87) suffered from back trouble and psychological problems, and spent his twenties pursuing a variety of studies in an effort to discover the equilibrium he craved, becoming a competent pianist and artist and acquiring a knowledge of sociology and physics. After reading *The Universal Constant in Living*, he decided he had found the key to his problems, and resolved to go to England to learn from F.M. During his lessons, lasting almost two years from July 1951 to May 1953, he kept a diary which brings the octogenarian F.M. vividly to life. At their first meeting, Binkley was struck by his 'warmth, intelligence and vitality', which belied his years, and the sense of 'timelessness' in his teaching room, which felt as if nothing had changed in it since 1914.[9] (F.M. had in fact contrived this atmosphere, arranging the room as if it were a stage set, with a ticking grandfather clock, eye-catching *objets* on the mantelpiece, and Edwardian décor and furnishings.) As his lessons proceeded, Binkley found most of his troubles being sorted out; and he was entranced by Alexander's talk, which he 'boswellised'. ('Why, Mr Binkley, when I am teaching you, as I do now, I am able to convey to you what I want to convey, because as I touch you, and guide you with my hands in carrying out my instructions, I myself am going up! up! up!'[10]) Binkley finally entered the training course in the summer of 1953, an event which he had been happy to delay as it meant he would see little more of F.M., who no longer concerned himself with training.

Louise Morgan approached F.M. in 1953 with a view to writing a book about his Technique. Her first impression was of his extraordinary youthfulness. 'His back is as straight as a young acrobat's, and he gives the impression of a vitally alive personality at least a generation younger than his actual [eighty-four] years.'[11] Of her subsequent experience with him, she wrote: 'Alexander made it clear to me that I had missed much of the pleasure of living . . . One wonderful day, I found myself walking, sitting down and getting up in a new way. It was like moving on a cloud . . . The sensation is indescribably satisfying and invigorating . . . I am now unable to conceive how I managed to live before I discovered Alexander.'[12] These gushing tributes, along with her willingness to accept uncritically everything he told her about his life and work, suggest that, like many women before her, she had become infatuated with F.M. Her book, *Inside Yourself*, came out soon after his eighty-fifth birthday in January 1954 and amounted to a glowing advertisement for his work – though the first printing had to be withdrawn owing to legal threats from Lord Horder, whom she had described as one of F.M.'s supporters, whereas he was in fact a contemptuous opponent who had offered his support to Jokl in the libel case.*

F.M.'s last years were tinged with melancholy. He experienced the loss of many old friends, including the three women who, next to Margaret Goldie, had been closest to him – his sister Amy (distressed by the row between her brother and her daughter Marjory) in 1951; Ethel Webb in 1952; Jack Vicary (still only in her early sixties) in January 1955. The lease of 16 Ashley Place came to an end in 1953, and its renewal entailed an enormous rent increase. This was a blow to F.M.; but after forty years, as he wrote to Jones, he felt that he 'could not leave this place and the atmosphere that has been created in it'.[13] Instead, he decided to sell Penhill:

* See p. 207.

but this proved no easy matter, as he faced a long battle to obtain the planning permission which would give his twenty acres a substantial value. The sale was finally realised in March 1955, F.M. keeping the cottage and its garden for his continued use.

F.M. had been the eldest of eight children to reach adulthood; but of the others, only one was left – the youngest, Beaumont. 'Monty' was a colourful rogue, whose blackmarketeering activities during and after the war had got him into trouble both with the police and criminal gangs. F.M. nevertheless retained a soft spot for his remaining sibling, who was the last link with his early life in Australia, and young enough to be his son. He invited him to live in the basement flat at Ashley Place and the cottage at Penhill, and showed an avuncular interest in his two infant sons by his recently married third wife.

In 1955, after the death of his beloved Jack and the sale of Penhill, F.M. seems to have fallen into a depressive state. He remarked to Skinner that 'the work would come to an end when he went'.[14] He appeared to lose confidence even in the loyal quartet of teachers who had stood by him. By a will made around 1950, it had apparently been his intention to leave them his teaching practice, the lease of Ashley Place and the copyright in his books. However, on 25 July 1955, under the influence of Beaumont, he signed a new and final will which made no mention of his work, his devoted assistants, or even Margaret Goldie, his partner in life. Apart from providing a legacy of £100 to his adopted daughter Peggy Fraser (whom he had hardly seen since the war), and an annuity of £260 to his son John Vicary, its sole beneficiaries were Beaumont and his family. Originally, F.M. named Margaret Goldie and Walter Carrington as his executors; but when he came to sign, he crossed out the name of Carrington and substituted that of Beaumont.[15]

He continued to enjoy racing, writing to Mungo Douglas that his two days at Ascot that June had been 'the best I have ever known there'.[16] At the end of September, he attended a race meeting at Alexandra Palace. He had a bad day; it was cold and wet, and he caught a chill; afterwards he ate a hot lobster dinner at the Café Royal, which gave him indigestion. That night, he suffered a mild heart attack. He seemed to be recovering well, when, on the morning of 10 October 1955, while lying in bed at Carlisle Mansions chatting to the nurse, he quite suddenly died, ten weeks short of his eighty-seventh birthday. He was cremated without ceremony, and his ashes scattered: he wanted no grave or monument.

Epilogue

Since F.M.'s death, his Technique has enjoyed varied fortunes. He had shocked his secretary John Skinner by suggesting that the practice of it might not long survive him; and through his change of will, and failure to make arrangements for the future, he seems to have done his best to ensure this. The rascally Beaumont was left in charge at Ashley Place: he knew little about the work, and made it clear that he was only interested in it as a means of making money for himself. As F.M.'s four assistants refused to go along with his plans, they were told to leave at Easter 1956; the following year, after they had re-established themselves in former dressing rooms of the Dominion Theatre in Bainbridge Street, Beaumont took them to court in an outrageous (and unsuccessful) attempt to shut down their teaching, claiming that they were not entitled to practise as Alexander teachers without his consent. (Had he succeeded, he would presumably have threatened to sue all the other teachers, many of them struggling, unless they agreed to give him a cut of their earnings.)

Beaumont induced Patrick Macdonald to return from Cardiff to teach at Ashley Place (which he continued to do until the lease ended and the property was demolished in 1970). This meant that there were now four rival centres of the Technique, each barely acknowledging the others and teaching and training teachers according to slightly different methods: Macdonald at Ashley Place; the Barlows at Albert

Court; Neil at Lansdowne Road; and Carrington, Goldie, Skinner and Stewart at Bainbridge Street. Beaumont's ludicrous lawsuit had aired before the world the schisms within the movement. Fortunately, a degree of harmony was restored during the early 1960s. The premature death of Neil in 1958 brought about the demise of his unorthodox variant of the Technique, Walter and Dilys Carrington eventually taking over his premises in Lansdowne Road, where they established the Constructive Teaching Centre to carry on F.M.'s original methods. The Barlows meanwhile revived the Society of Teachers of the Alexander Technique (STAT), which had been in a state of suspended animation since 1948; during the next few years, it was joined by virtually all teachers and active supporters of the work, thus reuniting the Alexander community as a single family and introducing much-needed professional regulation.

While one problem had been solved, another had arisen, for the mid-1960s saw an alarming decline of public interest in the Technique, resulting in a dwindling of both pupils and trainees. At a STAT meeting in 1967, the view was expressed that, unless something happened to revive interest soon, the work might, by the end of the century, exist only as a memory. That such a revival did indeed occur was largely due to the dedication of individual teachers, who kept going through hard times, building up reputations through their achievements. The Barlows, the Carringtons and Macdonald acquired international renown, students coming to train with them from many parts of the world, often setting up their own training courses on their return to their own countries. A number of personalities involved in training performing artists and sportsmen became interested in the Technique, which thus began to be introduced into other areas of teaching.

If one event may be said to mark a turning point in the history of the Technique after Alexander, it was the address of Nikolaas Tinbergen (1907–88), Professor of Animal Behaviour at Oxford, on receiving his Nobel Prize in December

1973. Like Coghill and Dart before him, Tinbergen was fascinated by the Technique and its implications for his own work; and although his introduction to it had been recent, he devoted almost half his lecture to it. He declared that F.M.'s 'story of perceptiveness, of intelligence, and of persistence, shown by a man without medical training, is one of the true epics of medical research and practice', and that, after just a few lessons, he could 'already confirm some of the seemingly fantastic claims made by Alexander and his followers, namely, that many types of underperformance and even ailments, both mental and physical, can be alleviated, sometimes to a surprising extent, by teaching the body musculature to function differently'.

There are now some 4000 registered teachers of the Alexander Technique practising in various parts of the world, all able to trace their training in an apostolic succession back to F.M. or A.R. In Britain and elsewhere, the Technique has become an integral part of the teaching of actors, dancers, singers and instrumental musicians, and is increasingly used in the training of sportsmen (notably in the equestrian field). If one includes students of these disciplines as well as private pupils, the number of those who have had some useful experience of the Technique may now run into millions – not to mention those who have benefited from other techniques and therapies (such as Feldenkrais and Gestalt*) which owe something to Alexander. Although the reason for its effectiveness is still not fully understood in scientific terms, few years go by without some distinguished scientist identifying

---

* Moshe Feldenkrais (1904–84) had lessons with F.M., who later considered that Feldenkrais had 'stolen' some of his ideas. Fritz Perls (1893–1970), the founder of Gestalt Therapy, makes a dozen approving references to F.M. in his book *Ego, Hunger and Aggression* (1942), written and published when he was living in South Africa: it seems likely that he took lessons from Irene Tasker, or knew people who had. (See Roger Tengwall, 'A Note on the Influence of F. M. Alexander on the Development of Gestalt Therapy', in *Journal of the History of the Behavioural Sciences*, January 1981.)

F.M. as the forerunner of important discoveries of our own time, notably in the field of neurology.

In his book *Feet of Clay* (1996), the late Anthony Storr discusses the characteristics which tend to be common to 'gurus' who found 'cults'. He considers a variety of figures,* ranging from unquestioned benefactors to criminal psychopaths, and concludes that they all conform to a basic pattern, along the following lines. The 'guru' goes through some traumatic early experience, getting over which he makes his 'discovery'. He then reinvents himself, concealing aspects of his background. He finds it difficult to form normal relationships, and tends to have followers rather than friends; but he has no difficulty winning adherents to his cause thanks to the magnetism of his personality. In particular, women throw themselves at his feet. He becomes absorbed in his teaching to the exclusion of other interests, and believes that it provides the answer to almost everything and the key to human salvation. He writes books which outsiders find curious, but the faithful accept as the Gospel. He tries to show (usually with faulty reasoning) that the truth of what he teaches is susceptible of proof. He sees the world in terms of believers and non-believers, the saved and the damned. He becomes obsessed with control, tolerating no dissent or deviation among his followers, and often ends up suffering from paranoia, trusting no one.

Although Storr's book does not mention Alexander, all these 'guru' characteristics may be said to apply to him. For F.M. was not just a teacher who discovered a method: he believed that his method was of universal application, that it provided the solution to all the world's ills, that it ought

---

* They include Gurdjieff, Rudolf Steiner, Freud and Jung, St Ignatius of Loyola, the Baghwan, and the American cult leaders Jones and Koresh who incited their followers to commit suicide. Though he does not discuss them in detail, Storr also suggests that his conclusions largely apply to messianic political leaders such as Lenin and Hitler, and even the founders of scientific movements such as Newton and Einstein.

to be practised by everyone. He saw himself as the Messiah of the new faith of 'correct use' and 'means-whereby'; his four books, with their special language and stern admonitions, constituted the Bible of the new creed. Jokl's article was ignorant and intemperate, but there was a grain of truth in his suggestion that F.M. led a cult based on the reverence of himself and the demonisation of anyone who cast doubt on his ideas.

However, F.M. differed from most other founders of cultish movements in four significant and salutary respects. First, there is the strictly practical nature of his basic teachings, which bring immediate tangible benefits to anyone who takes a lesson. As he used to say when his ideas were compared to those of other teachers, such as Gurdjieff: 'That's all very well – but do they have a technique?' (It is true that his books expound a philosophy which may be regarded as largely speculative – but as James Harvey Robinson wrote in his famous essay, one need not accept the philosophy in order to experience and benefit from the practical technique.)

Secondly, although F.M. was extremely proprietorial about his discoveries, he was also exceptionally modest. He always asserted that they were discoveries which might have been made by anyone, for they contained nothing arcane. In his more optimistic moments, he looked forward to a time when everyone practised his work as a matter of course and regarded it as the most natural thing in the world, puzzling over the fact that it had taken so long to discover and that its discovery was due to one man. There is something touching about his humility whenever someone considered to be brilliant, such as Dewey or Huxley, saw the great point of his teachings.

Thirdly, although F.M. recognised that people have much in common in the way they function and behave, and need to organise themselves into societies in order to survive and progress, he was only really interested in them as individuals. No doubt owing to the Protestant atmosphere in which he was brought up, he believed that each man has to take responsibility for himself and find the solution to his problems within himself; and these beliefs permeated both his life and his teachings. Hence his insistence on the cumbersome title *Constructive Conscious Control of the Individual*, lest it be thought that the 'control' he advocated had any connection with the mass movements which were establishing a hold at the time. This intense individualism (reminiscent of that of C. G. Jung, another thinker of Protestant background) at least partly explains the paradox that, while F.M. sought 'followers' and may be said to have led a 'movement', he always refused to set up any kind of institution to carry on his work.

Lastly, there is the remarkable fact that F.M., almost alone of the notable innovators of his time, had no discernible precursors. It is difficult to think of many distinguished scientists or philosophers whose teachings do not build to some extent on the previous work of others. But Alexander – apart from his training as an elocutionist and reciter, which taught him certain fairly obvious things about breathing, vocalisation and posture – had nothing to build on. He encountered a problem, in terms which no one seems to have considered before; he was determined to find the solution, even if he had to do so entirely on his own; and with extraordinary pertinacity and single-mindedness, and only occasional help (generally relating to the expression rather than the substance of his ideas), he carried on working out that solution for the rest of his life. Perhaps the last word should be with his mother, who wrote to him proudly on 25 October 1904: 'It is indeed wonderful what you have accomplished, and to think how you studied it all out for yourself.'

Notes

Frederick Matthias Alexander's four books and their years of first publication are:

Man's Supreme Inheritance (London, 1910; New York, 1918)
Constructive Conscious Control of the Individual (1923)
The Use of the Self (1932)
The Universal Constant in Living (1941)

During F.M's lifetime they appeared in several editions in both London and New York, the differences between editions sometimes being substantial. (The original American publisher was in each case Dutton; the first three titles were originally published in London by Methuen, the fourth by Chaterson, a firm established by F.M.'s pupil F. C. C. Watts with the purpose of keeping his writings in print.) I have used the excellent editions of *Man's Supreme Inheritance* (1996) and *The Universal Constant* (2000) annotated by Jean Fischer and published by his Mouritz company, which include in each case a history of the changes made in previous editions. For *Constructive Conscious Control* I have used the 1987 Gollancz paperback edition, and for *The Use of the Self*, the 1984 edition by Centreline Press (a Dutton imprint).

1. Tasmania

1   Questionnaire completed by F.M. for Ron Brown, *c.* 1950 (made available to the author by the late Tony Spawforth). Brown was then working on a biographical essay to use as an introduction to his book 'Alexander and the Doctors', but intended in time to write a full biography of F.M.; he fell ill shortly afterwards, and the first book was never completed, the second never begun.

2   For example, writing to Irene Tasker from New York on 22 October 1940, he remarks, referring to an argument over terms with his US publisher Macrae: 'Half-Scot against Whole Scot is a bit uneven, and I may not win.' According to Walter Carrington, F.M. usually referred to his alleged Scottish background in offering a tot of whisky to a guest.

3   J. A. Evans, *Frederick Matthias Alexander: A Family History* (Phillimore, 2001), Part 1. All information about F.M.'s forebears in this chapter derives from this excellent book by his great-niece.

4   Quoted in Rosslyn McLeod, *Up From Down Under: The Australian Origins of Frederick Matthias Alexander and the Alexander Technique* (published by the author, 1994, with subsequent editions and supplements), pp. 22–3.

5   Evans, *A Family History*, p. 59.

6   Anthony Trollope, *Australia and New Zealand* (1873), Vol. II, pp. 1–2.

7   For information on F.M.'s childhood, and life generally in north-western Tasmania during the period, I am again indebted to Evans, *A Family History* (Chapter 6), as well as to Rosslyn McLeod's *Up From Down Under*, and Margaret Long's series of articles 'Friends of Alexander' in the journal *Direction*.

8   Quotations from F.M. in this chapter are mostly from his fragment of autobiography written for Ron Brown's benefit around 1950, included in the collection of his *Articles and Lectures* edited by J. M. O. Fischer (Mouritz, 1995).

9   Walter Carrington, *A Time to Remember: A Personal Diary of*

Teaching the Alexander Technique in 1946 (Sheildrake Press, 1996), pp. 24–5 (entry for 16 May 1946).

10 *Ibid.*, p. 65 (entry for 30 September 1947).

11 McLeod, *Up From Down Under*, p. 28.

12 Carrington, *A Time to Remember*, p. 65.

13 Autobiographical fragment.

14 Autobiographical fragment; Carrington, *A Time to Remember*, p. 65.

15 McLeod, *Up From Down Under*, pp. 31–2.

16 Carrington, *A Time to Remember*, p. 65.

17 Evans, *A Family History*, p. 86.

18 Autobiographical fragment.

2. Australia

1 As with Chapter 1, this chapter owes extensive debts to three published works – Evans, *A Family History* (Chapters 7–9); McLeod, *Up From Down Under*; and F.M.'s fragment of autobiography.

3 Quoted in McLeod, *Up From Down Under*, p. 40.

4 *Ibid.*, pp. 40–1.

5 Full text of poem given in *Direction*, Vol. I, No. 7 (1991), p. 293.

6 Information from Walter Carrington.

7 Carrington, *A Time to Remember*, entry for 16 May 1946.

8 'Elocution as an Accomplishment' in the *Mercury*, 9 July 1894 (reprinted in Fischer [ed.], *Articles and Lectures*).

9 Quoted in McLeod, *Up From Down Under*, p. 48.

10 See 'A Respiratory Method' (1905), reprinted in Fischer (ed.), *Articles and Lectures*.

11 What follows is largely based on the edition of F.M.'s pamphlet published in Sydney in 1900 (Walter Carrington archives).

12 The Reverend E. Handel Jones. Other clergymen who furnished testimonials were the Reverend John Vance, a Presbyterian minister; Prior Thomas Kelly of the Carmelites; and the Principal of the Baptist Theological College, who had retained F.M. to teach thirty of his students.

13 Robert Young to F.M., 30 June and 28 August 1904.

14 Quoted in McLeod, *Up From Down Under*, p. 53.

15 Autobiographical fragment.

16 Owen interview with Patrick Macdonald, June 1961.

17 Article published 12 December 1903 (reprinted in Fischer [ed.], *Articles and Lectures*).

18 Betsy Alexander to F.M., 14 August and 23 October 1904.

19 Betsy to F.M., 25 October 1904.

20 Betsy to F.M., 9 May 1905.

21 Betsy to F.M., 26 April 1904.

22 Betsy to F.M., 23 August 1904.

23 Betsy to F.M., 6 and 20 February 1905.

24 Betsy to F.M., 18 September 1904.

25 Betsy to F.M., 23 August 1904.

26 Betsy to F.M., 26 June 1904.

27 A.R. to F.M., 28 January 1905.

28 Betsy to F.M., 26 April 1904.

29 Betsy to F.M., 10 June 1904.

30 A.R. to F.M., 8 November 1904.

31 Robert Young to F.M., 10 October 1904.

32 Betsy to F.M., 12 September 1904.

33 Robert to F.M., 28 August 1904.

34 Robert to F.M., 10 October 1904.

35 Betsy to F.M., 19 June 1904.

36 Betsy to F.M., 18 July 1904.

37 Betsy to F.M., 14 August and 23 October 1904.

38 A.R. to F.M., 29 June 1904.

39 Robert to F.M., 23 August 1904.

3. London

1 Young to F.M., 28 August 1904.

2 Information from Walter Carrington.

3 Betsy to F.M., 26 June and 23 August 1904.

4 F.M. described this meeting in a note he wrote in 1950 to serve

as a foreword to 'Alexander and the Doctors': see Fischer (ed.),
Articles and Lectures, XXVII.

5 Young to F.M., 30 June 1904: 'Just got your wire re Spicer.
Glorious from the start, dear boy. Told Dr McKay who is very
pleased indeed to hear of it.'

6 Young to F.M., 13 November 1904.

7 Betsy to F.M., 11 December 1904.

8 Young to F.M., 1 January 1905.

9 Fischer (ed.), *Articles and Lectures*, VI.

10 *Daily Express*, Wednesday 19 October 1904, p. 5.

11 Young to F.M., 1 January 1905.

12 A.R. to F.M., 3 January 1905.

13 Information from Walter Carrington.

14 A.R. to F.M., 14 November 1904: '. . . we all sincerely hope you
will be able to thoroughly cure Miss Brayton . . .'

15 Lily Brayton to F.M., 26 January 1906. This is one of a collection of 'letters from eminent London artistes [*sic*]' which F.M.
printed on a single page of a pamphlet he published in 1909; the
page is reproduced in fascimile on the jacket of Fischer (ed.),
Articles and Lectures.

16 Young to F.M., 1 January 1905.

17 Young to F.M., 23 November 1904: '. . . your present sphere is
better than "the life of an actor" with its attendant hardships.
You may later in life go in a bit for it, but really it seems such
a blessed lottery . . .'

18 Information from Walter Carrington.

19 Carrington, *A Time to Remember*, entry for 11 November 1946.

20 *Ibid*.

21 'Letters from eminent London artistes' (see n. 15 above).

22 Ron Brown's notes. See also Frank Pierce Jones, *Freedom to
Change* (Mouritz, 1997), Chapter 3: 'Sir Henry Irving used to
keep [F.M.] in the wings while he was on stage in order to have
his professional help between acts. Alexander told me that he
used to sit with a book in his hands, threatening to throw it at
Irving if he pulled his head back while speaking. "He knew that
I would do it, too," he added.'

23   Carrington, *A Time to Remember*, entry for 29 March 1946.

24   H. B. Irving's letter quoted by Fischer in *Articles and Lectures*, pp. 292–3.

25   'Letters from eminent London artistes' (see n. 15 above).

26   Matheson Lang, *Mr Wu Looks Back* (1940), pp. 85–6.

27   'Letters from eminent London artistes' (see n. 15 above).

28   Young to F.M., 28 August 1904: 'Now what do you think you are really going to do with your Book? For my part I think you ought NOT to publish it. If you do you give away your theory, and more than that, you do not – so I consider, I may be wrong – explain your theory in such a way as to encourage favourable criticism of it as SOMETHING ENTIRELY NEW.'

29   Young to F.M., 13 November 1904.

30   Fischer (ed.), *Articles and Lectures*, V.

31   *Ibid.*, VII.

32   *Ibid.*, VIII.

33   *Ibid.*, IX.

34   *Ibid.*, Appendix B.

35   Lulie Westfeldt, *F. Matthias Alexander: The Man and his Work: Memoirs of Training in the Alexander Technique, 1931–34* (Allen & Unwin, 1964), p. 70 of Mouritz edition of 1998.

36   Leonard Woolf, *Sowing* (1960), pp. 101–2.

37   Fischer (ed.), *Articles and Lectures*, XI.

38   *Ibid.*, XII.

39   Quoted in Goddard Binkley, *The Expanding Self: How the Alexander Technique Changed My Life* (STAT Books, 1993), p. 48.

40   Information from Walter Carrington.

41   F.M. to Irene Tasker, 3 July 1941.

42   Edward Owen's interview of John Skinner, 13 November 1961.

43   Young to F.M., 10 October 1904: 'I can understand how lonely you feel in London and you can appreciate how I feel here . . .'

44   Betsy to F.M., 12 September 1904.

45   The text of Leeper's Report is given in the first issue of *Direction*, and in McLeod's *Up From Down Under*, pp. 73–80. Walter Carrington's archives also contain the MS (undated) of an interesting article by McLeod on the subject of the Report.

46 Fischer (ed.), *Articles and Lectures*, XIII–XIV.

47 *Ibid.*, XVI.

48 *Ibid.*, XVI, p. 293.

49 These and other interesting details are included in Appendix I to Jean Fischer's admirable 1996 edition of *Man's Supreme Inheritance*.

50 *Man's Supreme Inheritance*, Chapter IV.

51 *Conscious Control*, Chapter I.

52 For an excellent account of F.M.'s fallacious views on evolution and related subjects, see Jean M. O. Fischer's two-part article 'F. M. Alexander and Evolution' in *Direction*, Vol. 1, Nos. 6 and 7.

53 *Man's Supreme Inheritance*, Chapter III.

54 *Conscious Control*, Chapter III.

55 *Man's Supreme Inheritance*, Chapter I.

56 Included in Appendices D and E of the 1996 edition.

57 For this and the following two paragraphs, see Evans, *Family History*, Chapters 10–11.

58 *An Examined Life: Marjory Barlow . . . in conversation with Trevor Davies* (Mornum Time Press, 2002), p. 85.

59 Information from Walter Carrington.

60 Jones, *Freedom to Change*, Chapter 5.

61 On 3 February 1913, Margaret wrote from Rome to her parents in New York that she would be attending the Mardi Gras festivities the following day with 'Miss Tasker and Miss Webb, two very nice English girls'. Unfortunately no letters home from her subsequent sojourn in London, during which she took lessons with F.M., seem to survive. (Letters from Margaret Naumburg to Max and Thérèse Naumburg in Naumburg Papers, University of Pennsylvania.)

4. America

1 Information from Walter Carrington.

2 'Biographical Sketch' in Brown, 'Alexander and the Doctors' (MS).

3 F.M.'s preface to the 1955 edition of *Constructive Conscious Control of the Individual*.

4   Evans, *A Family History*, p. 157.

5   'Biographical Sketch' in Brown, *Alexander and the Doctors*.

6   I am most grateful to Sue Fox of New York for her research into the elusive Margaret Naumburg. Particularly illuminating are the obituary article 'Margaret, Naumburg and Florence Cane: A Family Portrait', in *American Journal of Art Therapy*, Vol. 22, July 1983, and the biographical outline by Amey Hutchins accompanying the online catalogue of Margaret's papers at the University of Pennsylvania.

7   Margaret Naumburg, *The Child and the World: Dialogues in Modern Education* (New York, Harcourt Brace & Co., 1928); pp. 259–71 (F.M. mentioned by name, p. 265).

8   *Man's Supreme Inheritance*, Part I, Chapter VII; pp. 75–83 in the Mouritz edition of 1996.

9   Dewey's 'Introductory Word' to *Man's Supreme Inheritance*, 1918 edition.

10   Irene Tasker, *Connecting Links* (Sheildrake Press, 1978), p. 13.

11   Evans, *A Family History*, pp. 159–60. This is possibly the crippled girl whom F.M. describes in *Constructive Conscious Control of the Individual* (Part II, Chapter II, Illustration IV), whose parents demanded a demonstration of what F.M. could do with her. Once he had successfully demonstrated how she might be helped to walk again, the girl gave expression to her faulty sensory appreciation by exclaiming: 'Oh Mummie, he's pulled me out of shape.'

12   For the Greenwich Village Group, see Gorham Munson, *The Awakening Twenties: A Memoir-History of a Literary Period* (Louisiana, 1985), and Clive Fisher, *Hart Crane* (Yale, 2002).

13   *Man's Supreme Inheritance* (editions of 1918 and later), Part One, Chapter VIII.

14   Jones, *Freedom to Change*, Chapter 8.

15   Barlow, *An Examined Life*, p. 182.

16   Information from Walter Carrington.

17   *Ibid*.

18   F.M. to Edith, March–April 1917.

19   Edith to F.M., 1 January 1918.

20   F.M. to Edith, undated (probably late 1914).

21   Edith to F.M., 1 January 1918.

22   *Man's Supreme Inheritance*, Part One, Chapter VIII.

23   Tasker, *Connecting Links*, pp. 11–13.

24   Quoted by Eric David McCormack in *Frederick Matthias Alexander and John Dewey: A Neglected Influence* (presented as a university thesis 1958 and published by NASTAT, 1992), p. 39: McCormack adds in a footnote that he heard this anecdote both from Dewey's widow and Frank Pierce Jones.

25   Quoted in Jay Martin, *The Education of John Dewey* (2002), p. 286.

26   Jones, *Freedom to Change*, Chapter 11.

27   McCormack, *Alexander and Dewey*, pp. 47–8.

28   *Ibid.*, pp. 49–57.

29   *Man's Supreme Inheritance*, Part One, Chapter VIII.

30   F.M. to Waldo Frank, 18 August 1916, in Frank Collection, University of Pennsylvania.

31   Tasker, *Connecting Links*, pp. 13–15.

32   These changes are listed by Jean Fischer in Appendix J to the Mouritz edition.

33   *Man's Supreme Inheritance* (editions of 1918 and later): Part One, Chapter V.

34   *Ibid.*, Part One, Chapter VIII.

35   F.M. to Edith, 7–8 April 1917.

36   Included in Jean Fischer (ed.), *The Philosopher's Stone: Diaries of Lessons with F. Matthias Alexander* (Mouritz, 1998).

37   Randolph Bourne, 'Making Over the Body', included in Mouritz edition of *Man's Supreme Inheritance* as Appendix G.

38   'John Dewey's Reply to a Reviewer of *Man's Supreme Inheritance* in *The New Republic*, 11 May 1918', included in the prefatory material of later editions of *Man's Supreme Inheritance*.

39   Stephen C. Rockefeller, *John Dewey* (1991), p. 305. Dewey may have been stung to this intemperate outburst by the fact that Bourne had been one of the most ardent literary critics of American involvement in the war.

40   Evans, *A Family History*, p. 167.

41   Jones, *Freedom to Change*, pp. 34–5.

42   Quoted by F.M. in *The Universal Constant in Living*, Chapter X.

43   Evans, *A Family History*, p. 172.

44   *British Medical Journal*, 24 November 1923.

45   Jones, *Freedom to Change*, pp. 37–9.

46   *New Republic*, 24 January 1923.

47   *Constructive Conscious Control of the Individual*, p. 2.

48   *Ibid.*, Part III, Chapter III.

49   'Unreliable Sensory Appreciation as a Universal Defect' (pp. 22–3 in the Gollancz edition).

50   Essay-like footnote on pp. 59–60 of the Gollancz edition.

51   Jones, *Freedom to Change*, pp. 40–1.

52   *Constructive Conscious Control of the Individual*, Part I, Illustration III.

53   *Ibid.*, Part IV.

54   Edward Owen's interview with John Skinner.

55   Binkley, *The Expanding Self*, p. 47.

56   See Jones, *Freedom to Change*, pp. 44–5, 104–5.

5. Progress

1   Not much is known about F.M.'s career as an owner and trainer, except that he was closely associated in these activities with both A.R. and their friend and pupil Sir Hugo Cunliffe-Owen (who had bought a baronetcy from Lloyd George in 1920).

2   Evans, *A Family History*, pp. 176–8.

3   F.M.'s description in Appendix to *The Use of the Self*.

4   Tasker, *Connecting Links*, p. 20.

5   Part II, Chapter I.

6   Tasker, *Connecting Links*; Edward Owen's interview with Margaret Goldie, 22 February 1962.

7   Quotations from Magnus's lectures in Walter Carrington's paper *The Work of Professor Magnus and the F. M. Alexander Technique* (written in about 1950 but only published by STAT Books in 1994).

8 For early suggestions of a link between F.M. and Magnus, see Dr Macleod Yearsley's article 'Man's Future', in *Literary Guide and Rationalist Review*, October 1925; Dr Peter Macdonald's presidential address to the Yorkshire Branch of the BMA, 'Instinct and Functioning in Health and Disease' in *BMJ*, December 1926; and Anthony Ludovici in *Man: An Indictment* (1927).

9 Carrington, op. cit.

10 F.M.'s first known employment of this term, as well as his first known reference to Magnus, occurred in a lecture delivered to the Child-Study Society in February 1925, 'An Unrecognised Principle in Human Behaviour' (included in Fischer [ed.], *Articles and Lectures*, as No. XXIII).

11 Lord Lytton's privately published diary (Knebworth Archive).

12 Lytton to his mother, 18 November 1926 (Knebworth Archive).

13 *Ibid.*, 13 December 1926.

14 Ibid., 7 October 1926.

15 Ludovici's politics are examined in two interesting articles by Dan Stone: 'The Extremes of Englishness: The "Exceptional" Ideology of Anthony Mario Ludovici', in *Journal of Political Ideologies*, Vol. 4, No. 2, pp. 191–218; and 'The English Mistery, the BUF, and the Dilemmas of British Fascism', in *Journal of Modern History*, Vol. 75, No. 2 (June 2003), pp. 341ff.

16 This account comes from Ludovici's *Religion for Infidels* (1961), the relevant extracts from which are included in Jean Fischer's collection *The Philosopher's Stone*.

17 *Ibid.*

18 Anthony M. Ludovici, *Man: An Indictment* (1927), p. 355.

19 *Ibid.*, pp. 313–14.

20 *Ibid.*, p. 355.

21 R. D. Best, 'Conscious Constructive Criticism of Mr F. M. Alexander's New Technique' (1941), Chapter 1 (MS in Walter Carrington archives).

22 *Ibid.*

23 *Ibid.*

24 She is probably 'Example III' in Chapter V of *The Use of the Self*, a young woman suffering from strain who is enabled by lessons with F.M. to complete her teachers' training.

25 Jones, *Freedom to Change*, pp. 44–5, 104–5; Westfeldt, *Alexander: The Man and his Work*, p. 39 of Mouritz (1998) edition.

26 See footnote on pp. 59–60 of Gollancz paperback edition.

27 Included in Appendix to *The Use of the Self*.

28 *Ibid.*

29 Edward Owen's interview with John Skinner, 13 November 1961.

30 *The Use of the Self*, Chapter V.

31 *Ibid.* (alluding to Lord Dawson's address to the House of Commons on 24 February 1926, reported in the *Lancet*).

32 *Ibid.*

33 As he lamented in letters to Waldo Frank during the autumn of 1936 (Frank Collection, University of Pennsylvania).

34 The fullest and most interesting account, though coloured by her strongly negative feelings towards F.M., is Lulie Westfeldt, *F. Matthias Alexander, The Man and his Work: Memoirs of Training in the Alexander Technique, 1931–34* (1964; 2nd [Mouritz] edition 1998). Other published recollections include Marjory Barlow (*née* Mechin), *An Examined Life* (Mornum Time Press, 2002); George Trevelyan, *Why I Took Up Alexander's Work* (included in Jean Fischer [ed.], *The Philosopher's Stone* (Mouritz edition, 1998); Erika Whittaker (*née* Schumann) in the *Alexander Journal*, No. 13 (1993); and Kitty Wielopolska (*née* Merrick), *Never Ask Why* (2001). Patrick Macdonald and Irene Stewart spoke of their experiences when interviewed by Edward Owen in 1961, Max Alexander when he addressed the NASTAT AGM in Chicago in 1992.

35 See especially Westfeldt, *Alexander: The Man and His Work*, Chapter 4.

36 For the division into groups, see Barlow, *An Examined Life*, pp. 196–7.

37 Edward Owen's interview of Macdonald, 4 June 1961.

38 Barlow, *An Examined Life*, p. 26.

39 Westfeldt, *Alexander: The Man and His Work*, pp. 45–6.

40 For F.M.'s Shakespeare productions of 1933–4, see especially Westfeldt, Chapter 7 (and appendices to Mouritz edition).

41 Owen interview.

42 *Daily Telegraph*, 14 November 1934 (quoted in Appendix E to Mouritz edition of Westfeldt).

43 For an account of the Second Training Course, see *Walter Carrington on the Alexander Technique in discussion with Séan Carey* (Sheildrake Press, 1986).

44 Tasker, *Connecting Links*, pp. 22–3.

45 *Ibid.*, pp. 20–2.

46 Westfeldt, *Alexander: The Man and His Work*, pp. 38–9, 65–7.

47 A good account of Huxley's involvement in the Technique is contained in Jones, *Freedom to Change*, Chapter 7.

48 Grover Smith (ed.), *Letters of Aldous Huxley* (1969), pp. 399–400 (Maria Huxley to Eugene F. Saxton, 21 February 1936).

49 *Eyeless in Gaza*, Chapter XLIX.

50 *Ibid.*

51 *Ibid.*, Chapter II.

52 *Ibid.*, Chapter XXIII.

53 F.M. to Waldo Frank, 16 August 1936 (Frank Collection, University of Pennsylvania): 'Aldous Huxley has been one of a number of very interesting pupils. Ere this you probably have seen his book "Eyeless in Gaza" in which he mentions one's name & puts into the mouth of Miller expressions which are in accord with our philosophy and our procedures.'

54 Owen's interview with John Skinner.

55 Copy of letter from Aldous Huxley to Robert Best from Llano, California, 10 July 1942, in Robert Best file, Walter Carringon archives.

56 Jones, *Freedom to Change*, p. 53.

57 Carrington, *A Time to Remember*, entry for 29 May 1946.

58 Evans, *A Family History*, pp. 195–7.

59 Preface to *London Music in 1888–89 as heard by Corno di Bassetto* (Constable, 1937), reprinted in Eric Bentley (ed.), *Shaw on Music: A Selection from the Music Criticism of Bernard Shaw*

(Doubleday, 1955). ('Corno di Bassetto' had been Shaw's pseudonym as a music critic.)

60   Note of Isobel, Lady Cripps, dated 22 July 1943 in Cripps Papers (kindly made available by Professor Peter Clarke).

61   Cripps's evidence in the South African libel case (see Chapter 7).

62   Westfeldt, *Alexander: The Man and His Work*, Chapter 6.

63   Jones, *Freedom to Change*, Chapter 11 (quoting a letter from Dewey to Jones).

64   Reproduced in *The Universal Constant in Living* as Appendix D.

65   Copy of letter dated 15 August 1942 from John Hilton to Robert Best in Best file, Carrington archives.

66   Reproduced in *The Universal Constant* as Appendix B.

67   See F.M.'s preface to original edition of *The Use of the Self*.

68   The letter is reproduced in Chapter II of *The Universal Constant*: Jean Fischer in his (Mouritz) edition of 2000 provides excellent notes on all the signatories.

69   Copies of correspondence in possession of Missy Vineyard, Amhurst, Massachusetts.

70   Westfeldt, *Alexander: The Man and His Work*, p. 48.

71   *Ibid.*, p. 95.

72   F.M. to Irene Tasker, January 1939 (Carrington archives).

73   Jones, *Freedom to Change*, Chapter 8.

74   Westfeldt, *Alexander: The Man and His Work*, p. 51.

75   Barlow, *An Examined Life*, p. 136.

76   Owen's interview with John Skinner.

77   Owen's interview with Patrick Macdonald.

78   *Ibid.*

79   Walter Carrington's preface to the Mouritz (2000) edition of *The Universal Constant*.

80   Quoted in Walter Carrington, *The Foundations of Human Well-Being: A Comparative Study of the Work of F. Matthias Alexander and of Dr G. E. Coghill on the Problem of Human and Animal Behaviour* (completed March 1941; published by STAT Books, 1994), p. 16.

81   G. E. Coghill to F.M., 4 June 1939; quoted in *The Universal Constant*, Chapter VI.

82   F.M. to Irene Tasker, 11 April 1939.

83   *Ibid.*, 11 June 1939.

84   Coghill to F.M., 4 June 1939.

85   *Walter Carrington on the Alexander Technique in discussion with Séan Carey*, pp. 42–3.

86   F.M. to Irene Tasker, 19 February 1939.

87   *Ibid.*, 19 March and 29 July 1939.

88   *Ibid.*, 26 March 1939.

89   *Ibid.*, 3 September 1939.

6. War

1   For F.M.'s treatment of 'S.B.'s' injured leg, which Dr McDonagh considered 'the best example of [his] work', see *The Universal Constant in Living*, Chapter II, Example G.

2   F.M. to Irene Tasker, 21 April 1940.

3   *Ibid.*, 14 October 1939.

4   *Ibid.*, 29 March 1940.

5   See *The Universal Constant*, Chapter III, Part II, where F.M. publishes an article by Aldous Huxley welcoming the acceptance of F.M.'s methods by the army. In a letter published in the *BMJ* on 16 November 1940, Dr Andrew Murdoch stated that he had heard from Wand-Tetley that changes to army training in line with F.M.'s principles had been implemented the previous July. F.M.'s letters to Irene Tasker reveal that Hilton had inspired Wand-Tetley to make these changes. In 1947, giving evidence for the defence in F.M.'s South African libel case, Wand-Tetley denied that F.M. had ever had any influence on army training; but an army medical officer subsequently confirmed to Walter Carrington that the changes mentioned by Murdoch had indeed taken place. The whole affair is explained in Jean Fischer's note 85 to the Mouritz edition of *The Universal Constant*.

6   F.M. to Irene Tasker, 13 March 1940.

7   *Ibid.*, 1 June 1940.

8   Information from Walter Carrington.

9   F.M. to Irene Tasker, 23 May 1940.

10 *Ibid.*, 11 June 1940.

11 *Ibid.*, 16, 22 and 28 June 1940.

12 *Ibid.*, 10 July 1940.

13 F.M. to Walter Carrington, 10 July 1940.

14 *Ibid.*, 7 September 1940.

15 F.M. to Carrington, 7 September, and Irene Tasker, 15 September 1940.

16 Jones, *Freedom to Change*, Chapter 8.

17 F.M. to Carrington, 7 September 1940.

18 F.M. to Irene Tasker, 22 January and 3 February 1940.

19 F.M. to Carrington, 22 February 1941.

20 Carrington, *A Time to Remember*, pp. 49–50.

21 F.M. to Irene Tasker, 22 July 1941.

22 ' The Educational Methods of F. M. Alexander' by G. E. Coghill, published as a prefatory 'Appreciation' in *The Universal Constant*.

23 Jones, *Freedom to Change*, Chapter 7.

24 'Introductory Notes' to the Mouritz edition (2000).

25 Aldous Huxley, 'End-Gaining and Means Whereby' in the *Saturday Review of Literature*, 25 October 1941 (reproduced in Mouritz edition of *The Universal Constant* as Appendix J).

26 F.M. to Carrington, 24 January 1942.

27 In conversation with the author.

28 Jones, *Freedom to Change*, Chapter 9.

29 *Ibid.*, Chapter 8.

30 F.M. to Carrington, 6 January 1942.

31 F.M. to Irene Tasker, 14 November 1941.

32 *Ibid.*, 29 November 1940.

33 *Ibid.*, 23 March 1942.

34 Jones, *Freedom to Change*, Chapters 8 and 9.

35 F.M. to Carrington, 30 October 1940.

36 F.M. to Irene Tasker, 15 December 1941.

37 F.M. to Carrington, 11 November 1942.

38 F.M. to Irene Tasker, 22 February 1942.

39 F.M. to Mungo Douglas, 1 June 1943.

40 *Ibid.*, 25 February 1943.

41 F.M. to Frank Pierce Jones, 18 October 1942.

42 F.M. to Douglas, 5 January 1944.

43 *Ibid.*, 4 August and 6 November 1943.

44 *Ibid.*, 5 January 1944.

45 Barlow's evidence in *Alexander v. Jokl*, 16–17 February 1948.

46 F.M. to Jones, 22 October 1944. Dr Drew's letter in the *Medical Press and Circular* ('The Work of F. M. Alexander and the Medical White Paper') is reproduced in *Knowing How to Stop: An Introduction to the Work of F. Matthias Alexander* (Chaterson, 1946).

47 F.M. to Douglas, 29 July 1943.

48 *Ibid.*, 16 December 1943.

49 F.M. to Jones, 22 October 1944.

50 F.M. to Douglas, 15 April 1945.

51 *Ibid.*, August 1945.

52 F.M. to Jones, 7 February 1945.

53 Carrington archives.

54 F.M. to Jones, 16 September 1946.

55 Carrington, *A Time to Remember*.

56 *Ibid.*, 12 March and 11–17 April.

57 *Ibid.*, 4 March.

58 *Ibid.*, 1 April.

59 *Ibid.*, 12, 29 and 30 July.

60 *Ibid.*, 16–30 September.

61 *Ibid.*, 19 June and 12 November.

62 *Ibid.*, 9 May.

63 *Ibid.*, 25 March and 13–14 September.

64 *Ibid.*, 29 March ('the South African business is fairly safe now, even if it comes to trial'), 24 May, 3 June, and entries for July (when F.M.'s South African solicitor Berrangé visited him in London).

7. Trial

1   The main source on the background to the case consists of the proceedings in the case itself. The author has not seen the complete

material (said to run to half a million words), but has read the very detailed daily reports published in the South African press at the time, copies of which exist in Walter Carrington's archives. These archives also contain other interesting material – the copy of the offending article read by F.M., preliminary documentation in the case, transcripts of the judgments, press comment and some correspondence. Walter Carrington himself has provided further details.

2   Extracts from Hall's address are given as F.M.'s first appendix to *The Universal Constant in Living*.

3   Tasker, *Connecting Links*.

4   Jokl to Dr Malherbe, 3 May 1943 (quoted in cross-examination of Jokl).

5   Quoted in Jones, *Freedom to Change*, Chapter 10.

6   Barlow evidence.

7   F.M. to Douglas, 3 November 1944.

8   *Ibid.*, February 1945.

9   Jones, *Freedom to Change*, Chapter 10.

10 F.M. to Douglas, 14 December 1945; Cripps's evidence.

11 All three matters are discussed in Carrington, *A Time to Remember* (the notes by Jean Fischer being of excellent value as always).

12 *Ibid.*, 25 July 1946.

13 Quoted in Jones, *Freedom to Change*, Chapter 10.

14 F.M. to Carrington (undated but probably August or September 1947).

15 F.M. to Douglas, February 1946.

16 F.M. to Jones, 20 January 1948.

17 F.M. to Irene Tasker, 26 October 1947.

18 Barlow evidence.

19 F.M. to Irene Tasker, 19 January 1948.

20 Carrington's description of Pirow in *A Time to Remember*, 25 March 1946.

21 F.M. to Irene Tasker, 29 February 1948.

22 *Ibid.*, 20 March 1948.

8. Finale

1 Much of the information in this chapter derives from the recollections (published and unpublished) of Walter Carrington, and Edward Owen's notes of his interviews in 1960–1 with Carrington, Margaret Goldie, Patrick Macdonald, John Skinner and Irene Stewart.

2 F.M. to Douglas, 12 July 1949.

3 F.M. to Jones, 9 December 1949.

4 F.M. to Douglas, 7 February 1949.

5 *The Times*, 22 January 1949.

6 *Daily Telegraph*, 28 October 1950.

7 Copy of letter from Marjory Barlow to F.M., 12 April 1950, in Cripps Papers.

8 Heated correspondence regarding these events is contained in a file deposited by the Alexander teacher Sidney Holland in Walter Carrington's archives.

9 Binkley, *The Expanding Self*, pp. 37–8 (diary entry for 11 July 1951).

10 *Ibid.*, p. 51 (entry for 17 October 1951).

11 Louise Morgan, *Inside Yourself* (1954), p. 11.

12 *Ibid.*, p. 34.

13 F.M. to Jones, 11 September 1953.

14 Owen's interview with Skinner, 13 November 1961.

15 Will of F.M. in English Probate Registry; Edward Owen's interview of Beaumont Alexander, 29 July 1962 (Beaumont making no secret of the fact that he had persuaded F.M. to change his will).

16 F.M. to Douglas, 24 September 1955.

Index